The Hebrew Word for 'sign' and its Impact on Isaiah 7:14

The Hebrew Word for 'sign' and its Impact on Isaiah 7:14

MARK D. SCHUTZIUS II

WIPF & STOCK · Eugene, Oregon

THE HEBREW WORD FOR 'SIGN' AND ITS IMPACT ON ISAIAH 7:14

Copyright © 2015 Mark D. Schutzius II. All rights reserved. Except for brief quotations in critical publications or reviews, no part of this book may be reproduced in any manner without prior written permission from the publisher. Write: Permissions, Wipf and Stock Publishers, 199 W. 8th Ave., Suite 3, Eugene, OR 97401.

Wipf & Stock
An Imprint of Wipf and Stock Publishers
199 W. 8th Ave., Suite 3
Eugene, OR 97401

www.wipfandstock.com

ISBN 13: 978-1-4982-1831-3

Manufactured in the U.S.A.   07/24/2015

To my wife, Faith. This would not have been possible without her support, love, and prayers during the long days and nights of research.

Contents

Introduction | ix

1 The Purpose of Miracles in the Old Testament | 1
2 Etymology and Usage of אוֹת | 14
3 Etymology and Usage of מוֹפֵת | 56
4 Functional Differences between אוֹת and מוֹפֵת | 74
5 Historical Interpretations of Isaiah 7:14 | 88
6 Isaiah's Use of אוֹת | 115
7 Conclusion | 133

APPENDIX A
Occurrences of אוֹת in the Old Testament
with Miraculous or Non-Miraculous Results | 139

APPENDIX B
Occurrences of מוֹפֵת in the Old Testament
with Miraculous or Non-Miraculous Results | 142

APPENDIX C
Interpretations of Isa 7:14 by Modern Scholars | 144

Bibliography | 147

Introduction

THE WRITERS OF THE Old Testament used the Hebrew word אוֹת (ŏt) seventy-nine times in fourteen books.¹ Out of all of these occurrences, the most controversial passage where this word appeared in the Old Testament is in Isa 7:14. The controversy surrounding this text centers on the interpretation of אוֹת and עַלְמָה ('almâ). For example, some scholars contend that the passage did not contain a predictive element; therefore, the interpretation of the text only pertained to the writer's time.² In contrast, other scholars claim that the text had a predictive nature and may have referred to a future event.³ If the text did have this predictive element, then what was the writer of the text foreseeing? For example, did the fulfillment take place in the writer's time, or at some point in the future? These questions and others surround the debate of this text.

The nature of biblical inspiration is one reason that this single verse has attracted so much attention. For example, evangelicals typically see a predictive element in the text. Furthermore, the writer of the Gospel of Matthew applied the verse to the birth of Jesus in Matt 1:22–23. As a result, if Isa 7:14 is not a prediction, then the integrity of Matthew's gospel could be in question. If the verse is not foretelling anything, then the writer of Matthew was apparently mistaken when he applied it to Jesus' birth. Consequently, one's position on Isa 7:14 may reflect one's view of the inspiration of the book of Isaiah and the Gospel of Matthew.

---

1. Brown, Driver, and Briggs, *Lexicon*, s.v. אוֹת. Hereafter, the author will refer to this source as BDB. Also see Koehler and Baumgartner, *Lexicon*, s.v. אוֹת; Gesenius, *Gesenius' Hebrew*, s.v. אוֹת.

2. See Durousseau, "Isaiah 7:14b," 175–80.

3. Machen, *Birth*, 288–90.

Introduction

The debate surrounding the prophetic nature of this passage often revolves around the translation of the Hebrew word עַלְמָה ('almâ). Some scholars translate the word, "young woman."[4] Others maintain the correct translation is "virgin."[5] A number of works provide support for both positions. If the word truly meant "virgin," then there is evidence for a miraculous prophecy. However, if the word only meant "young woman," then there was no supernatural connotation and only a small window for a predictive element to be present within the verse. Neither side in the scholarly discussion has produced conclusive data to settle the issue.

This book examines the text from a different perspective. Rather than discuss the various possibilities for the translation of עַלְמָה, this book attempts to analyze the implications of the word אוֹת for the interpretation of Isa 7:14. Typically, translators render the word as "sign." As a result, a general translation of Isa 7:14 would be: "Therefore the Lord himself will give you a sign [אוֹת]. Behold, the virgin shall conceive and bear a son, and shall call his name Immanuel." This book endeavors to determine whether careful analysis of the presence of אוֹת in this passage can shed new light on the interpretation of the verse.

Scholars who have produced works on the verse seldom adequately deal with the presence of אוֹת.[6] Instead, they give attention to other aspects of the verse. For example, the most debated issue is the translation of עַלְמָה. Most works analyze the usage of אוֹת in specific contexts, but few have provided an extensive analysis on how the writers of the Old Testament used the word. In fact, few works examine the presence of אוֹת in Isa 7:14.

The authors of the Old Testament used אוֹת broadly. This book examines how biblical writers used it and what they intended it to mean in various contexts. This book also examines the cognate words in other languages in order to help determine what the word meant in the Ancient Near East.

Because Isa 7:14 is such a controversial verse, this book aims to contribute to a more thorough understanding of the passage. Scholars have dealt extensively with the interpretation of the verse. Still, no work exists that provides conclusive evidence that has settled the debate.[7] This book

---

4. Wegner, "Virgin Births," 471–76. Also see Dennert, "Isa 7:14," 98; Kamesar, "Isaiah 7:14," 51–75.

5. See Bultema, *Isaiah*, 108; Motyer, *Isaiah*, 84–5; Leupold, *Isaiah 1–39*, 155–7; Smith, *Isaiah 1–39*, 213; Young, *Isaiah*, 286–8.

6. See Box, *Isaiah*; Douglas, *Isaiah*; Mauchline, *Isaiah*. Each of these authors examines the translation of עַלְמָה but does not mention the significance of אוֹת.

7. Feinberg, "Virgin Birth and Isaiah 7:14," 11–12.

INTRODUCTION

explores the various ways that the writers of the Old Testament utilized אות in an attempt to determine if there is a relevant pattern in Scripture that revolves around the nature of signs. For instance, K. H. Rengstorf has observed:

> If they [signs] are also symbolical actions, it may be seen clearly from the use of אות for them that they are autonomous acts after the manner of divine signs and that they thus have an intrinsic quality of proclamation, so that one must not regard them merely as aids to the delivery of the divine message.[8]

Rengstorf correctly noted that some signs in Scripture have a divine "quality of proclamation."[9] An examination of the evidence will help determine whether certain signs were coincidental or intentional. This evidence will be a factor in the interpretation of Isa 7:14.

A possible intentional sign occurred in Judg 6:17, where Gideon asked the Angel of the Lord for a sign (אות) as proof of his identity. Another occurrence appears in 2 Kgs 20:8–9, when Hezekiah asked God for a sign (אות) to prove that God would heal him. The author researches these passages and other passages where אות appears in order to determine if there is a relevant pattern to the Isa 7:14 discussion.

The writer also examines the New Testament usage of σημεῖον, which is the Greek equivalent for אות. William Dennison noted how the author of the Gospel of John used the word:

> John uses the word *semeion* in the sense of "pointer" and "mark" in the full sense of the formal character of the word; it preserves the richness of the word carried over from the Old Testament. Not only does it preserve it, but enriches it into the full dimensions of messianic and eschatological expectations wrought by the presence of Jesus Christ in the New Testament.[10]

According to Dennison, it appears that the authors of the New Testament may have used σημεῖον similarly to how the authors of the Old Testament used אות. The author attempts to analyze how writers used the Greek word within the New Testament and examines the ramifications this research may hold for the interpretation of Isa 7:14.

---

8. Rengstorf, *TDNT*, s.v. σημεῖον.
9. Ibid.
10. Dennison, "Miracles as 'Signs,'" 192.

Introduction

The Greek word σημεῖον also appears in extrabiblical Greek writings. The author researches the usage of the word in Classical Greek works, apocryphal books, and the Septuagint in order to determine how those writers employed the word in early Greek culture. If parallels exist between the usage of σημεῖον and the usage of אוֹת in the Old Testament, there may be new evidence for a clearer interpretation of the verse.

Research on this subject is justified on several grounds. First, the authors of the Old Testament used אוֹת seventy-nine times in fourteen books. Thus, the writers were familiar with the word and used it in various ways, depending on the context.[11] For instance, the writers often used the word in reference to ordinary objects, such as a banner.[12] They also used the word in reference to symbolic actions performed by some of the prophets.[13]

Second, the Old Testament authors frequently used the word in texts that contained miraculous events. Because the Old Testament authors used the word in several different ways, disagreements exist about the intended meaning. For example, Brian Dennert has argued, "While a sign (אוֹת) can be miraculous, it does not *require a miracle*, only something that prompts belief in God."[14] Dennert correctly observed that the use of the word does not necessitate a miracle. Still, in other instances the word seemingly refers to a miraculous event.[15] Thus, it will be necessary to determine if objective evidence can confirm when the authors used the word in reference to the miraculous and when they used it in reference to an ordinary object.

Third, no recent work examines all the usages of אוֹת in the Old Testament. Several authors have dedicated their research to studying individual uses of the word in various passages, but most studies do not demonstrate extensively how the word functioned in the Old Testament.[16] Therefore, it will be necessary to examine all of the various ways the authors of the Old Testament used the word.

---

11. Cf. Gen 1:14; 9:12, 13, 17; Exod 3:12; 12:13; 13:9, 16; 31:13, 17; Num 16:38; 17:10; Deut 6:8; 11:18; Judg 20:38; 2 Kgs 19:29; Job 21:29; Isa 19:20; 20:30; 37:30; 38:22; 55:13; 57:8; 66:19; Jer 32:44; Ezek 12:6, 11; 14:8; 20:12, 20; 24:24, and 27.

12. Cf. Gen 1:14; Num 2:2; Josh 4:6; 1 Sam 2:34.

13. Cf. Ezek 4:3.

14. Dennert, "Isa. 7:14," 98. Italics added. Still, there are times when the word appears to reference miraculous events. See Gen 4:15; Exod 4:8, 9; 8:23; Duet 4:34; 6:22; 13:1, 2; 28:46; 1 Sam 2:34; Neh 9:10; Ps 105: 27; and Jer 32:20.

15. Ibid.

16. See Khoo, "Sign of the Virgin Birth," and Porúbčan, "Word 'ôt in Isaia 7:14," 144–59.

INTRODUCTION

The fourth justification is the inspiration of the text. If Isa 7:14 referred to a miraculous birth, possibly even the birth of Jesus, then it provides strong support for the divine inspiration of the text. The implication is that the author of the verse predicted a supernatural event centuries before it took place. If the birth was not miraculous, then the author of Matthew incorrectly applied it to Jesus' birth. Therefore, it will be necessary to determine if the author of Isa 7:14 intended the verse to be used in such a manner.

The final justification for this investigation is the controversy surrounding the interpretation of Isa 7:14. Since scholars began questioning the meaning of the verse, critical and conservative scholars have debated its interpretation. The author of this book provides fresh objective data that sheds new light on the interpretation of Isa 7:14.

The book logically falls into seven chapters. In chapter 1, the author examines the Old Testament concept of miracles. This chapter helps determine the purpose of miracles in the Old Testament and shows their significance in the Bible. The chapter does not set out to prove that miracles actually occurred. Instead, the author examines how the writers of these events interpreted them.

In chapter 2, the author provides an analysis of the etymology and usage of אוֹת. This chapter reveals the history of the word and how it functioned in the Old Testament. The writer considers how the authors of the different genres of the Old Testament employed the word. For instance, the word appears in the Law, the Prophets, and the Writings. This chapter also determines how various Semitic and Greek words compare to the Hebrew word אוֹת.

Chapter 3 examines the etymology and usage of מוֹפֵת. Translators typically render the word as "wonder." The word is often parallel to אוֹת and carries a similar meaning. In fact, the two words used together create a common phrase used in Scripture—"signs and wonders." The author gives a brief history of מוֹפֵת and examines how the authors of the Old Testament used it in relation to אוֹת. The chapter also considers the Greek equivalent in order to understand its role in ancient literature.

In the fourth chapter, the author seeks to uncover the functional differences between אוֹת and מוֹפֵת. Since the two words are similar in meaning and consistently appear side by side, it will be necessary to determine how and why certain authors chose to use a specific word in a particular context. For example, in some instances, an author may employ מוֹפֵת to

xiii

Introduction

describe an event. Yet, that same author may also use אות at a different time in reference to the same event. Were these two words synonymous, or did the writer intentionally use them differently because of their functionality?

Chapter 5 considers the historical interpretations of Isa 7:14. The author summarizes the interpretations of how the author of the Gospel of Matthew used Isa 7:14. The researcher focuses on the interpretations of the early church fathers, popular exegetes of the Middle Ages, the Reformers, the Puritans, and selected modern-day scholars.

In chapter 6, the author examines the use of אות in the book of Isaiah. The author considers each time the word appears in the book of Isaiah. The focus of this chapter gradually narrows to analyze the use of the word in Isa 7:11–14. At this point, the author seeks to determine what the word meant in that context. It will also be necessary to identify the audience the sign was meant for and the various interpretations of the sign. For example, did the prophet declare the sign would be for his current generation, Ahaz, or someone else?

The final chapter concludes by reviewing the implications of the book's results. An analysis of the evidence determines whether this research provides any new data concerning the authorship of Isaiah, the interpretation of Isa 7:14, and the use of Isa 7:14 in Matt 1:22–23.

1

The Purpose of Miracles in the Old Testament

THE FIRST STEP IN the process of this book is to determine the purpose of miracles in the Old Testament. Furthermore, it is necessary to define a miracle.[1] Charles Hodge stated, "The word miracle is derived from *miror*, to wonder, and therefore signifies that which excites wonder . . . it may be used to designate any extraordinary event adapted to excite surprise and rouse attention."[2] C. S. Lewis noted that a miracle was "an interference with nature by supernatural power."[3] Charles Moule identified a miracle as "a work beyond the power of man."[4] Werner Schaffs added, "All the biblical miracles have in common the fact that they depart from the commonplace."[5] The fact that the biblical writers believed that this type of event was possible is a central foundation to this book.

If the biblical writers believed that certain events were miraculous, then they also recorded those events for a reason. The purpose behind the

---

1. It is not within the scope of this book to discuss the scientific and religious views of miracles, but for a detailed discussion of this topic, see Mavrodes, "Miracles," 333–46; Remus, "Magic or Miracle," 127–56; Knight, "Conception of Miracle," 355–61; Newman, "Miracle," 63–7; DeWolfe, *Theology*, 66; Pritchard, "Miracles," 97–109.

2. Hodge, *Theology*, 1:617.

3. Lewis, *Miracles*, 10.

4. Moule, *Miracles*, 23. Also see Pannenberg, "Miracle," 759–62.

5. Schaaffs, *Miracles*, 18.

events brings new meaning to the interpretation. For example, Schaffs went on to say:

> Most "modern" theologians regard the miracles as myths, i.e., as implausible, virtually fantastic accounts. They hold that these myth-miracles originated in the culture of the ancient Israelite communities and in the mythological conceptions of early Christian congregations ... Just as the experimental findings are embedded in a good theory of physics, and the two are inseparable, so the miracles are embedded in the distinctive miracle-language of the Bible, inspired by the Holy Spirit, and the language is inseparable from the miracles.[6]

Schaffs aptly understood the importance of knowing why the biblical writers recorded certain events. Furthermore, those writers used language that helped reveal whether they believed an event was miraculous or not.[7]

This author is not interested in proving or disproving whether miracles ever occurred in Scripture. Rather, the author is only examining some of the various events the biblical writers believed contained a supernatural element. The writers recorded specific events with a purpose in mind. For example, they may have believed the event fulfilled a promise or demonstrated God's power.

MIRACLES DEMONSTRATING GOD'S POWER

If the authors of the Old Testament recorded seemingly miraculous events in their writings, it is necessary to examine how those events functioned within the context of their appearance. The writers recorded numerous examples of specific miraculous events to demonstrate God's power and authority to a given audience.

God's Judgment

The writers of the Old Testament may have viewed miracles as a way to reveal the power of God to Israel and the surrounding nations. Many Ancient Near Eastern religions believed that the god of the nation revealed his

---

6. Ibid., 22.
7. Landrum, "Miracle," 52.

The Purpose of Miracles in the Old Testament

power by fighting for them in battle.[8] For instance, Merenptah claimed to have received divine confirmation that he would be victorious over the invading Sea Peoples in the thirteenth century BC. The day before the battle, he received a vision from the god Ptah granting him the sword of victory.[9]

Logically, the authors of the Old Testament also believed the God of Israel fought on their behalf. It also seems logical that these authors supposed that God demonstrated his divine wrath through his influence over the elements.[10] By doing so, he confirmed his power over any other deities.[11] As a result, the biblical writers recorded events that they believed God orchestrated to reveal his power. The writers undoubtedly believed the events were miraculous.

The Flood

One example of God's judgment is the flood.[12] The event is a popular and controversial display of God's divine retribution. According to Gen 6:5–7, God chose to flood the earth based on the wickedness of humanity. Kenneth Matthews wrote:

> The justification for the calamity is the complete moral corruption of the human family and the defilement of the earth. The repetition of "corrupt," occurring three times in vv. 11–12, underscores God's appraisal of the human condition and proves the legitimacy of the extreme penalty he will invoke.[13]

According to Matthews, God's judgment was intentional, and it demonstrated his authority over creation.

Scholars disagree about the nature of the flood. Most evangelical scholars claim the narrative provides a historical account of a global disaster that was miraculous.[14] Critical scholars argue for a localized flood

---

8. Merrill, *Kingdom*, 81.
9. As cited by Oppenheim, *Interpretation*, 251.
10. Knight, "Conception of Miracle," 358.
11. Sabourin, "Miracles," 30.
12. This book cannot adequately address the nature of the flood. For more information, see Froede, "Record," 40–43; Northrup, "Noahic Flood," 173–79; ibid., "Part Two," 181–85.
13. Matthews, *Genesis 1–11:26*, 359. Also see Rushdoony, *Genesis*, 70.
14. See Schiermeier, "Oceanography," 718–19; Austin and Wise, "Pre-Flood/Flood Boundary," 38–39.

The Hebrew Word for 'sign' and its Impact on Isaiah 7:14

or even approach the text as a myth.[15] Again, in order for this event to be miraculous, it required a global flood; all other floods have a naturalistic explanation.

Scholars have presented material in support of both types of floods. William Barrick argued:

> It is abundantly clear from the language of the Flood narrative that the disruption of the earth's surface was comprehensive and global. Such a description is not dependent upon the imposition of questionable etymological analyses for the individual terms employed in the passage. Individual words in and of themselves make no direct contribution to the task of determining the geologic consequences of Flood mechanisms. Rather, such contributions must be founded upon the sounder semantic clues provided by phraseology, literary devices, and context—the collective impact of the entire narrative.[16]

Barrick noted that the entire narrative is important to understanding the nature of the flood. The narrative seems to indicate a global flood, which would make it an event orchestrated by God to bring divine judgment. It would also indicate that the writer believed the event actually took place as a result of divine intervention.[17]

Sodom and Gomorrah

The destruction of Sodom and Gomorrah is another event in Scripture that shows God's judgment.[18] Genesis 19:24–25 states, "Then the Lord rained on Sodom and Gomorrah sulfur and fire from the Lord out of heaven. And he overthrew those cities, and all the valley, and all the inhabitants of the cities, and what grew on the ground."[19] Matthews commented, "The author calls on the description of Noah's flood to describe this deluge by fire at Sodom

---

15. See Von Rad, *Genesis*, 118–21; Putter, "Sources," 137; Emerton, "Flood Narrative in Genesis, pt 1," 401–20; ibid., "Flood Narrative pt 2," 1–21.

16. Barrick, "Implications," 260. For a list of one hundred different reasons for understanding the flood as a global catastrophe, see Morris and Whitcomb, "Flood," 204–13; Morris, *Genesis*, 683–86.

17. Pritchard, "Miracles," 100.

18. For an excellent discussion on the possible location of this city, see Van Hattem, "Sodom and Gomorrah," 87–92; Harland, "Sodom and Gomorrah," 17–32.

19. Unless noted otherwise, all Scripture references are taken from The Holy Bible: English Standard Version, known as the ESV.

... Twice v. 24 attributes the fiery destruction to the Lord's initiative. This heaven's rain cannot be explained solely as a natural phenomenon, such as an earthquake; it was exceptional, never again repeated."[20] Matthews observed the appearance of divine judgment in the text and suggested that this judgment was intentional.

This book cannot adequately examine every aspect of this event—miraculous or otherwise—but instead concerns itself with determining how the author of the passage viewed the event. The narrative seems to indicate that the destruction of the city was a direct result of God's divine wrath and judgment on sin.[21] James McKeown stated, "This [the city's destruction] continues the theme that began with the curse on the ground as a result of Adam's sin: the welfare of the ground and its vegetation are adversely affected by the rebellion of human beings against God's will."[22] The author of the text indicated that the people's sin was the reason for God's judgment on the city, just as in the flood narrative. The destruction represented his divine wrath and his judgment on the people of Sodom and Gomorrah. Overall, it is difficult to argue that the author did not believe the event was miraculous.

Jericho

Like the account of the flood and the destruction of Sodom, the story of Jericho carries a tone of God's judgment upon a sinful people. The author of Josh 6 records the events that unfolded as Israel approached the city. Like other events that appear to contain a miraculous connotation, some scholars dispute the historicity of the Jericho account. John Garstang and J. B. E. Garstang held the event was historical and concluded that the city fell in the fifteenth century BC. Their findings indicated that the walls of the city fell outward rather than downward.[23] The implication of his conclusion is that the walls fell in an abnormal manner, thus giving some validity to the Joshua account.

---

20. Matthews, *Genesis 11:26–50:26*, 241.

21. For more on the theological reason God may have judged the city, see Freytag, "Sodom and Gomorrah," 55–69; Peters, "Difficult Passages," 38–52; Lytton, "Sodom and Gomorrah," 31–55.

22. McKeown, *Genesis*, 109.

23. Garstang and Garstang, *Jericho*, 120.

In contrast, Kathleen Kenyon argued that Garstang and Garstang misread the information at Jericho.[24] She claimed that the city fell in the fourteenth century BC.[25] Her conclusions removed any possibility of Israelite involvement in the city's downfall.[26] The archeological evidence is inconclusive, but Garstang and Garstang's initial discoveries appear most accurate, based on the Egyptian scarabs of Amenhotep III they discovered at the site.[27]

Israel was on the verge of taking over the promised land. They suffered God's punishment by wandering in the desert and hoped to see the power of God revealed in the defeat of the city of Jericho. God's instruction seems to indicate that the destruction was not due to their military strength, but from his own divine intervention (Josh 6:2–7). Charles Pfeiffer asserted, "there are two facts related in the capture of the city by Joshua which should be illuminated by excavations. First, it is indicated that the walls fell down flat, apparently in a major disruption which caused them to tip down the slope of the mound."[28] Pfeiffer referred to specific aspects of this event that indicate the original author saw it as miraculous. The text appears to declare God's sovereignty over the Canaanites and assure Israel that God was with them in their conquest. The text also describes the event as God's righteous judgment upon those who did not worship him.

God's Providence

The Old Testament relates particular events that appear miraculous and refer to God's providence. While the judgment events attract more attention, the providential intervention of God is equally important in the story of Israel's development. For instance, God's providential care over the Israelites insured that they would become the nation he promised to Abraham, Isaac, and Jacob.

---

24. Kenyon, *Jericho*, 260.

25. Ibid.

26. If the city fell ca. 1300 BC, then neither the early date nor the late date for the Exodus would allow Israel to be entering the promised land during this time period.

27. Garstang and Garstang, *Jericho*, 119.

28. Pfeiffer, *Archaeology*, 308.

The Purpose of Miracles in the Old Testament

Manna and Quail

One example of God's miraculous providence for Israel is the provision of food and water as Israel wandered in the wilderness (Exod 15:22–27; 17:1–7). After the Israelites left Egypt, they continuously faced scenarios that caused them to question God's plan (Exod 15:24; 16:2–3; 17:2). They complained about their need for water and food; thus, the author of the text indicates that God interceded on several occasions. Exodus 16:1–36 records a scenario wherein God provided manna and quail.[29] According to the text, God caused a flake-like bread to form on the ground each morning and caused quail to cover the camp each evening so that the Israelites had enough food for the whole nation (Exod 16:13–14).

This book cannot prove that this event took place; rather, the record of the event itself demonstrates that the writer viewed the circumstances as miraculous.[30] The author of the text indicates that the food proved God's faithfulness and his ability to establish Israel as his people. Douglas Stuart observed, "God was teaching them [Israel] a concept: that he was their ultimate provider, the one who from heaven gave them not necessarily what they expected but what they really needed."[31] According to Stuart, the bread assured Israel of God's power and authority. Joshua 5:12 reveals that the bread only lasted as long as the people needed it; upon entering into Canaan, the bread ceased to appear (Josh 5:12).

Elijah and the Ravens

Another example of an event that implies God's miraculous provision is the account of ravens feeding Elijah.[32] The author of 1 Kgs 17:2–7 recorded that God told Elijah to remain in an area by a brook called Cherith. Elijah was to wait there for food that God commanded the ravens to bring him. The account is brief, but it is a demonstration of how the author of Joshua viewed God's sovereignty over nature.

---

29. There is some debate about the nature of this food. Some scholars claim that the word came from the Egyptian *menu*, meaning "food." Others suggest that it comes from the Hebrew *menhu*, meaning "What is it?" See Jacob, *Exodus*, 452; Fields, *Exodus*, 343–44.

30. Janzen, *Exodus*, 115–18.

31. Stuart, *Exodus*, 372. Also see Youngblood, *Exodus*, 82–85; Meyer, *Exodus*, 186–90.

32. Brueggemann, *Kings*, 211–12. Also see Voss, *Kings*, 113–14.

An important aspect of the account revolves around the nature of ravens: they are not normally gatherers but typically act as scavengers.[33] This detail adds even more to the significance of the event. Peter Leithart noted, "When Elijah crosses the Jordan into the wilderness, Yahweh's power does not cease. Yahweh is Lord of the wilderness as well as the garden, and he provides for his prophet, preserving the carrier of the word of God in a dry and thirsty land."[34]

Of course, some scholars argue for a more naturalistic approach.[35] For instance, there is some debate that the word עֹרְבִים (ʾō rē bim), typically translated "raven," may be referring to merchants of some sort who passed by the area to drink the water.[36] The argument does not seem to be credible, since the writers of the Old Testament used the word consistently in reference to birds (cf. Gen 8:7; Lev 11:15; Deut 14:14; Job 38:41).

Another common claim from scholars who take a naturalistic approach is that this type of story was prevalent in Ancient Near Eastern texts. Richard Nelson stated, "The story of Elijah and the ravens reflects the common folktale motif of the hero being fed by the beasts and reminds the reader of the canonical traditions of wilderness feeding."[37] The credibility of this story is easy to question because of the extraordinary nature of what took place. Nevertheless, the author of the text seems to see the event as miraculous. In fact, after the water in the stream dried up, verses 8 and 9 state, "Then the word of the Lord came to him [Elijah], 'Arise, go to Zarephath, which belongs to Sidon, and dwell there. Behold, I have commanded a widow there to feed you.'" It appears that even after the natural elements could no longer sustain Elijah, God intervened again for his provision.[38]

Miracles Confirming Divine Calling

Thus far, it seems the authors of the Old Testament viewed specific events as miraculous. Some events were a result of God's judgment, and others were for provision. There were also events with a miraculous connotation

---

33. Fretheim, *Kings*, 97.
34. Leithart, *Kings*, 127. Also see House, *Kings*, 213.
35. See Lockyer, *Miracles*, 110.
36. *BDB*, s.v. עָרַב.
37. Nelson, *Kings*, 109.
38. House, *Kings*, 214–15.

that confirmed a divine calling from God.[39] For example, Exod 4:1–17 records an account of such instances. In Exod 3, God revealed himself to Moses. The author of the text indicates that God planned to deliver Israel from Egypt.[40] Immediately upon hearing that God wished to use Moses as a major part of this event, Moses sought something that would prove God had sent him.[41] God's response was to provide Moses with three actions he could perform as this proof. In Exod 4:8–9, God called these events, אֹתוֹת (signs).

Moses' Staff

The first of these proofs is the transformation of Moses' staff. The author of Exod 4:2–5 records how God gave this symbol of assurance to Moses. First, God commanded Moses to throw his staff on the ground. Moses did so, and the staff immediately became a serpent. Scholars debate the nature of this event. For instance, some scholars claim that it was a common trick in Egypt.[42] Pinching a nerve in the back of the snake's neck caused the snake to become rigid. Others argue that this was not a trick, but a true miracle.[43]

The author of Exod 4:3 recorded Moses' reaction. The text states that Moses ran from the snake, which seems to indicate it was not a trick.[44] Where he first saw his staff, he then saw something that threatened his life (Exod 4:3). Verse 4 provides God's next command to Moses. God told him, "Put out your hand and catch it by the tail" (Exod 4:4). Godfrey Ashby noted, "nobody with any experience of snakes would attempt to grasp one by the tail; it would immediately whip round and bite. A snake has to be grasped by the back of the head."[45] Ashby is correct in his observation. Furthermore, the nerve that causes snakes to become rigid is behind the head. Moses' obedience to God's command seems to demonstrate his faith.[46] The

---

39. Habershon, *Miracles*, 110–11.

40. Davis, *Gods of Egypt*, 76. This book cannot adequately address the issue of the authorship of the Pentateuch. For more on this issue, see Christensen and Narucki, "Authorship," 465–71; Enns, "Authorship," 385–403.

41. Motyer, *Exodus*, 76–77.

42. See Fretheim, *Exodus*, 69–70; Longman, *Exodus*, 104; Hyatt, *Exodus*, 82.

43. See Stuart, *Exodus*, 129–30; Jacob, *Exodus*, 84–85.

44. Meyer, *Exodus*, 60; Youngblood, *Exodus*, 35; Fields, *Exodus*, 110.

45. Ashby, *Exodus*, 25.

46. Motyer, *Exodus*, 77.

event confirmed to Moses a specific purpose. It also appears to be miraculous, and it verified God's word.[47]

Moses' Leprous Hand

The next proof that God gave to Moses was the transformation of his hand. In Exod 4:6, God told Moses to place his hand inside his cloak; upon doing so, Moses' hand was stricken with leprosy. Verse 7 states that God told Moses to put his hand back inside his cloak. After Moses followed this command, God restored his hand to its original state. Based on the language of the text alone, it is difficult to argue that the author did not see it as miraculous.[48] Ronald Clements stated, "There is no obvious physical explanation for the change."[49]

Again, God tested Moses' faith by commanding him to place his hand back inside his cloak (Exod 4:7). This command probably went against all of Moses' understanding of the disease. By placing his infected hand back inside the cloak, he would have given the disease an opportunity to spread. Yet when God restored his hand to its normal condition, it confirmed that God's word was trustworthy. Both transformations were further confirmation to Moses that God had ordained him for this mission.[50]

Water Turned into Blood

According to Exod 4:8–9, God also gave Moses one final proof of his divine commissioning—the transformation of water into blood. The author wrote, "If they will not believe even these two signs or listen to your voice, you shall take some water from the Nile and pour it on the dry ground, and the water that you shall take from the Nile will become blood on the dry ground" (Exod 4:9). Thus, the final proof also seemed to be miraculous. Benno Jacob stated, "This was a powerful sign, for it transformed the life-giving water into blood and so imitated death."[51] The transformation

---

47. Stuart, *Exodus*, 129.
48. Meyer, *Exodus*, 61.
49. Clements, *Exodus*, 27.
50. Stuart, *Exodus*, 130–31.
51. Jacob, *Exodus*, 87.

of water into blood functioned in the same manner as the two previous proofs God provided.[52]

The text demonstrated God was in control and he was going to deliver the people as he had promised. Walter Brueggemann added, "The text grows out of the powerful signs, but the signs themselves continue to have power because they are embedded in and mediated by the text. The text and its interpretation are to bring the people to believe and to have life."[53] In every instance, God told Moses that the miracles were to show Israel that he had called Moses to lead the people out of Egypt (cf. Mark 16:20). However, some biblical writers also recorded seemingly miraculous events for other purposes.

Miracles Fulfilling a Covenant

The Birth of Isaac

Some events confirmed divine calling or demonstrated the judgment of God, while others fulfilled covenants.[54] For instance, God made a covenant with Abraham that he would be the father of a great nation even though he had no children at the time (Gen 15:1–21; 17:7–14). Abraham was one hundred years old, and his wife, Sarah, was ninety. Abraham seemed to understand the improbability of fathering a child at that age. In fact, Gen 17:17 states, "Then Abraham fell on his face and laughed and said to himself, 'Shall a child be born to a man who is a hundred years old? Shall Sarah, who is ninety years old, bear a child?'" Abraham may have laughed for joy, but he also seemed to have doubts.[55] Abraham knew that God's intervention was necessary for them to become parents.

The author of Gen 21:12 stated that God fulfilled his promise to Abraham by allowing Sarah to conceive and bear a son, Isaac. James Smith affirmed, "Incredible though it seemed, a man of one hundred and a woman of ninety were about to become parents. In this period of Bible history, procreation at these ages was indeed a miracle."[56] Terence Fretheim added, "The distinct divine acts in v. 1 (cf. Luke 1:68) stress that God has

---

52. Motyer, *Exodus*, 79.
53. Brueggemann, *Exodus*, 721.
54. Hubbard, "Hope," 39.
55. Matthews, *Genesis 11:26–50:26*, 205–56.
56. Smith, *Pentateuch*, Gen 17:15–22.

made Isaac's birth possible. The first verb (*paqad*, various translations are possible) links this act of God with Exodus events, showing the import of Isaac for the larger divine purpose."[57] Isaac's birth was foundational for the Israelite people. His birth literally helped form the nation. The author of Hebrews also believed that Isaac's birth was miraculous (Heb 11:8–12). Hebrews 11:12, says, "Therefore, from one man, and him as good as dead, were born descendants as many as the stars of heaven and as many as the innumerable grains of sand by the seashore." It seems clear that the writer of Hebrews also interpreted the birth as miraculous. Furthermore, the author of the Abraham narrative in Gen 18:13–14 believed that Isaac's birth was not ordinary. The text states, "The Lord said to Abraham, 'Why did Sarah laugh and say, "Shall I indeed bear a child, now that I am old?" Is there anything too hard for the Lord?'" (Gen 18:13–14). It appears the author of the text interpreted the event as miraculous; thus, the birth of Isaac confirmed the covenant made between Abraham and God.

The Plagues on Egypt

The author of the book of Exodus records that God's covenant with Israel provides the basis for the plagues that came upon Egypt.[58] Exodus 2:24–25 says, "And God heard their groaning and God remembered his covenant with Abraham, with Isaac, and with Jacob. God saw the people of Israel— and God knew." The author of the text indicates that God knew Israel was suffering and he had not forgotten his covenant. According to Exod 3:20, the plagues were the determining factor in Israel's release from Egypt.[59] The verse states, "So I will stretch out my hand and strike Egypt with all the wonders that I will do in it; after that he will let you go" (Exod 3:20). It appears that the plagues also demonstrated God's power (cf. Deut 11:1–4).[60] In fact, Exod 7:5 records, "The Egyptians shall know that I am the Lord, when I stretch out my hand against Egypt and bring out the people of Israel

---

57. Fretheim, *Genesis*, 486. Also see Wenham, *Genesis*, 75. Wenham agreed that Isaac's birth was divinely orchestrated.

58. Block, "Plagues," 519–20.

59. Roderick, "Exodus," 21–26.

60. It is not within the scope of this book to discuss the individual significance of the plagues brought on Egypt. For a detailed analysis of the plagues in relation to the gods of Egypt, see Kilpatrick, "Against the Gods of Egypt"; Davis, *Gods of Egypt*; Hoffmeier, "Arm of God," 378–87.

The Purpose of Miracles in the Old Testament

from among them." Thus, the plagues functioned as an act of judgment and a response to the fulfillment of a covenant.[61]

There are different interpretations of the plagues. For instance, some scholars see a naturalistic explanation for their occurrence,[62] others consider them myth,[63] and some see them as miraculous.[64] Regardless of one's interpretation, the text seems to record them as miraculous events with an intentional purpose. In fact, the plagues confirmed God's ability to fulfill his covenant, and they were a motivation for the Israelites to remain faithful (cf. 1 Chr 16:12). Moses later reminded the people of their knowledge of the plagues as a demonstration of God's power (Deut 29:2–3). After he recalled all that God had done for them, Moses said, "Therefore keep the words of this covenant and do them, that you may prosper in all that you do" (Deut 29:9).

CONCLUSION

These examples demonstrate that the authors of the books of the Old Testament viewed some events as miraculous and believed these events accomplished a specific purpose. In some circumstances, the miracles proved God's power over another nation. Some events, like the flood, showed God's might over nature. Other miracles revealed God's providence for his people. God intervened in the course of nature for the wellbeing of his followers. Finally, the Old Testament authors recorded seemingly miraculous events that confirmed a covenant.

These miracles are not an exhaustive list. Nevertheless, these texts reveal that the authors of the Old Testament apparently believed that some of the events fell outside the laws of nature. The authors included such events because they conveyed specific messages about God's interaction with humanity. The writers also used precise words to label an event as miraculous. Thus, it is necessary to analyze אות in order to determine if its usage may or may not reveal an event to be supernatural. The evidence will help determine whether the author of Isa 7:14 intended the verse to be miraculous.

---

61. Eakin, "Plagues," 474.

62. See Benjamin and Mangel, "Ten Plagues," 17–34; Fretheim, "Historical Disaster," 385–96; Wilson, *Signs and Wonders*; Moss and Stackert, "Darkness," 362–72.

63. See Bailey, "Plague Narratives," 7–17; Van Seters, "Plagues," 31–39; Childs, *Exodus*, 146–51.

64. See Meyer, *Exodus*, 16–27; Motyer, *Exodus*, 113–25; Bruckner, *Exodus*, 70–75.

2

Etymology and Usage of אוֹת

As mentioned earlier, the authors of the Old Testament used אוֹת seventy-nine times.[1] Most of these occurrences are in the Law and the Prophets. The author of Exodus used the word sixteen times, which is more than any other book. The writer of the book of Deuteronomy used the word in twelve instances, and the author of the book of Isaiah used it eleven times. K. H. Rengstorf noted, "The present H[ebrew] T[ext] contains 79 אוֹת times, twice in the same verse at Ex. 4:8 and also Ps. 74:4. About half of all the ref. are in the Pentateuch (39) and another quarter in the major prophets Is., Jer. and Ez. (19)."[2] The word appeared in all genres of the Old Testament and had significant usage throughout the books of the Old Testament.

A common translation of אוֹת is "sign," but it may also convey "banner" or "mark" (cf. Num 2:2 and Gen 9:12–13, 17).[3] F. J. Helfmeyer said, "The etymology of 'ōth is wholly uncertain. If the tav may be regarded as an original feminine ending, possibly it is derived from the root 'vh, which, however, means 'to wish, to desire.'"[4] One source noted that the word carried the idea of a "token, proof . . . [or] as marker of seasons."[5] Benjamin Davies claimed the word might mean, "Impression, engraving, mark, a

---

1. *BDB*, s.v. אוֹת.
2. *TDNT*, s.v. σημεῖον.
3. *BDB*, s.v. אוֹת.
4. *TDOT*, s.v. אוֹת.
5. Clines, *Dictionary*, s.v. אוֹת.

characteristic."⁶ Regardless of the translation, there seems to be a broad range of meaning.

The authors of the books of the Old Testament used the word in close connection to miraculous events. In fact, James Swanson noted that the word meant "a miracle to confirm faith."⁷ Benno Jacob added, "When God spoke of such signs, they always violated natural order. They were intended as proof of God's might for those who doubted or were afraid. They should and might occur, but could not appropriately be considered as 'guarantees' for the future."⁸ In addition, the word occurs in reference to "signs, [or] omens promised by prophets as pledges of certain predicted events."⁹ Robert Alden added, "Most of the seventy-nine occurrences of 'ôt refer to 'miraculous signs.' All the plagues on the Egyptians are called signs."¹⁰

Thus, the word carried two predominate meanings in the Old Testament. The first was an ordinary marker or signal. The second might signify some sort of divine action.¹¹ In order to understand how the author of Isa 7:14 used the word, a thorough analysis of the development and various nuances of the word is necessary.

THE USE OF אות FOR ORDINARY OBJECTS OR EVENTS

The first analysis will examine how authors used the word to denote a simple marker. The authors of the Old Testament used the word in reference to ordinary objects in several instances. For example, Brian Dennert said, "While a sign (אות) can be miraculous, it does not require a miracle, only something that prompts belief in God."¹² Dennert accurately acknowledged that אות does not require a miracle. In fact, the authors of the Old Testament used the word to refer to ordinary events and markers quite often. In

---

6. Davies, *Lexicon*, s.v. אות. Also see Clark, "Signs," 201–9. Clark makes a connection between the usage of signs in the apocryphal Wisdom of Solomon and the Gospel of John.

7. Swanson and Nave, *Nave's*, s.v. "sign."

8. Jacob, *Exodus*, 63.

9. *BDB*, s.v. אות.

10. *TWOT*, s.v. אות.

11. For an in-depth discussion on this subject, see Amorim, "Selected Miracles in the Gospels," 16–30.

12. Dennert, "Isa 7:14," 98.

most instances, the sign revolved around a symbolic action of some sort. Rengstorf observed:

> Typical of their form as presented in the tradition is that they take place by a divine injunction which demands obedience, and that they are combined with an interpretation. It is significant for their interpretation that eyewitnesses are almost always mentioned or tacitly assumed, and that they have a definite purpose. If they are also symbolical actions it may be seen clearly from the use of אות for them that they are autonomous acts after the manner of divine signs and that they thus have an intrinsic quality of proclamation, so that one must not regard them merely as aids to the delivery of the divine message.[13]

Thus, it appears that some actions carried a special meaning but were not necessarily miraculous.[14] In order to determine the differences between miraculous and non-miraculous events, it is necessary to examine how the word appears in the Law, the Prophets, and the Writings.

The Law

The word אות appears six times in the book of Genesis. The first occurrence is appears in Gen 1:14, in the context of the creation narrative. The verse reads, "And God said, 'Let there be lights in the expanse of the heavens to separate the day from the night. And let them be for signs [אתת] and for seasons, and for days and years" (Gen 1:14). The word seems to designate the lights as markers. Kenneth Matthews stated, "The narrative stresses their [sun, moon, and stars] function as servants, subordinate to the interests of the earth. They are to differentiate day and night and to distinguish the seasons, days, and years."[15] Matthews interpreted the word to be a descriptor of how the sun, moon, and stars would function. The author seemed to use the word to give a major purpose of the celestial atmosphere.[16]

---

13. *TDNT*, s.v. σημεῖον.
14. Ibid.
15. Matthews, *Genesis 1–11:25*, 154.
16. Cf. Jer 10:2. The author of Jeremiah used the word in connection to the same celestial atmosphere. He states that the nations worship them as idols and consider them to be deities. The nations' behavior directly contradicted God's designation of the sun, moon, and stars in Gen 1:14. In this context, God clearly labeled them as markers or signals to the changing of the seasons; they were not something to be worshipped above him.

The word reappears in Gen 9:12–13 and 17 in reference to the covenant God made with Noah after the flood. Verse 17 reads, "God said to Noah, 'This is the sign [אוֹת] of the covenant that I have established between me and all flesh that is on the earth.'" God designated the rainbow as the sign of the covenant. The bow itself functioned as a reminder to anyone who saw it that God promised not to flood the earth in that manner again (Gen 9:11). The bow also does not seem to be miraculous. Apparently, after rain became a regular part of the earth's environment, God designated this natural event as a sign to humanity of his covenant with Noah.[17]

The next occurrence of the word is in Gen 17:11. In this context, the author used אוֹת in reference to the mark of circumcision. God said that the mark would be "a sign [אוֹת] of the covenant between me and you [Abraham]" (Gen 17:11). Here, the word denotes a physical mark on a person's body. In fact, Gerhard Von Rad wrote,

> Thus, according to the sense of this passage, circumcision is only the act of appropriation, of witness to the revelation of God's salvation, and the sign of its acceptance. This distinguishes this covenant from the covenant with Noah; it is for a definite circle of men and demands their obedience.[18]

The sign does not appear to be supernatural in this context. It served as an indicator that a person was in covenant with God. The usage here is a typical example of how the authors of the Old Testament used the word to describe a simple marker. The important factor about its appearance is that God did not give the sign directly to Abraham. Instead, he indicated that the mark of circumcision would serve as a sign. The distinction between God designating something as a sign and God providing something as a sign becomes a key difference in the understanding of how the word functioned elsewhere in Scripture.

The first occurrence of the word in Exodus is one of the most controversial. In chapter 3 of Exodus, God revealed himself to Moses and promised to bring the Israelites out of Egypt. In Exodus 3:11, Moses responded with a question of his own worthiness to be the vessel God would use. God answered in verse 12 by saying, "But I will be with you, and this shall be a sign [אוֹת] for you, that I have sent you: when you have brought the people out of Egypt, you shall serve God on this mountain." Scholars disagree

---

17. Hughes, *Genesis*, 147–48.
18. Von Rad, *Genesis*, 201.

about the interpretation of the sign. Brevard Childs stated, "The problem of interpreting the sign in v. 12 has long been felt. The real difficulty of this verse lies in determining exactly the nature of the sign and how it functions in the narrative."[19]

Childs noted that the majority of scholars interpret the sign as what would follow—the worship on the mountain.[20] Childs claimed that the grammatical construction is a strength for this interpretation, though he ultimately discredited it. He said, "The difficulty of this view is that the sign would only confirm the word after the mission had been accomplished, which does not satisfy the biblical definition of a sign."[21] Jacob added, "We would expect a guarantee to mention something current, not a distant future event. What should encourage him till that time?"[22]

The difficulty for most scholars lies in their interpretation of how a sign should function in Scripture. Childs argued that a sign must always be an immediate authentication of a promise.[23] However, it is difficult to prove that a sign must occur immediately after a promise. The interpretation is a subjective understanding of the functionality of a sign. In fact, Douglas Stuart concluded:

> The fulfillment sign for Moses' call was a successful exodus followed by arrival at Mount Sinai and worship there by all the people ("you will worship" is plural). This is significant because it is not merely measurable by movement from one place to another but also by their movement from one faith to another. They would get to Sinai, but more importantly they would get to saving belief in the only true and living God. Fulfillment signs require faith since they promise proof to follow after an interval of time rather than immediately; in doing so they encourage faith.[24]

---

19. Childs, *Exodus*, 56.

20. Ibid., 56–57. Cf. Spero, "Pharaoh's Three Offers," 95. Spero notes the dialogue between Moses and Pharaoh in Exod 9:24–26. In this text, Pharaoh finally granted Moses permission to leave Egypt, but stipulated that his people must leave their herds behind. Moses replied that they needed the livestock to offer sacrifice and that they would not know explicitly how until they reached the mountain, referring back to Exod 3:12. Thus, this would prove that Moses anticipated meeting God again on Sinai.

21. Ibid., 57.

22. Jacob, *Exodus*, 62. Also see Pixley, *Exodus*, 20.

23. Childs, *Exodus*, 56.

24. Stuart, *Exodus*, 119.

Stuart's interpretation seems most accurate; thus, the sign was not miraculous. The sign served as an authentication of a promise to Moses and the Israelites.

Exodus 12:13 includes another occurrence of אוֹת. In the passage, God instructed the Israelites to slay a lamb and spread its blood on the doorposts and lintels of their homes (Exod 12:7). Then God said, "The blood shall be a sign [אֹת] for you, on the houses where you are. And when I see the blood, I will pass over you, and no plague will befall you to destroy you, when I strike the land of Egypt" (Exod 12:13). The blood of the lamb was a sign for the Israelites. God told the Israelites that he would pass over them if he saw the blood, but the blood did not act as a sign to him; the sign was for the people.

God designated the blood as a sign to fulfill his promise that the plague would not harm them. Bruckner observed, "This culminating sign was not for the pharaoh, however, but for the people. The people received the miracle when they accepted the Lord's offer of grace, protection, and lordship by placing the blood on their doorposts."[25] Even if the people did not obey by spreading the blood on the doorposts and lintels of their homes, the blood still functioned as a sign.[26] Those who did not obey would witness the protection of those who did. Thus, the sign demonstrated God's faithfulness and proved his spoken word, but it was not necessarily miraculous according to the parameters set earlier.

The word appears again in Exod 13:9 and 16. These verses occur in the context of God's establishment of the Feast of Unleavened Bread. After God gave the description of the feast, he said the feast would be a sign to the Israelites when they observed it. The language is ambiguous because God stated that the sign would be "on your hand and as a memorial between your eyes" (Exod 13:9). Walter Brueggemann provided an interpretation of what God meant by this strange distinction. He said:

> The tradition knows, perhaps from very specific experience, that present-tense well-being causes disregard of past-tense tribulation. Moreover, such forgetting causes a disregard of dependence on Yahweh and a sense of one's independence, autonomy, and self-sufficiency. Thus the festival intends to keep Israel in touch with a more difficult past, so that it will know that its

---

25. Bruckner, *Exodus*, 111.
26. Fox, "Ninth Plague," 219.

present situation properly evokes wonder and gratitude, and not self-congratulations.[27]

Brueggenmann's interpretation seems to be accurate, and it explains the curious usage of the word in this context. Thus, the feast acted as a sign due to its presence in the Israelites' lives.[28] It would be common to their way of life; it was synonymous with seeing their hand on a daily basis.

The author used אות with the same connotation in Exod 13:16. In this verse, the sign referred back to the consecration of the firstborn. The writer described the process of setting apart the firstborn in verses 11 through 13. In verse 14, the Lord predicted a question that would be asked by the children of the Israelites. When asked why they followed these commandments, the parents would respond with the story of redemption from Egypt (Exod 13:15). Finally, God explained that the process served as a sign of his faithfulness. Brueggemann continued, "The answer, which the child would never guess ahead of time, is that the festival is practiced because of what Yahweh did in the exodus."[29] The word functioned in the same manner as when it appeared in reference to the Feast of Unleavened Bread.

The final individual use of the word in Exod is 31:12 and 17. The context of the passage is the designation of the Sabbath day. God gave Moses specific words he was to speak to all the people. He said, "Above all you shall keep my Sabbaths, for this is a sign [אות] between me and you throughout your generations that you may know that I, the Lord, sanctify you" (Exod 31:13).[30] The word functioned in a similar manner in verse 17, but the focus was on the creation account.

In verse 13, the sign pointed to the sanctification of Israel. C. F. Keil and Franz Delitzsch noted, "It was therefore a holy thing for Israel, the desecration of which would be followed by the punishment of death, as a breach of the covenant."[31] By keeping the Sabbath holy, the people were reminded that God made them holy. The sign in verse 17 was still the Sabbath, but its second function reminded them that God created the heavens

---

27. Brueggemann, *Exodus*, 786.

28. Cf. Deut 6:8 and 11:18. The word functioned in the same manner in these passages.

29. Brueggemann, *Exodus*, 786.

30. Cf. Ezekiel 20:12 and 20. The author of Ezekiel used the word in reference to this verse. The context is God reminding Israel that he gave the Sabbath to them as a sign so that they might remember who sanctifies them.

31. Keil and Delitzsch, *Pentateuch*, 218–19. Also see Alexander, "Exodus," 116.

Etymology and Usage of אוֹת

and the earth in six days (Exod 31:17). As a result, the usage of the word was similar to its function in Genesis. Often it served as an indicator or as a symbolic event. It is clear that the word carried a broad meaning.

In Num 2:2, the word emerges again in reference to an ordinary object. In the passage, the word designated the tribal markers for the Israelites during their encampment. The verse reads, "The people of Israel shall camp each by his own standard [אוֹת], with the banners of their fathers' houses. They shall camp facing the tent of meeting on every side" (Num 2:2). James Smith observed, "Each tribe had its own standard. Tradition says that these standards matched the color of the twelve precious stones which represented each tribe on the breastplate of the high priest."[32] Again, there was nothing extraordinary about these banners. In reality, the author of the text used the word similarly to how modern English writers might.[33] The banners were literally signs that provided tribal boundaries for Israel. They were not miraculous in any way.

The author of Num 16:38 used אוֹת in the context of the rebellion of Korah. After God judged those who followed in this rebellion, he commanded Moses to take the censers of the men who died and to cover the altar with them. He said, "for they offered them [the censers] before the Lord, and they became holy. Thus they shall be a sign [אוֹת] to the people of Israel" (Num 16:38).

Apparently, these men's censers became a regular part of Israel's life. Adding them to the altar meant that everyone who saw them remembered the consequences of challenging God's authority.[34] Keil and Delitzsch stated, "Through this application of them [the censers] they became a sign, or, according to ver. 39, a memorial to all who drew near to the sanctuary, which was to remind them continually of this judgment of God, and warn the congregation of grasping at the priestly prerogatives."[35] In this sense, God designated an ordinary object as a sign to serve as a reminder of a past event, and it did not have a miraculous element.

---

32. Smith, *Pentateuch*, Num 1:52–2:34.
33. *TDOT*, s.v. אוֹת.
34. Cole, *Numbers*, 270.
35. Keil and Delitzsch, *Pentateuch*, 110–11.

The Prophets[36]

Writers outside of the first five books of the Law also used the word in several instances. The first occurrence is found in Josh 2:12, in the context of the two Israelite spies in Jericho. The two men sought to avoid capture, and Rahab provided shelter for them. Before they left her presence she said, "Now then, please swear to me by the Lord that, as I have dealt kindly with you, you also will deal kindly with my father's house, and give me a sure sign [אות] that you will save alive my father and mother, my brothers and sisters, and all who belong to them, and deliver our lives from death" (Josh 2:12–13). The sign that Rahab requested was a token of assurance that these two men would spare her and her family when the Israelites invaded the city.[37] In response, the two men told Rahab to tie a scarlet cord outside of her house and to gather her family on the day of the battle (Josh 2:18). If she met these conditions, the Israelites would spare Rahab and her family. The covenant with the two men acted as the sign, but it was nothing more than a formal agreement (Josh 2:19).

The writer of the book of Joshua used the word again shortly after this encounter with Rahab. In this text, Joshua informed the Israelites that the memorial they built was a sign (אות) for their children (Josh 4:6). The sign was a reminder for the Israelites that God brought them into the promised land by crossing the Jordan.[38] The memorial did not have a supernatural element. It stood as a marker for future generations and reminded Israel of what God had done.

The author of 1 Sam 2:34 used אות in the context of a prophet's words to Eli, the high priest. He told Eli that his two sons, Hophni and Phinehas, would die on the same day. Their death would serve as a sign to Eli that he and his family would no longer be anointed by God for the priesthood. Robert Bergen said:

> As a result of the house of Eli's sins, the Lord would "cut short" their "strength." The practical outworking of this judgment was twofold. First, the current generations of Eli's family would suffer penalties: Eli himself would witness distress in the Lord's dwelling,

---

36. This book will follow the Hebrew canonical order.
37. Smith, *History*, Josh 2:8–21.
38. Soggin, *Joshua*, 145.

and Eli's sons, Hophni and Phinehas, would die on the same day, a sign confirming the reality of God's judgment.[39]

According to Bergen, the death of Hophni and Phinehas initiated the downfall of that family line. There does not seem to be a miraculous connotation to their death. Their death confirmed to Eli that God had removed his lineage from the priesthood.

In 1 Sam 10:7 and 9 the author used אות in reference to the confirmation of Saul's anointment as king of Israel. The text reads, "Now when these signs [אתות] meet you, do what your hand finds to do, for God is with you" (1 Sam 10:7). The previous verses described these signs.[40] Samuel told Saul the signs would confirm his anointment.[41] Bergen wrote, "This replay of events in Saul's life would underline the significance of his encounter with Samuel and at the same time confirm the veracity of the divine word spoken through the prophet."[42] Again, the signs themselves did not seem to have a miraculous nature; instead, they acted to confirm what the prophet had already stated. In addition, God did not give them to Saul; Samuel simply designated certain future events as signs.[43] Thus far, each instance has referred to an event or object that became a sign by designation. God did not directly give any of these signs, which will be an important consideration as this book moves forward.

The author of 2 Kgs 19:29 used אות in reference to specific events that would take place after the Assyrians' defeat in Israel. The verse occurred in the context of the siege of Jerusalem by Sennacherib. The Assyrian king seemed to have Hezekiah at the point of surrender when Isaiah prophesied the victory of Israel. At the end of the lengthy polemic against Assyria, the prophet stated that a fruitful harvest would be in Israel's future (2 Kgs 19:29).

The fruitful years would be a sign to the nation that it would recover from the invasion. Paul House asserted, "Here the sign is a natural event that will occur when the Assyrians leave. It will take two full years for the land to be replenished after the invasion, but in the third year all will be well

---

39. Bergen, *Samuel*, 83. Also see Payne, *Samuel*, 300.

40. Also see 1 Sam 14:10, where the author used אות in a similar fashion. The text describes the encounter between the Philistines and Jonathan. The Philistines' response was a sign to Jonathan that he would be victorious in the battle.

41. Robinson, *Samuel*, 60.

42. Bergen, *Samuel*, 128.

43. Brueggemann, *Samuel*, 22–23.

again . . . The sign means Judah has been healed from what appeared to be a terminal illness."[44] Again, the author designated the event as a sign, and it was not miraculous.

The writer of Ezekiel used the word in reference to ordinary events on two different occasions. The first was God's command to Ezekiel to lie on his side as a representation of the siege of Jerusalem (Ezek 4:3). God told Ezekiel that his actions would be a sign for Israel of the upcoming judgment. There does not appear to be any evidence of the supernatural in Ezekiel's actions. Thus, the author used the word in the same manner as the previous authors.

In the second instance, God designated anyone who refused to repent from their idolatry as a sign to others that he would judge them (Ezek 14:8). Again, there appears to be nothing miraculous about this sign. The author used the word in the same manner as the other non-miraculous passages.

The Writings

The word also appears in the Writings of the Old Testament. The author of Job only used the word once, and in a unique manner. The context is Job's reply to the prosperity of the wicked. The text reads, "Have you not asked wayfaring men, and do you not recognize their witness [אֹתֹתָם]?" (Job 21:29 NASB). It appears that the author used the word in reference to the testimony of the "wayfaring men." John Hartley stated, "In turn Job answers their supposed objection with a question, a question that seeks to demonstrate that the friends have not accepted the signs or evidence that travelers offer from what they have seen."[45] There does not seem to be anything out of the ordinary in this passage, nor is there a miraculous connotation. The author employed the word in a unique fashion, but the word still functioned in the same manner. It acted as an authentication of what the travelers said.[46]

The word appears three times in the book of Psalms in reference to ordinary objects or events. The author used אוֹת in Ps 74:4 and 9 in the context of a plea about Israel's enemies trampling over her people. In verse 4, the author specifically mentioned the temple, writing, "Your foes have roared in the midst of your meeting place; they set up their own signs [אֹתֹתָם]

---

44. House, *Kings*, 370.
45. Hartley, *Job*, 320–21. Also see *TDOT*, s.v. אוֹת.
46. Alden, *Job*, 227.

Etymology and Usage of אות

for signs [אֹתוֹת]" (Ps 74:4). It appears the word only represented ordinary artifacts or worship symbols. For example, Geoffrey Grogan stated, "The people's praise has been replaced by the enemy's ugly roar, the temple's divine symbols by military standards, the reverence of worshippers for the fabric of God's house by the sound of destructive tools."[47] Grogan observed that the enemy had replaced the holy symbols of God with their own signals of triumph.

The word reappears later in Ps 86:17. In this context, the psalmist requested a sign of God's favor. It reads, "Show me a sign [אוֹת] of your favor, that those who hate me may see and be put to shame because you, Lord, have helped me and comforted me" (Ps 86:17). It seems that the author of this psalm understood the force of the word. In fact, he asked God directly for the sign as a demonstration of his faithfulness.[48] If provided, the sign from God would prove to the psalmist's enemies that God was with him. The text never answers the question of whether or not God gave the sign; thus, there does not appear to be any miraculous sense to the word.

Rabbi Sholomo Yitzchaki (Rashi) took a different approach to the text. He stated, "However, the Holy One Blessed be He did not need to show the sign during his [King David's] lifetime but rather in the lifetime of Solomon his son when the gates [of the Temple] stuck to each other and would not open until he said, 'Do not reject Your anointed one; remember the loyalty of Your servant David.'"[49] Rashi's interpretation implies the possibility of a miraculous event connected to the request in this psalm, but there is not sufficient evidence to substantiate this claim.

Overall, these passages provide corroboration that authors of the Old Testament used אוֹת to refer to ordinary events or ordinary objects. Again, many of these events were symbolic and did not contain any miraculous connotation. One author summarized, "Though these signs are unmistakably connected externally with the manticism of the ancient Orient, one cannot refer to them as oracular signs. They are signs or symbols, but not magical or mantic actions."[50] Thus, when the authors of the Old Testament used the word in this manner, the sign did not have a miraculous connotation, but it still held a certain degree of significance. These passages also help demonstrate the broad sense of meaning the word carried, depending

---

47. Grogan, *Psalms*, 135–36. Also see Smith, *Psalms*, Ps 74:4.
48. Ross, *Psalms*, 234.
49. Gruber, *Psalms*, 557.
50. *TDNT*, s.v. σημεῖον.

The Hebrew Word for 'sign' and its Impact on Isaiah 7:14

on the context. As noted, the authors of the Old Testament also used the word in close connection to miraculous events. As a result, an analysis of these passages is also necessary.

THE USE OF אוֹת FOR A MIRACULOUS EVENT

Due to the nature of this chapter, it is essential to analyze the use of אוֹת in reference to miraculous events. Alden affirmed, "The word 'sign' either signifies the unusual event itself or in some way points to that unusual event."[51] Alan Amorim observed, "As God was revealing Himself, He used signs to prove and authenticate his person. These miraculous deeds were not a magic trick or an exhibition on the part of the Lord, but they served as a means to an end."[52] Amorim noted that some signs seemed to serve a more distinct purpose than others.

As noted earlier, the authors of the Old Testament used the word almost eighty times. In many instances, the use of the word denoted some sort of divine action. K. H. Rengstorf observed:

> If they [signs] are also symbolical actions it may be seen clearly from the use of אוֹת for them that they are autonomous acts after the manner of divine signs and that they thus have an intrinsic quality of proclamation, so that one must not regard them merely as aids to the delivery of the divine message.[53]

Helfmeyer added, "Like all of God's works, his signs are intended to impart knowledge, and thus they are the 'imperative components of the affirmation of knowledge.'"[54] Thus, it appears that some events occurring in conjunction with אוֹת may have been the result of divine activity. Paul Achtemeier added, "Signs may be miraculous and spectacular, as in the case of those performed by Moses before the people of Israel to demonstrate that God had sent him to them or before Pharaoh for the same purpose."[55] The difficulty lies in determining how the sign functioned and what it meant to those who witnessed it.

---

51. *TWOT*, s.v. אוֹת.

52. Amorim, "Selected Miracles in the Gospels," 16. Also see Spencer, "Symbolizing," 324.

53. *TDNT*, s.v. σημεῖον.

54. *TDOT*, s.v. אוֹת.

55. Achtemeier, *Harper's*, s.v. "sign."

The Law

Authors of the Law, the Prophets, and the Writings all used אות in reference to several events. Each one of these instances helps reveal more information about the word and its significance in the Old Testament. For example, the first appearance of the word in connection with the result of divine activity is the mark that God gave Cain after he murdered his brother Abel. The author of Gen 4:15 wrote, "So the Lord said to him, 'Therefore whoever kills Cain, vengeance will be taken on him sevenfold.' And the Lord appointed a sign [אות] for Cain, so that no one finding him would slay him" (Gen 4:15 NASB). In this context, the word described the type of mark that Cain received from God.

The sign may have provided safety for Cain, possibly to keep the violence from spreading in his family. Matthews wrote, "Perhaps the answer is that by the 'sign' God prevents the spread of bloodshed that otherwise would escalate."[56] The author of the text never described the sign, which has led to varied interpretations. Kent Hughes wrote, "The nature of Cain's sign has been the result of endless speculation. Some have supposed a tattoo, others, a special hairstyle. One of the ancient rabbis argued that the sign was a dog that accompanied Cain on his wanderings."[57] Regardless of what the sign was, the important factor is that God provided it for Cain, thereby interceding in the affairs of humankind. Even if the sign was a change in Cain's appearance, it seems God changed Cain's appearance in miraculous fashion. Furthermore, God directly provided this sign to Cain, which is different from God designating something as a sign.

As previously discussed, God provided Moses with three seemingly miraculous proofs of his calling to return to Egypt. The author of Exod 4:8, 9, and 17 referred to these events as signs. In fact, אות appears in each of these verses.[58] Again, God directly provided these signs for Moses as confirmation of his calling to return to Egypt. The narrative reveals that Moses requested proof of his calling to show the Israelites, and God obliged by giving him these signs.

The next instance of אות in the Law is found in Exod 8:23. In this context, the plagues had already begun. Again, the author of the plague

---

56. Matthews, *Genesis 1–11:26*, 278.

57. Hughes, *Genesis*, 107.

58. Also see Exod 4:28, 30, and 7:3. The word appears again in these first two verses in the same manner and in reference to the plagues in 7:3, which this book will discuss later.

The Hebrew Word for 'Sign' and its Impact on Isaiah 7:14

narrative certainly seemed to consider them to be miraculous. In addition, the author consistently referred to them as signs. Stuart stated:

> The Hebrew term most often used in what we call the plague accounts, however, is 'ot, a word usually connoting "miraculous sign." What Moses recorded in the book of Exodus is actually a series of eleven miraculous signs having in common their indication of God's sovereignty over Egypt, the Egyptians, and their Pharaoh—the final one in the series being an especially great sign both of his sovereignty and of judgment: the imposition of death upon the firstborn of people and animals among the Egyptians ... Thus the signs of sovereignty must not be understood as ends in themselves but as lead-ins to God's great deliverance of his people from bondage to the greatest superpower of their day, a deliverance that was completed only when the Egyptian army was destroyed and Pharaoh's heart broken.[59]

In addition, Randall Bailey wrote, "the familiar 'otot umopatiim, signs and wonders is used ... in these passages, however, the signs and wonders are those miracle or magical actions which are performed ... in order to show him the mighty power of YHWH."[60]

By Exod 8:23, the water had turned into blood, the frogs had come upon the land, and the lice had invaded the homes of the Egyptians. In Exod 8:20–23, God told Pharaoh that he was going to cause a plague of flies on Egypt.[61] This plague was unique because God caused a division between the Egyptians and the Israelites. The division served an important purpose. God said, "But on that day I will set apart the land of Goshen, where my people dwell, so that no swarms of flies shall be there, that you may know that I am the Lord in the midst of the earth" (Exod 8:23).

In Exod 8:23, God said the sign would occur on the following day. The division served as a sign to Pharaoh that God was more powerful than

---

59. Stuart, *Exodus*, 185–86.

60. Bailey, "Plague Narratives," 7–17. While this author does not agree with Bailey's view of the authorship of Exodus, he does affirm Bailey's observation for the purpose of the plagues. In contrast, some scholars do not interpret the plagues as miraculous. See Fretheim, "Plagues," 385–96; Also see Eakin, "Plagues," 473–82; Block, "Plagues," 519–26; Luyster, "Exodus," 155–70; Van Seters, "Plagues," 31–39.

61. There is some confusion about the translation of הֶעָרֹב. The word has traditionally been translated as "flies" due to the Septuagint translation of "dog flies." Overall, the truest sense of the word is some sort of flying insect. For more on this, see Jacob, *Exodus*, 266–67.

he was.⁶² James Bruckner added, "This is the first time knowing God 'in the earth' is mentioned, but not the last (9:14, 29). It is a creational theme concerning knowledge of the creating Lord in the whole world, beginning in Egypt."⁶³ When the flies swarmed the Egyptians but left the Israelites untouched, Pharaoh saw the power of God. Tammi Benjamin and Marc Mangle added, "The text itself provides considerable support that the plagues are to convey a knowledge of God to all who witness them or hear about them."⁶⁴ God provided this division as a sign to Pharaoh. The division appears to be miraculous, and it was evidence of God's power and authority in the land of Egypt.

The next occurrence of the word is in Exod 10:1–2. It appears before the eighth plague, the plague of locusts. God spoke to Moses and said, "Go in to Pharaoh, for I have hardened his heart . . . that I may show these signs [אֹתֹתַי] of mine among them . . . that you may know that I am the Lord" (Exod 10:1–2). The author of the text referred to the plagues as signs, and their purpose was to show the Israelites and Pharaoh that God was more powerful than any Egyptian deity.⁶⁵ Kirk Kilpatrick noted:

> Even the "eye" (עֵין) of the land, the sun, was darkened by the locusts (Exodus 10:15), thus foreshadowing the ninth plague. As a reference to the sun over Egypt, this was a fitting poetic allusion, considering the widely known solar associations with the cult of Horus ("eye of Horus").⁶⁶

God provided the signs so the Egyptians and the Israelites would look to their fulfillment as confirmation of God's words.

In Num 14:22–23, the author of the book referred back to the plagues as signs. The verse reads, "None of the men who have seen my glory and my signs [אֹתֹתַי] that I did in Egypt and in the wilderness, and yet have put me to the test these ten times and have not obeyed my voice, shall see the land that I swore to give to their fathers" (Num 14:22–23). In this context,

---

62. This fact is especially important when one remembers Pharaoh's statement in Exod 5:2, where he said, "Who is the Lord, that I should obey his voice and let Israel go? I do not know the Lord, and moreover, I will not let Israel go." Also see Roderick, "Exodus," 21–22.

63. Bruckner, *Exodus*, 83.

64. Benjamin and Mangel, "Ten Plagues," 17.

65. For more on this, see Davis, *Gods of Egypt*, 128–33; and Hoffmeier, "Arm of God," 378–87.

66. Kilpatrick, "Plagues," 94.

God pronounced a death sentence on those Israelites who repeatedly complained about their condition.

The plagues served as one of the major reasons that God denounced the Israelites' faith. The unbelieving Israelites were evidently supposed to see the plagues as a true demonstration of God's power and his faithfulness. Smith noted, "God expressed to Moses his disappointment with the lack of faith in Israel even after all of the miraculous signs which he had performed in their midst. The Lord expressed his intent to strike down Israel and build a new and even greater nation of Moses."[67] According to Smith, the plagues functioned as signs before and after the Israelites left Egypt.[68]

Later in Num 17:10, the word occurs again in the context of the budding of Aaron's staff. God commanded that the leader of each tribe place his staff in the tent, and the one that budded would be the leader of the priests. The following day, Moses found that Aaron's staff had "produced blossoms, and it bore ripe almonds" (Num 17:8). Immediately after the discovery, God told Moses, "Put back the staff of Aaron before the testimony, to be kept as a sign [אוֹת] for the rebels, that you may make an end of their grumblings against me, lest they die" (Num 17:10). The staff apparently served as a constant reminder to the people that God had chosen Aaron and his family for the priesthood.[69] In fact, as David Stubbs stated:

> Both the authority of Moses and Aaron were being challenged. To put an end to this, the leaders of the tribes were now instructed to bring a staff with their name written on it, and they as well as Aaron were to place their staves in front of the covenant of the tabernacle. The staff that sprouted would be a sign from God about "who is his, and who is holy, and who will be allowed to approach him." The next day, Aaron's staff sprouted . . . That such a test was conducted at all shows that not just anyone could fill the role of high priest; its miraculous nature suggests that a special calling or anointing was required.[70]

---

67. Smith, *Pentateuch*, Num 13:1–14:38.

68. This usage is common. In fact, the plagues are referred to this way consistently throughout the book of Deuteronomy. See Deut 4:34; 6:8, 22; 7:19; 11:3; 26:8; 29:3; 34:11. In each of these instances, the author referred to the plagues as signs. They were to be a constant reminder to Israel that God intentionally brought the Israelites out of Egypt, demonstrating his power to deliver them.

69. Harrison, *Numbers*, 243–45.

70. Stubbs, *Numbers*, 149. Also see Naylor, *Numbers*, 185.

ETYMOLOGY AND USAGE OF אות

Again, God provided this sign directly to the people, and the author of the text evidently considered the event to be miraculous.

The author of Deut 13:1–2 used the word in the context of God's warning against idolatry. The text reads, "If a prophet or a dreamer of dreams arises among you and gives you a sign [אוֹת] or a wonder, and the sign [אוֹת] or wonder that he tells you comes to pass, and if he says, 'Let us go after other gods,' which you have not known, 'and let us serve them,' you shall not listen to the words of that prophet" (Deut 13:1–2). Eugene Merrill stated:

> A "sign" or a "wonder" was any kind of supernatural deed or act that was done to authenticate its performer as a representative of deity . . . But such displays of power could also be performed by false prophets, thereby making it impossible to rely upon these alone as criteria for determining truth. This is why the sign or wonder had to be tested against the message of the prophet, for only when the message was consistent with the whole range of divine revelation could the accompanying miracles be given credibility.[71]

The text implies that a false prophet was capable of performing something miraculous to verify his prophecy. According to Merrill, the determining factor for a prophet's credibility revolved around his guidance on worship. If such a prophet proposed the worship of a false god, then regardless of his sign, Israel was to ignore him and even put him to death (Deut 13:5).[72]

These passages have helped shed light on the way the authors employed the word in reference to miraculous events within the Law. Thus far, God was the author of these signs. His activity in providing these signs helps distinguish these events from others that do not share their supernatural nature. This pattern occurs in the Prophets as well.

The Prophets

As noted earlier, the author of Joshua used אות in 2:12 and 4:6 in reference to ordinary objects. The use of the word in Josh 24:17 is different because it refers to the plagues on Egypt. In fact, the word appears to function in the same manner as when the author of Deuteronomy used it to speak of the

---

71. Merrill, *Deuteronomy*, 231.
72. Also see Von Rad, *Deuteronomy*, 96.

plagues. Joshua 24:17 says, "For it is the Lord our God who brought us and our fathers up from the land of Egypt, out of the house of slavery, and who did those great signs [אתות] in our sight and preserved us in all the way that we went."[73] Again, the author of this verse used the word in reference to the plagues.

In this context, the people responded to Joshua's challenge to fear and serve God. Their response indicates they understood the importance of the plagues as signs from God. David Howard asserted:

> The people rose to Joshua's challenge and promised to serve the Lord, not other gods (vv. 16, 18) . . . The Israelites saw (r'h) in these signs the hand of God, just as God had said that they had seen (r'h, v. 7). Joshua had suggested that perhaps it was evil in their eyes to follow the Lord (v. 15), but they insisted that they did see things aright now, and they would serve him.[74]

The fact that the plagues are specifically mentioned and referred to as signs reinforces Howard's argument.

The author of Judg 6:17 recorded another similar instance of the word. In this passage, the Angel of the Lord visited Gideon. He told Gideon that God was going to remove the yoke of oppression caused by the Midianites (Judg 6:11–16). After the angel told Gideon that he would be the one to lead Israel against Midian, Gideon asked for a sign to confirm his calling. Gideon's request was, "If now I have found favor in your eyes, then show me a sign [אות] that it is you who speak with me" (Judg 6:17). It appears that Gideon wanted verification that God was truly speaking with him.[75] After preparing a meal for the angel, Gideon placed it on a rock. When the angel touched it with his staff, fire consumed the food (Judg 6:21).

Daniel Block observed that Gideon understood the connotation of the sign. Block wrote, "Gideon does not only demand a sign of Yahweh/the messenger but also dictates the nature of the sign . . . While the narrative offers no interpretation of the act, its significance is clear: when a deity consumes the meal a worshiper has brought, this is a sign the latter has found favor in the deity's sight."[76] The sign was not a marker or something

---

73. Also see Jer 32:20–21. The word appears in the same manner in these two verses and directly references the plagues in Egypt.

74. Howard, *Joshua*, 436.

75. Wood, *Judges*, 206–7. Also see Schneider, *Judges*, 105–7; Hamlin, *Judges*, 94.

76. Block, *Judges*, 262–63. For more on the interpretation of this sign as a miracle, see Gunn, *Judges*, 94; McCann, *Judges*, 64; Webb, *Judges*, 148; Brensinger, *Judges*, 82.

of that nature. Rather, it appears the sign was miraculous. Paul Enns added, "The Hebrew word for sign denotes a miracle as a pledge or attestation of divine presence or interposition. The same Hebrew word is used in Exodus 4:8–9, 30 with reference to the miraculous signs in Israel's deliverance from Egypt."[77] Gideon requested a sign, and God obliged by providing one to confirm his calling.

Most scholars affirm that the event appears to be supernatural. For example, J. Alberto Soggin stated, "Here the sign belongs in the sphere of the cult and, one might say, to an earlier phase: the deity has to consume, root *'akal*, literally 'eat,' the offering in a particular manner."[78] John Gray added:

> The "sign," or manifestation of the ultimate power of God in the world of sensible phenomena, authenticates a practical divine command. The phenomenon was often quite natural, miraculous only in respect of coincidence with man's need and the action of God, but in view of the supernatural power so authenticated it tended to be related, especially in saga, as also supernatural.[79]

Although both authors argued that the event might have never taken place, they still acknowledged that it contained a miraculous element.[80] Even Gideon's reaction reinforces this idea. After the fire consumed the food, Gideon said, "Alas, O Lord God! For now I have seen the angel of the Lord face to face" (Judg 6:22).

Another example occurs in 2 Kgs 20:8 and 9, a passage that recounts the illness and healing of Hezekiah. The author of 2 Kgs 20:1 described Hezekiah as being sick to the point of death. The sickness caused Hezekiah to weep, and he called upon God for healing (2 Kgs 20:1–3). God heard his cries and told Hezekiah that he would add fifteen years to his life (2 Kgs 20:5–6). Although Hezekiah believed God's promise, he asked for a sign to confirm it.

Isaiah responded that Hezekiah might ask for one of two signs. The first was for the shadow to lengthen on the steps of Ahaz, and the second was for the shadow to shorten (2 Kgs 20:9). Robert Cohn noted, "Hezekiah requests a sign that he will be healed and, when given the choice of an easy or more difficult miracle, he chooses the latter, involving apparently the

---

77. Enns, *Judges*, 63. See also Martin, *Judges*, 84–85.
78. Soggin, *Judges*, 121. Also see Burney, *Judges*, 191; Simpson, *Judges*, 27–28.
79. Gray, *Judges*, 286.
80. Soggin, *Judges*, 121.

reversal of time by the shortening of a shadow."[81] This reversal of time was clarification that God would heal Hezekiah as he had promised.[82] More than the healing itself, the author emphasized the event that confirmed Hezekiah's recovery.

Moreover, Paul House observed, "Though he [Hezekiah] chooses the far more difficult latter sign, it does occur. His healing thereby takes on miraculous proportions."[83] Peter Leithart added, "Isaiah promised a sign that represents what happened to Hezekiah. His life was moving toward evening, but the Lord reversed the lengthening shadow and gave him a new life."[84] Thus, not only was Hezekiah's healing apparently miraculous, but the reversal of time was also equally supernatural. Furthermore, God provided the sign directly to Hezekiah; he did not designate a future event. This has been an important distinction in determining whether a sign contained a miraculous element.

The final time the word appears in the Prophets is in Jer 44:29. In this context, the author of the text recorded a polemic against Israel. The entire chapter revolves around how God was going to bring judgment on Israel. In verse 29, God declared he would give them a sign of confirmation that this judgment would take place as he said. The verse reads, "This shall be the sign [אוֹת] to you declares the Lord, that I will punish you in this place, in order that you may know that my words will surely stand against you for harm" (Jer 44:29). Apparently, God was going to judge Israel by allowing Babylon to conquer them. F. B. Huey stated:

> In order to emphasize the certainty of punishment of the Jews in Egypt, the Lord gave a sign ... Pharaoh Hophra would be handed over to his enemies as a sign, just as the Lord had handed Zedekiah over to Nebuchadnezzar ... On one occasion Hophra confidently declared, "Not even a god can move me from my throne."[85]

According to Huey, God's deliverance of the pharaoh was a sign that confirmed God's judgment on the nation. The Israelites understood that God had already declared them defeated; thus, their actual defeat would be a complete confirmation of what God had already said. Interestingly,

---

81. Cohn, *2 Kings*, 142.

82. Cf. Voss, *Kings*, 204–5. Voss does not interpret this sign as a miracle.

83. House, *Kings*, 373. Also see Brueggemann, *Kings*, 523; Davis, *Kings*, 302–3; Nelson, *Kings*, 244–45; Fretheim, *Kings*, 205.

84. Leithart, *Kings*, 260.

85. Huey, *Jeremiah*, 370.

God appears to be orchestrating the Israelites' defeat. Thus, the actual sign would seemingly be a miraculous intervention on God's part.

The Writings

As noted, the Law and the Prophets both contain instances in which authors employed אות. According to this author's research, authors used the word in reference to a miraculous event four times in the Writings (Neh 9:10; Ps 78:43; 105:27; 135:9). In each of these instances, the authors addressed the plagues. For example, Ps 78:42–43 reads, "They did not remember his power or the day when he redeemed them from the foe, when he performed his signs [אותות] in Egypt and his marvels in the fields of Zoan." This usage is similar to the author of Deuteronomy's references to the plagues. In both instances, the plagues were a reminder to Israel of what God performed in Egypt on their behalf.[86] Hans-Joachim Kraus wrote, "Again and again, the psalm-singer turns to the wonders of the initial period—the signs in Egypt and the wonders of the fields of Zoan. Now especially the plagues are mentioned in vv. 44ff."[87] Apparently, the plagues were to be a constant reminder of God's power and faithfulness within Israelite history.[88]

Other than the Psalms, אות also appears in the book of Nehemiah. Once again, the usage is in reference to the plagues. Nehemiah states, "And you saw the affliction of our fathers in Egypt and heard their cry at the Red Sea, and performed signs [אותות] and wonders against Pharaoh and all his servants and all the people of his land, for you knew that they had acted arrogantly against our fathers" (Neh 9:9–10). In this context, the people of Israel confessed their sins to God and referred back to their deliverance from Egypt. God gave the plagues as signs, and it appears that Israel consistently recalled these signs as a visual demonstration of God's power over the Egyptian pantheon.

These examples demonstrate that the authors of the Old Testament used אות in reference to miraculous events. The determining factor in whether or not the event was miraculous was how the sign appeared. When God *designated* something as a sign, the object or event was not necessarily miraculous, but when God *gave* the sign, it was miraculous. Overall, the

---

86. Also see Ps 105:27 and 135:9. Both of these passages refer to the plagues in the same manner. For more on these passages, see Margulis, "Plagues," 491–96.

87. Kraus, *Psalms*, 129.

88. Broyles, *Psalms*, 324.

use of the word seems to call attention to an event or object. As Robert Alden summarized, "The word 'sign' either signifies the unusual event itself or in some way points to that unusual event."[89] In order to develop a full understanding of the Old Testament usage of אוֹת, an analysis of the Semitic cognates is also necessary.

SEMITIC COGNATES OF אוֹת

Aramaic

The Aramaic language resembles Hebrew but is nevertheless distinct in certain respects. The authors of the Aramaic portions of the Old Testament used the cognate אָת ('at) similarly to the way the authors of the Hebrew sections used אוֹת. For instance, Rengstorf noted, "אָת, the Aram[aic] equivalent of אוֹת, occurs three times in Dan. at 4:2–3; 6:28, and in different ways all three ref[erences] confirm the picture we now have of the biblical אוֹת."[90] The picture Rengstorf noted is the way אוֹת often refers to an event with a miraculous connotation.

The authors of the Aramaic sections of the Old Testament used the word three times (Dan 4:2–3; 6:27). Ludwig Koehler and Walter Baumgartner said these instances occurred as "a sign confirming the truth of an earlier statement... a miraculous sign, which proves someone's ἐξουσια."[91] The author of Daniel used the word similarly to the other passages mentioned. Robert Vasholz asserted that "about ninety percent of the Aramaic vocabulary in Daniel occurs in fifth-century texts or earlier and maintains that words appearing in the fifth century presuppose their existence in the sixth century."[92] Thus, the use of the word in the book of Daniel helps shed light on the development of the Aramaic equivalent of אוֹת.

The author of Dan 4:2 and 3 recorded Nebuchadnezzar's recognition of Daniel's God as being the true God in heaven. In the text, Nebuchadnezzar proclaimed, "It has seemed good to me to show the signs [אָתַיָּא] and wonders that the Most High God has done for me. How great are his signs [אָתוֹהִי], how mighty his wonders! His kingdom is an everlasting kingdom,

---

89. *TWOT*, s.v. אוֹת.

90. *TDNT*, s.v. σημεῖον.

91. Koehler and Baumgartner, *Lexicon*, s.v. אוֹת.

92. Vasholz, "Daniel," 315–21. For an excellent discussion on the Aramaic of Daniel, see Kitchen, "Daniel," 31–79. Cf. Wesselius, "Daniel," 194–209; Driver, "Daniel," 110–19.

and his dominion endures from generation to generation" (Dan 4:2–3). At this point in the book of Daniel, Nebuchadnezzar was near the end of his reign.[93] He had seen the work of God in several events, and had come to acknowledge that many of the things he had seen were miraculous (e.g., Dan 2:17–45; 3:13–30).

Just as the plagues were a demonstration of God's power over Egypt, these events revealed the might of God to Nebuchadnezzar. Stephen Miller observed:

> Both "signs" and "wonders" describe miraculous manifestations (cf. 6:27) and occur again in the next verse. Yahweh had employed miracles in order to demonstrate his reality and power to Nebuchadnezzar. Not only the earlier fiery furnace episode, but even the experience related in this account was a wondrous sign to the king.[94]

According to Miller, Nebuchadnezzar saw these signs as miracles. In addition, Robert Anderson stated, "The 'signs and wonders' to which the king refers in v. 2 and again in the doxology (v. 3), might well serve as a reminder of the great deeds of God demonstrated in the previous chapter."[95]

The writer of Dan 6:27 recorded the words of King Darius after he discovered that God saved Daniel in the lion's den. In this text, the king proclaimed, "He [God] delivers and rescues; he works signs [אָתִין] and wonders in heaven and on earth, he who has saved Daniel from the power of the lions" (Dan 6:27). The author used the same Aramaic word here to distinguish this event as a sign. Again, Miller wrote, "Both 'signs' ('atin) and 'wonders' (timhin) refer specifically to miracles . . . The purpose of miracles is set forth in this passage. Miracles are not wrought by God to 'show off' but to demonstrate to a lost world that he is the true God and should be honored."[96] Miller asserted that the miracle in this situation was for the audience's benefit. The Aramaic usage of the word in the Old Testament seems to reinforce the idea that the cognate functioned in a similar way as אוֹת.[97] Examining the Akkadian language may reveal even more about how authors of ancient Near Eastern texts used the word.

---

93. Miller, *Daniel*, 128.
94. Ibid., 129.
95. Anderson, *Daniel*, 40.
96. Miller, *Daniel*, 189.
97. *TDNT*, s.v. σημεῖον.

The Hebrew Word for 'sign' and its Impact on Isaiah 7:14

Akkadian

The Akkadian writing system differs vastly from Hebrew, but it was a cognate language to Hebrew during the Old Testament period. Authors of Akkadian texts used the cognate *ittu* similarly to the way Old Testament authors used אות. Rengstorf argued, "The fact is that practically no light at all is shed on the historical understanding of the term by connecting it with the Akkadian *ittu*."[98] Nevertheless, a possible translation of the word is "good omen."[99] Some authors of certain Akkadian texts even used the word in reference to divine action. The similar usage seems to provide an objective bridge between the two words.

One author used it in reference to signs from the gods. For instance, another text stated, "He [the god] showed his propitious sign to my people."[100] The author did not describe the sign, but it was apparently something supernatural. Another text read, "My lord (i.e., the river god) has given me (lit. shown) a sign, now would my lord amplify the sign he has given."[101] Again, there is no description of the sign, but there is a direct reference to the deity providing the sign. Still another text stated, "The signs occurring in the sky as well as those on the earth give us signals, heaven and earth bring us omens in the same way, they are not released separately (because) heaven and earth are interconnected."[102] These signs seem to have a direct correlation to divine activity, which would coincide with some signs in the Old Testament.

Furthermore, the Akkadian creation epic known as the *Enuma Elish* states, "I [Marduk] [have appointed] a sign, follow its path, approach and give judgment."[103] In this text, the Akkadian account of creation refers to the moon as the sign that Marduk provided. Although this evidence is not conclusive, several authors apparently used the word in a similar fashion to the Hebrew word. Perhaps an analysis of the Greek word σημεῖον will reveal more about the interpretation of אות.

---

98. Ibid.
99. Tawil, *Akkadian*, 9.
100. Oppenheim, *I and J*, s.v. "*ittu*."
101. Ibid.
102. Tawil, *Akkadian*, 8.
103. Speiser, "Creation Epic," 1, 28.

THE USE OF ΣΗΜΕΙΟΝ[104]

The Greek language is still further separated from Hebrew than Akkadian. Yet the translators of the Septuagint (LXX) translated the Old Testament Hebrew into Greek, and the New Testament writers quoted the Greek Old Testament on numerous occasions. In addition, authors of classical Greek works also used the word. Thus, an examination of how Greek authors used the equivalent will shed light on the meaning of σημεῖον, the word used to translate אוֹת for the Greek-speaking world.

Etymology

The Greek word, σημεῖον (sēmeion), functioned in a similar manner as אוֹת. The etymology of the word is uncertain, but its usage is clear. Rengstorf noted, "σημεῖον is a development of σῆμα . . . It shares with σῆμα/σᾶμα the sense of 'sign,' 'characteristic,' 'mark,' with its many nuances. Etymological research has hardly reached any assured results regarding the original sense of the word."[105] Although the etymology is unclear, authors used the word consistently in their writings. Translators commonly render the word as "A sign, a mark, token," but it could also mean "a sign from the gods, [or] an omen."[106] Thus, the word initially shows several parallels to its Hebrew counterpart.

Joseph Thayer defined σημεῖον as a "sign, prodigy, portent, i.e., an unusual occurrence transcending the common course of nature."[107] William Arndt and F. Wilbur Gingrich stated the word could mean a "miracle of divine origin, performed by God himself, by Christ, or by men of God."[108] Evidently, σημεῖον could carry the same connotations as אוֹת. Thayer went on to say that the word could refer to "miracles and wonders by which God authenticates the men sent by him, or by which men prove that the cause they are pleading is God's."[109] According to Thayer, the word functioned

---

104. For more on the development of this word, see Charlier, "La Notion du Signe," 434–48.
105. *TDNT*, s.v. σημεῖον. Also see McCasland, "Signs," 150.
106. Liddell, *Lexicon*, s.v. σημεῖον.
107. Thayer, *Lexicon*, s.v. σημεῖον.
108. Arndt and Gingrich, *Lexicon*, s.v. σημεῖον.
109. Thayer, *Lexicon*, s.v. σημεῖον.

The Hebrew Word for 'sign' and its Impact on Isaiah 7:14

in the same way as אות. An analysis of the development of σημεῖον will disclose more about how the word functioned in ancient texts.

Development

Classical Usage[110]

Homer

Historians traditionally credit Homer with writing the *Iliad* and the *Odyssey*. Although he did not use σημεῖον, he did use σῆμα, which, as noted earlier, eventually morphed into σημεῖον. The word appeared first in the *Iliad* as a reference to the lightning of Zeus at the beginning of the expedition against Troy. According to these ancient writings, the Greek gods often helped humankind determine which decision they should make.

A key event in the fourth book of the *Iliad* provides a clear example of this type of divine interaction. The Achaeans and Trojans decided to allow a duel between Menelaus and Paris. After Menelaus defeated Paris, some sort of meteor passed through both armies.[111] Although the word for sign never appears in the text, apparently both armies perceived it as some sort of divine intervention on how to proceed. Hermann Frankel wrote, "Trojans and Achaeans see the miraculous sign and ask whether it signifies a new battle."[112] Thus, it seems that the author may have used the word for miraculous signs from the gods.

Later in the *Iliad*, the author used σῆμα to describe a specific sign from the gods. The text reads, "For he [Zeus] lightened on our right shewed forth signs [σήματα] of good."[113] In this context, the signs from Zeus were a good omen to those who witnessed them because they assured the witnesses that he was aware of the upcoming conflict.

Homer also applied the word to ordinary objects. For example, in Hector's challenge to the Achaeans, there is a mark used to distinguish who would fight. The author used σῆμα to describe that mark.[114] This event does not seem to have a supernatural element. Interestingly, the author did not

110. The author has chosen specific writers who use the word in a more prominent manner. This selection is by no means exhaustive regarding the classical works.

111. Homer, *The Iliad*, 153–57.

112. Frankel, *Poetry*, 65.

113. Homer, *Iliad*, 77.

114. Ibid., 317.

record any supernatural activity either. This may suggest that even Greek authors understood that the presence of divine action determined whether a sign was miraculous.

The word appeared again later, when the author wrote: "And Zeus, son of Cronos, shows them signs [σήματα] upon the right with his lightnings, and Hector exulting greatly in his might rageth furiously, trusting in Zeus, and recketh not of men nor gods, for mighty madness hath possessed him."[115] Apparently, the signs provided Hector with confidence in the midst of the battle. Furthermore, the signs came directly from Zeus, and they had a miraculous element.

The author of the *Odyssey* used the word in the same manner. The writer first used the word in Odysseus' prayer to Zeus for a sign. Zeus answered Odysseus' prayer with a loud thunderclap, which the author described using the Greek word τέρας (*teras*). The thunder sparked the interest of a nearby girl who found the sound of thunder curious since there were no clouds in the sky.[116] The narrator wrote, "She now stopped her mill and spoke a word, a sign [σῆμα] for her master."[117] The sign was the spoken word from the girl, but the thunder was what enticed her to speak. Rengstorf provided a brief explanation of the event: "Related is the fact that in its whole range of usage σῆμα—and later σημεῖον—is orientated to a clear statement or assertion which holds good irrespective of explanations."[118] The usage of the word in these contexts demonstrates that it carried a wide variety of meanings, but it helped bring attention to a specific event.

Herodotus

Herodotus also used the early version of σημεῖον, but only in reference to some sort of monument. He wrote, "There is in Lydia the tomb [σῆμα] of Alyattes, the father of Croesus, the base whereof is made of great stones and the rest of it of mounded earth."[119] In this instance, the author used the word to describe an enormous tomb or monument. The writer did not record the presence of any divine activity, and the text seems devoid of

---

115. Ibid., 399.
116. Ibid., *Odyssey*, 281.
117. Ibid., 283.
118. *TDNT*, s.v. σημεῖον.
119. Godley, *Herodotus*, 123.

a supernatural element. This example is another illustration of the broad sense that the word carried in ancient literature.

Philo

The Jewish historian Philo used the word in his works. However, he rarely used it in reference to any sort of miraculous events. One author wrote, "Yet he [Philo] also uses *sēmeion* in wider Greek senses, e.g., for symptom or proof. In allegory it has the meaning 'pointer.' The Bible is for Philo a treasury of *sē meía*. Miracles, however, play little part in his usage."[120]

Josephus

Flavius Josephus, also a Jewish historian, wrote extensively about biblical events and provided a commentary on portions of Scripture. He also commented on various historical events. Throughout his works, there are several instances where he used σημεῖον. In one example, he wrote, "And when the Jews petitioned him again, he gave a signal [σημεῖον] to the soldiers to encompass them round, and threatened that their punishment should be no less than immediate death, unless they would leave off disturbing him, and go their ways home."[121] The signal that he referred to in this context does not seem to carry any sort of miraculous connotation; rather, it acted as a normal sign for an action to commence.

Another occurrence seems to point to some sort of supernatural event. The author wrote, "A false prophet was the occasion of these people's destruction, who had made a public proclamation in the city that very day, that God commanded them to get up upon the temple, and that there they should receive miraculous signs [σημεῖα] of their deliverance."[122] In this context, the author implied that these signs would be miraculous. The text contained a seemingly miraculous event, which the author attributed to divine activity.

In one final example, the author commented on the proofs that God gave to Moses at his commissioning. Josephus employed σημεῖον in referring to them as signs. He wrote, "Upon the wonder that Moses showed at

---

120. *TDNT*, s.v. σημεῖον.
121. Josephus, *Ant.*, 18.58.
122. Ibid., *Wars*, 6.285.

these signs [σημεῖα], God exhorted him to be of good courage."[123] The word functioned in the same manner as אות in the original passage, which reinforces the idea that σημεῖον might have been used interchangeably. Thus, a brief examination of the way the word appears in the Septuagint will help shed light on this possibility.

The Septuagint

The usage of σημεῖον in the Septuagint reveals the way that the translators of the Hebrew text interpreted אות. For example, the translators used σημεῖον consistently in their translation of אות. Rengstorf noted, "If in the LXX אות is normally transl.[ated] σημεῖον, this is adequate proof how close the two words are by nature. Σημεῖον shares fully with אות the distinctive feature that it applies more to the technical side of a process than its result."[124] It seems that when the translators chose to use σημεῖον in place of אות, they used the closest Greek word to convey the correct meaning.

Rengstorf later added, "LXX usage compels us even in instances where σημεῖον is used directly or indirectly for God's action to recognize quite unequivocally the formal character which is proper to the word by nature and which is only strengthened by its Semitic equivalent אות."[125] The translators evidently felt that σημεῖον was the best word to use in place of אות. The two languages differ in many ways, but σημεῖον seems to be synonymous. Furthermore, every previously analyzed Old Testament passage that contained אות used σημεῖον in the translation. Such consistency is substantial evidence that the translators understood the meaning of אות and employed the closest Greek word. To continue the development of this possibility, an analysis of how the authors of the apocryphal works used the word is necessary.

---

123. Ibid., *Ant.*, 2.274, 276, 280.
124. *TDNT*, s.v. σημεῖον.
125. Ibid.

The Hebrew Word for 'sign' and its Impact on Isaiah 7:14

Apocryphal Works

Wisdom of Solomon[126]

One occurrence of σημεῖον in the apocryphal works appears in the Wisdom of Solomon. The text reads, "[E]ven so we in like manner, as soon as we were born, began to draw to our end, and had no sign [σημεῖον] of virtue to shew; but were consumed in our own wickedness" (Wis 5:13 Cambridge Paragraph Bible).[127] The author did not seem to reference anything miraculous; instead, these words seem to reference an ordinary display of virtue.

The next appearance of σημεῖον seems to imply an event with a miraculous connotation. The author of the text wrote, "If a man desire much experience, she knoweth things of old, and conjectureth aright what is to come: she knoweth the subtilties of speeches, and can expound dark sentences: she foreseeth signs [σημεῖα] and wonders, and the events of seasons and times" (Wis 8:8). The conjunction with "wonders" (τέρατα) provides reasonable evidence that these signs may have had a miraculous connotation. Thus, the author's use of the word reinforces the support from the previously examined passages.

Sirach[128]

The author of the book of Sirach used σημεῖον in 42:18.[129] He wrote, "He seeketh out the deep, and the heart, and considereth their crafty devices; for the Lord knoweth all that may be known, and he beholdeth the signs [σημεῖον] of the world" (Sir 42:18).[130] In this context, the writer used the word in reference to the natural signs of the universe. Thus, this usage parallels those passages that refer to ordinary objects.

---

126. It is not within the scope of the book to discuss the authorship or original language of the Wisdom of Solomon. Rather, the author will assume that the Greek translations and writings are accurate. For more on this, see Purinton, "Wisdom of Solomon," 276–304; Reymond, "Wisdom of Solomon," 385–99; Baars, "Wisdom of Solomon," 230–33.

127. All other apocryphal quotations will be taken from the Cambridge Paragraph Bible unless otherwise noted.

128. Again, it is not within the scope of the book to address the authorship of this work. For more, see Baars, "Sirach," 280–81.

129. For the significance of Greek authorship, see Hartman, "Sirach," 443–51.

130. Cf. Sir 43:6–7.

ETYMOLOGY AND USAGE OF אות

In the next occurrence, the writer used the word with a miraculous connotation. He recorded, "By his words he caused the wonders [σημεῖα] to cease, and he made him glorious in the sight of kings, and gave him a commandment for his people, and shewed him part of his glory" (Sir 45:3). The translator chose to use "wonders" instead of "signs." The context of the passage revolves around the role that Moses played in Scripture. The language suggests that the word could be referencing the plagues in Egypt.

Second Maccabees

The writer of Second Maccabees used the word in 6:13, where he wrote: "For it is a token [σημεῖον] of his great goodness, when wicked doers are not suffered any long time, but forthwith punished."[131] This usage holds no miraculous connotation. The author referenced the destruction of Jerusalem when mentioning the token. Thus, the exile would seem to be the focus of the passage. The writer appears to be claiming that the exile was part of the judgment of God as a sign of his goodness.[132]

Baruch

The final appearance of the word in the apocryphal works occurs in Bar 2:11. The text reads:

> And now, O Lord God of Israel, that hast brought thy people out of the land of Egypt with a mighty hand, and high arm, and with signs [σημείοις], and with wonders, and with great power, and hast gotten thyself a name, as appeareth this day: O Lord our God, we have sinned, we have done ungodly, we have dealt unrighteously in all thine ordinances. (Bar 2:11)

The context of the verse is within the author's confession to God for the sins of the nation (Bar 2:1–20). The author refers to the events in Egypt as signs and wonders. As already noted, this was a common term for the plagues, and the author of this text seems to apply it in the same manner as the Old Testament authors. This usage coincides with other passages that

---

131. Also, see 2 Macc 15:35 and 3 Macc 6:32.

132. One could argue that the judgment on Israel was a miraculous event brought about as an act of God, but the text does not seem to indicate that it was to be perceived as miraculous.

use the word in reference to miraculous events. A brief examination of the way the authors of the New Testament used the word will help shed more light on the Greek word.

The New Testament

The Gospels

The authors of the New Testament Gospels used σημείοις forty-eight times.[133] According to this author's research, Matthew used the word thirteen times in his gospel. However, most of these occurrences involved the Jews asking Jesus for a sign. For instance, in Matt 12:39 the author wrote, "But he answered them, 'An evil and adulterous generation seeks for a sign [σημεῖον], but no sign [σημεῖον] will be given to it except the sign [σημεῖον] of the prophet Jonah.'" In this context, the Jews claimed that Jesus was performing work with the power of Beelzebul (Matt 12:27). In order to prove that his power was from God, the Pharisees asked him to provide some sort of sign.[134] Jesus did not perform a miracle at that time; rather, he referred to the sign of Jonah.

Some debate exists about what Jesus meant when he referred to the sign of Jonah. There are three traditional interpretations of the sign. Some scholars claim the sign was the resurrection of Jesus. Craig Blomberg asserted, "The only sign Jesus will provide, therefore, is the 'sign' that is Jonah. Jonah's languishing in the big fish for three days parallels the period of Jesus' death. But since Jesus would only remain dead for three days, the 'sign' must include his resurrection as well."[135] Blomberg interpreted the passage to refer to the resurrection of Jesus on the third day; thus, it functioned as the sign that God sent him.

Authors who hold to the second position assert that the sign was the death of Jesus. Scholars who hold this position claim that Jonah died in the belly of the fish, thus Jesus foretold his own death.[136] Both of these

---

133. Thayer, *Lexicon*, s.v. σημεῖον.

134. Hauerwas, *Matthew*, 123–24.

135. Blomberg, *Matthew*, 206. Also see Long, *Matthew*, 142; Turner, *Matthew*, 326–27; Osborne, *Matthew*, 485–86; Hobbs, *Matthew*, 157.

136. Hendrickson, *Matthew*, 532–23; Woodhouse, "Jesus and Jonah," 33–41; Hare, *Matthew*, 279.

positions have some credibility, but their weakness is in how Jonah was a sign to Nineveh. If Jonah himself was a sign to Nineveh, Jonah's death or resurrection would have made little difference to them, given that they probably never saw either occur.

The third position is that the sign revolved around Jesus' preaching. For example, Jonah went and preached to Nineveh in order to bring about their repentance, and Jesus preached repentance in the same way. Eugene Merrill stated:

> Since the Lord Jesus, according to both Matthew and Luke, spoke of Jonah as constituting in himself a sign to ancient Nineveh, a sign so persuasive that the population from king to peasant repented, something in Jonah's experience must be found to provide adequate explanation for his effectiveness. In Matthew attention is drawn to Jonah's having been in the belly of the fish for three days and three nights, but since Luke specifies that Jonah was a sign to Nineveh that experience in the fish must have been communicated to the Assyrian capital and have become to the Ninevites a sign that Jonah was a divine messenger. Such a sign would be particularly convincing to a people whose aetiology taught them that their city had been founded by a fish-god. The spectacular and timely arrival of Jonah among them created a curiosity and receptivity to his message that would have been possible in no other way. When the truth of the message of Yahweh was then proclaimed, the response was the repentance and faith recounted in the sacred text. Jesus, basing his own appeal for repentance on this account, argues *a fortiori* that if the pagan Ninevites repented at the preaching of the foreigner Jonah so much more ought his own generation to repent, "for a greater than Jonah is here."[137]

Merrill's argument is convincing, given that he considers all interpretations to be somewhat correct. Frederick Bruner took a similar position when he stated: "I wonder if all three opinions—Jesus' preaching, death, and resurrection—might unite in a fourth—Jesus himself in his historical career is God's sign, so that we do not have to choose a particular feature of his work."[138]

---

137. Merrill, "Sign of Jonah," 29–30.

138. Bruner, *Matthew*, 574. Cf. Matt 16:1, 2, 4; Mark 8:11, 12; Luke 11:29. The author of Luke seems to indicate that Jonah was indeed the sign. The grammatical construction of the sentence also strengthens this position. The structure is an appositional genitive, which would make the sentence read, "the sign of the prophet Jonah." The construction makes Jonah the focus of the sign. For more on this, see Turner, *Grammatical*, 60.

The real importance of this event is that both the Pharisees and Jesus understood σημεῖον to refer to some sort of authentication event. The event may or may not have been miraculous.[139] Regardless, the word carried a degree of prominence insofar as the author used it in reference to the Pharisees' request for proof of Jesus' authority. Furthermore, Jesus understood its significance and referred to another authentication event.

The author of Matthew used the word again in Matt 24:3 in the context of the signs that may come at the end of the age. He wrote, "As he sat on the Mount of Olives, the disciples came to him privately, saying, 'Tell us when will these things be, and what will be the sign [σημεῖον] of your coming and of the close of the age?'" (Matt 24:3). In this context, the disciples apparently referenced some sort of marker or signal that would indicate Jesus' return was imminent.[140]

One of the more controversial parts of the Gospel of Mark also contains a brief use of σημεῖον. The author of Mark 16:17–18 wrote:

> And these signs [σημεῖα] will accompany those who believe: in my name they will cast out demons; they will speak in new tongues; they will pick up serpents with their hands; and if they drink any deadly poison, it will not hurt them; they will lay their hands on the sick, and they will recover.[141]

The usage of the word in this passage seems to refer to the authentication events that surrounded those who were true followers of Jesus.[142] The author of Acts recorded several seemingly miraculous events that authenticated the apostles' authority (cf. Acts 2:5–13; 28:3–5).

The only other occurrences of σημεῖον in the Synoptic Gospels all seem to refer to simple objects or events. For example, the author of Luke used the word in reference to the clothes Mary wrapped Jesus in as a sign to the shepherds that he was the baby the angels had told them about (Luke 2:12). The writer of Matt 26:48 used the word in relation to the kiss Judas gave to Jesus as a sign to the men arresting Jesus that he was the one they

---

139. Cf. Luke 23:8. The word occurs here in reference to the sign that Herod hoped to see upon meeting Jesus. The usage seems to indicate that he expected some sort of miracle.

140. Cf. Matt 24:30; Luke 21:7, 11, 25. The word appears in each of these passages in a similar fashion.

141. See Brooks, *Mark*, 271–75 for a discussion on the authorship of this passage.

142. Williamson, *Mark*, 288. Also see Moloney, *Mark*, 361.

sought. These passages do not have a miraculous connotation, but they also do not suggest any divine activity.

The author of the Gospel of John used σημεῖον in a way that helps demonstrate a distinct quality of the word that the other gospels do not conclusively prove.[143] James Boice noted, "[I]n John a sign is always something that pointed to reality greater than itself."[144] Boice provided an insight into the way the author of John used the word.[145] It appears that the author understood the possibility of σημεῖον carrying a miraculous connotation; thus, he consistently used the word in connection with Jesus' miracles.[146]

The author of John consistently referred to Jesus' miracles as signs. Rengstorf remarked, "The distinctiveness of the Johannine use of σημεῖον is that here, both in the Gospel and Rev., the word has taken over the role which σημεῖον plays elsewhere in the NT and especially in the Synoptics, namely, as the exclusive term for certain miraculous events."[147] William Dennison added, "John uses the word *semeion* in the sense of 'pointer' and 'mark' in the full sense of the formal character of the word, i.e., it preserves the richness of the word carried over from the Old Testament."[148] Rengstorf and Dennison both conclude that the use of σημεῖον in John helps expose more about the purpose and meaning of אות.

The writer of John first used σημεῖον in reference to the miracle of water turned into wine at the wedding in Cana (John 2:11). The author wrote, "This, the first of his signs [σημείων], Jesus did at Cana in Galilee, and manifested his glory. And his disciples believed in him" (John 2:11). Immediately, the author of the passage referred to this event as a sign. Regardless of the validity of the account, the author of the text used σημεῖον as a way to bring attention to the event. Urban von Wahlde stated that the text's "purpose is to affirm that not only have the disciples seen the miracle (sign) and believed, but they have seen the glory of Jesus revealed in the sign."[149] Thus, the author of John used the sign to point to the authentication of Jesus as God.[150]

---

143. For more the word in John, see Mollat, "Le Semeion Johannique," 209–18.
144. Boice, *John*, 203.
145. Also see Wood and Marshall, *Dictionary*, s.v. "sign."
146. Cf. John 2:23; 3:2; 4:54; 6:2, 14, 26; 7:31; 9:16; 10:11; 11:47; 12:18; 12:37; 20:30.
147. *TDNT*, s.v. σημεῖον.
148. Dennison, "Miracles," 192.
149. Von Wahlde, *John*, 93.
150. Michaels, *John*, 48. This seemed to be the normal way the author of John

The Hebrew Word for 'Sign' and its Impact on Isaiah 7:14

The author of John used σημεῖον again in John 2:18–19, where he wrote, "So the Jews said to him, 'What sign [σημεῖον] do you show us for doing these things?' Jesus answered them, 'Destroy this temple, and in three days I will raise it up.'" The encounter here is similar to the account found in the Synoptics, but Jesus' answer in this instance is unique to this account. Evidently, the Jews sought some sort of sign to prove that Jesus was authoritative.[151] Jesus did not provide such a sign to appease their request, but he did refer to his own death (John 2:21–22). Gerald Borchert wrote, "Instead of giving the demanding Jews a magical proof, Jesus offered them a prediction concerning destruction and rising. If they had had ears to recognize it, they would have understood that the prediction could have served as a sign."[152] It appears that the word may have carried a miraculous connotation in this context.

The author of John used the word four times in chapter 6. The context is the crowd's confession that they believed God sent Jesus based on the signs that he performed. John 6:14 says, "When the people saw the sign that he had done, they said, 'This is indeed the Prophet who is to come into the world!'"[153] The narrator of the text continually reminds the reader that the Jews followed Jesus based on the miracles that he performed (John 6:2, 15, 26). As Francis Moloney summarized:

> [M]any came to Jesus when they saw the sign that Jesus did, but he did not entrust himself to them. The reader is aware that the people have not moved beyond the faith that originally drew them to follow Jesus, "because they saw the signs that he did" (6:2). They are still looking for a figure who would satisfy their needs and expectations.[154]

Apparently, the writer of John purposefully mentioned these signs as authentication of who Jesus was, and he reiterated that the crowds still rejected Jesus on many occasions. The signs were present, but it seems that the people may not have always recognized their ultimate purpose.

---

employed the word. Due to the brevity of this section, there is not sufficient space to analyze each instance of the word. Cf. John 2:23; 3:2; 4:54; 6:2, 14, 26; 7:31; 9:16; 10:11; 11:47; 12:18; 12:37; 20:30. The author of John employed a similar usage of the word in each of these passages.

151. Borchert, *John*, 165.
152. Ibid.
153. For a good analysis of this passage, see Hughes, *John*, 185–91.
154. Moloney, *Signs*, 37.

Overall, the word appears to be synonymous with the miracles recorded in the Gospel of John. Homer Hailey stated, "Of all the miracles done by Jesus, John selects seven which he weaves into his Gospel as signs, which testify to Christ's deity, and establish John's proposition that Jesus is the Christ."[155] In addition, the author of the book of Acts employed a similar usage.

Acts

According to this author's research, the author of Acts used σημεῖον thirteen times.[156] He also used it in a similar manner as the author of John. Peter's sermon on Pentecost made Jesus' miracles synonymous with signs. Peter said, "Men of Israel, hear these words: Jesus of Nazareth, a man attested to you by God with mighty works and wonders and signs [σημείοις] that God did through him in your midst, as you yourselves know" (Acts 2:22-23). It appears that the reference to the signs was a reminder of the miracles that Jesus performed in their midst, and thus that the miracles should have authenticated Jesus' claims.[157]

Just as the word referenced Jesus' miracles as authentication of who he was, the author of Acts also used the word synonymously with the miracles of the apostles. In Acts 2:42 he wrote, "And awe came upon every soul, and many wonders and signs [σημεῖα] were being done through the apostles."[158] The word seems to refer to the works performed by the apostles.[159] There is no clear indication as to what all of these works were, but they instilled a great amount of respect and fear in those who witnessed them. The narrator of the text seems to associate the works with signs in the same manner as the author of John. A brief look at the Epistles will continue the development of this chapter.

---

155. Hailey, *John*, 106.
156. *TDNT*, s.v. σημεῖον.
157. Polhill, *Acts*, 112.
158. Pelikan, *Acts*, 97–98.
159. Cf. Acts 4:16, 22; 8:6.

The Hebrew Word for 'sign' and its Impact on Isaiah 7:14

The Epistles

The authors of the Epistles do not use the word as often as the gospel writers, but it still occurs nine times in five different books.[160] The first significant occurrence is in 1 Cor 1:22, where the author wrote: "For Jews demand signs [σημεῖα] and Greeks seek wisdom."[161] The writer of the text used the word in reference to the miracles that the Jews sought in order to authenticate a claim given by a prophet. The usage is similar to the way the word appeared in the gospels. The author of this text understood that the word could refer to a possible miracle. In fact, he used it in order to contrast the wisdom that the Greeks sought. The signs that the Jews sought seemed to be a way for them to ignore who Jesus claimed to be. Roy Ciampa and Brian Rosner stated:

> Likewise, when Jews demand signs, or "miracles for proof" (TEV), that God is at work, this is not a legitimate, open-minded plea, but an obstinate insistence on a powerful confirmation of God's deliverance that renders faith unnecessary. Ironically, the cross is in fact a genuine sign and true wisdom from God (v. 24b).[162]

Both Ciampa and Rosner viewed the use of the word in this context as referring to some sort of miraculous proof.

The next occurrence worthy of examination is 2 Cor 12:12. The author wrote, "The signs [σημεῖα] of a true apostle were performed among you with utmost patience, with signs [σημείοις] and wonders and mighty works" (2 Cor 12:12). Again, the word seems to refer to the works performed as authentication of a true apostle. The text does not indicate whether these works were miraculous, but the word functioned in a similar way as the previously mentioned passages. Marvin Vincent said, "[T]he passage is remarkable as containing (what is rare in the history of miracles) a direct claim to miraculous powers by the person to whom they were ascribed."[163]

The author of 2 Thess 3:17 wrote, "I, Paul, write this greeting with my own hand. This is the sign [σημεῖον] of genuineness in every letter of mine; it is the way I write." The use of the word in this context demonstrates that, like אות, the word did not always reference a miracle or miraculous event. The narrator appealed to his own handwriting as the sign that he composed

---

160. *TDNT*, s.v. σημεῖον.
161. The word also appears in Rom 4:11 in reference to the sign of circumcision.
162. Ciampa and Rosner, *Corinthians*, 99.
163. Vincent, *Studies*, 3:357.

the letter. There does not seem to be any miraculous connotation to the sign whatsoever.

The writer of Heb 2:4 wrote, "[W]hile God also bore witness by signs [σημείοις] and wonders and various miracles and by gifts of the Holy Spirit distributed according to his will." Wonders (τέρασιν) and miracles (δυνάμεσιν) appear in conjunction with signs. It seems that each of these words may denote a different type of action. For example, is a "wonder" different from a "miracle," or are they different words to describe the same event? Kenneth Wuest clarified, "These miraculous manifestations were in the form of signs, 'a sign, mark or token miraculous in nature,' [and] wonders, 'something so strange as to cause it to be watched, miraculous in nature.'"[164] According to Wuest, these words all seem to describe the same events, but each word provides a unique perspective. The event witnessed as a sign may cause a different reaction in the viewer than the same event witnessed as a wonder.

Revelation

The writer of Revelation used σημεῖον seven times.[165] The author used the word in two distinct ways. The first way was to use it in reference to special events. For example, the writer of Rev 12:1 said, "And a great sign [σημεῖον] appeared in heaven: a woman clothed with the sun, with the moon under her feet, and on her head a crown of twelve stars."[166] The author used the word to indicate that the event he witnessed had special implications for those witnessing it.[167] John Walvoord wrote:

> Undoubtedly the sign provoked wonder, but the translation "a great sign" is more accurate, since John did not use the Greek word for wonder (*teras*). This was the first of a series of events called "signs" or "miracles." As signs they were symbols of something that God was about to reveal and usually contained an element of prophetic warning.[168]

---

164. Wuest, *Studies*, Heb 2:4.
165. *TDNT*, s.v. σημεῖον.
166. Cf. Rev 12:3 and 15:1.
167. Ford, *Revelation*, 188. Also see Shea and Christian, "Revelation," 269–92.
168. Walvoord, *Revelation*, 176.

According to Walvoord, the event functioned as a sign. It also had direct connection to divine activity and a miraculous connotation.

The second way the word appears is in reference to the works of false prophets and demons. Revelation 16:14 reads, "For they are demonic spirits, performing signs, who go abroad to the kings of the whole world, to assemble them for battle on the great day of God the Almighty."[169] The usage in this context seems to refer to the powerful works that these demonic spirits performed. The author used the word in a similar manner as other passages that referenced miracles; thus, it seems to be the best interpretation here.[170] Overall, the New Testament authors used the word consistently in their writings. It appears that they understood how the word could function to denote either a miraculous event or describe a simple object.

CONCLUSION

The research put forth of this chapter has demonstrated that the authors of the books of the Old Testament used אות in relation to ordinary objects or events. The research also provided numerous instances where writers used the word in reference to miraculous events. One key factor that seems to help distinguish the difference between miraculous and non-miraculous usage is the presence of divine activity. If God was the author of the sign, then the sign appeared to have a miraculous connotation. In contrast, there were several instances in which God designated certain objects or events as signs, but they never contained any supernatural element. The difference here is that God did not directly provide these things as signs; rather, he simply designated them to act as a sign for those who witnessed them.

The statistical evidence substantiates the idea that a God-given sign was miraculous. As noted, the authors of the Old Testament used אות seventy-nine times. In thirty-eight instances, there is evidence of direct divine activity by which God provided something as a sign. All thirty-eight of those occurrences contained a supernatural element.[171] In contrast, the remaining forty-one instances were designated as signs or symbolic actions that did not have a miraculous connotation.

The research also helped examine the various equivalents of אות. Out of these words, the Greek word σημεῖον was most useful in showing the

169. Cf. Rev 13:13, 14; 19:20.
170. Oakley, *Revelation*, 149.
171. See Appendix A.

Etymology and Usage of אוֹת

broad sense of the word. Authors of several classical works, several apocryphal works, and many authors of the New Testament all used the Greek equivalent similarly to the way the Old Testament authors used אוֹת. There were times when the word functioned to denote a miraculous event, and there were instances where the word only pointed towards an ordinary object or event. Again, even in the classical usage of the word, the presence of divine activity often dictated whether there was a supernatural element to the sign. Rengstorf summarized it best:

> This is, of course, esp[ecially] true when the subject of the σημεῖον is a divine person who in this way wants to tell a man something or to give him necessary information. In such cases the σημεῖον is more embracing than the oracle or dream but it also needs a relevant and competent explanation which will lead to correct understanding . . . If the ref[erence] is religious it may be a miracle. But it is this, not because it is called σημεῖον, but because in this case God is the author of the σημεῖον, as in other cases with a purely human ref[erence] men are the authors.[172]

Thus, a sign may or may not be miraculous, depending on the author and nature of the sign. Still, a brief examination of another common Hebrew word will further the development of this book.

---

172. *TDNT*, s.v. σημεῖον.

3

Etymology and Usage of מוֹפֵת

As already noted, אוֹת carried a broad range of meaning in the Old Testament. In contrast, the Hebrew word מוֹפֵת (*mopēt*) had a more focused meaning. Still, the two words had similar meanings and described the same event in certain circumstances.[1] In fact, the authors of the Old Testament used מוֹפֵת and אוֹת parallel to each other on eight different occasions.[2] In order to understand how the two words shared similar nuances but also had distinct qualities, a detailed analysis of מוֹפֵת is necessary.

The authors of the Old Testament used the word thirty-six times.[3] Fourteen of those times occurred in the Law (five times in Exodus and nine times in Deuteronomy).[4] The origin of the word is unclear. In fact, as one author noted, "This masculine noun is of no certain etymology. No verb or other noun uses the same root letters. However, the meaning of *mopēt* is not questioned. Often it is parallel to *ʾôt*."[5] William Holladay added that the word meant a "phenomenon in the skies."[6] Ernst Klein stated that it could refer to a "miracle, sign, proof, [or] demonstration."[7] Translators normally render the word as "wonder" or "miracle."

1. *TWOT*, s.v. מוֹפֵת.
2. Ibid.
3. *BDB*, s.v. מוֹפֵת.
4. Ibid.
5. *TWOT*, s.v. מוֹפֵת.
6. Holladay, *Lexicon*, s.v. מוֹפֵת.
7. Klein, *Hebrew*, s.v. מוֹפֵת. Also *BDB*, s.v. מוֹפֵת.

Etymology and Usage of מוֹפֵת

Over a century ago, H. W. F. Gesenius approached the origin of the word from a different perspective. He stated, "The true etymology was long unknown. However, I have now no doubt but that it should be referred to the root יָפָה [which means, "beautiful" or "fair"]; and that it properly means a beautiful or splendid deed."[8] The author of Judg 13:18 used a similar word that is in line with Gesenius' interpretation. In this text, 56. Manoah, the father of Samson, asked the Angel of the Lord his name. The angel responded, "Why do you ask my name, seeing it is wonderful [פֶּלִאי]?" (Judg 13:18). The Hebrew word, translated as "wonderful," is פֶּלִאי (pel'î), which is closely related to פֶּלֶא (pele'). The Old Testament authors used פֶּלֶא to refer to some sort of miracle.[9] In fact, the writers even used it in the same way they employed מוֹפֵת on several occasions.[10] Victor Hamilton observed:

> The basic meaning of the verb [פָּלָא] is "to be wonderful" and in the Hiphil "to cause a wonderful thing to happen." In the Piel, however, it means "to fulfil (a vow)," though this nuance is also present in two instances of pālā' in the Hiphil. Preponderantly both the verb and substantive refer to the acts of God, designating either cosmic wonders or historical achievements on behalf of Israel.[11]

Gesenius may have been correct in connecting the root of מוֹפֵת to יָפָה. When authors used מוֹפֵת, they may have been describing something beautiful and wonderful.

Context determined how the authors of the Old Testament used the word. The usage was similar to אוֹת.[12] Some circumstances carried a possible miraculous implication, while others appeared to be symbolic; thus, it will be necessary to examine the various ways authors used the word.

THE USE OF מוֹפֵת FOR SYMBOLIC ACTIONS OR EVENTS

First, it is necessary to examine how the word appeared in reference to symbolic actions or events. According to this author's research, this type of usage was less common than מוֹפֵת's use for a miraculous event. The authors of the Old Testament used the word in reference to a non-miraculous event

---

8. Gesenius, *Gesenius' Hebrew*, s.v. מוֹפֵת.

9. Hamilton, *TWOT*, s.v. פָּלָא. Cf. Exod 15:11; Ps 77:12, 15; 78:12; 88:11, 13; 89:6; 119:129; Isa 25:1; 29:14; Dan 12:6.

10. See Ps 77:15, 12; 89:6.

11. *TWOT*, s.v. פָּלָא.

12. *TWOT*, s.v. מוֹפֵת.

The Hebrew Word for 'sign' and its Impact on Isaiah 7:14

or object nine out of thirty-six times.[13] Furthermore, the word did not occur in this manner within the five books of the Law. Thus, the Prophets and the Writings are the primary focus for this portion of the chapter.

The Prophets

The first reference in the Prophets to a non-miraculous event or object is Isa 8:18. The author wrote, "Behold, I and the children whom the Lord has given me are signs and portents [מוֹפְתִים] in Israel from the Lord of hosts" (Isa 8:18). The author chose to use אֹתוֹת parallel to מוֹפְתִים, which implies that both words described the same thing. The author and his children were markers or ordinary symbols to Israel. The signs were not miraculous, but again, God did not give the signs directly to Israel.

God gave the children to the author, and when he named them, they became the symbols.[14] John Goldingay stated, "Isaiah has put his esteem on the line in the names of his children which make them signs and symbols."[15] Thus, מוֹפֵת and אוֹת had such close meanings that their usage sometimes overlapped.

The author of Isa 20:3 used מוֹפֵת again in a similar fashion. He wrote, "Then the Lord said, 'As my servant Isaiah has walked naked and barefoot for three years as a sign and portent [מוֹפֵת] against Egypt and Cush" (Isa 20:3). Again, the author used מוֹפֵת in reference to the symbolic actions of Isaiah walking naked and barefoot for three years. The author's use of the word did not indicate a miraculous facet of meaning. In fact, Gary Smith stated, "Isaiah's sign (his nakedness) depicts the Egyptians who will be taken into captivity by the Assyrians—naked and without sandals."[16] Isaiah's actions called attention to the possibility of a nation's destruction, but the act itself did not contain a supernatural element.

God commanded the prophet Ezekiel to perform similar actions in Ezek 12:6. The author wrote, "In their sight you shall lift the baggage upon your shoulder and carry it out at dusk. You shall cover your face that you may not see the land, for I have made you a sign [מוֹפֵת] for the house

---

13. See Appendix B.

14. The Hebrew text reads, הִנֵּה אָנֹכִי וְהַיְלָדִים אֲשֶׁר נָתַן־לִי יהוה לְאֹתוֹת וּלְמוֹפְתִים. A rough translation would be: "Behold, I and the children, which he gave to me, (namely) the Lord, are signs and are portents."

15. Goldingay, *Isaiah*, 69.

16. Smith, *Isaiah 1-39*, 367.

Etymology and Usage of מוֹפֵת

of Israel."[17] The language is similar to the language found in Isaiah. The prophet symbolically became a sign to Israel when he performed all of the actions God commanded him.

The actions themselves pointed towards a greater fulfillment, but they did not constitute a miraculous event. Lamar Cooper asserted:

> Ezekiel's actions demonstrated that he had some knowledge of Assyro-Babylonian battle tactics ... These actions provided a "sign" of coming destruction for Jerusalem and Judah. What the people refused to accept by word they witnessed in the symbolic actions of the prophet.[18]

Thus, the prophet's symbolic actions made him a sign to Israel, but they were not miraculous.

The final time the word appeared in the Prophets with a symbolic intention is Zech 3:8: "Hear now, O Joshua the high priest, you and your friends who sit before you, for they are men who are a sign [מוֹפֵת]: behold, I will bring my servant the Branch." In a similar fashion, Joshua and his friends symbolically represented something to those who saw them. In this case, the sign was not miraculous. James Smith stated, "These priests were 'men that are a marvelous sign.' The word can mean a special display of God's power, or a token of a future event. The term is used of men rousing the attention of the people to a coming event."[19] Smith interpreted the word to be symbolic in this context. The men represented something else to come, but nothing supernatural existed. Thus, the authors of these books used מוֹפֵת similarly to how other authors used אוֹת when they referred to something symbolic or non-miraculous.[20]

The Writings

The word only appeared once in the Writings in a non-miraculous sense, and it occurred in a similar fashion as in the Prophets. The author of Ps 71:7 used it in reference to himself.[21] The writer of the Psalm stated, "I have been as a portent [מוֹפֵת] to many, but you are my strong refuge" (Ps

---

17. Cf. Ezek 12:11; 24:24, 27.
18. Cooper, *Ezekiel*, 94.
19. Smith, *Minor Prophets*, Zech 3:8.
20. *TWOT*, s.v. מוֹפֵת.
21. Mays, *Psalms*, 235–36.

71:7). The author provided a symbolic sense of the word in this context. He described himself as something that conveyed a message to those around him. Rabbi Sholomo Yitzchaki (Rashi) argued that this verse functioned in the same way as Ezek 24:24.[22] James Mays added:

> The expression could mean a sign of God's favor or a manifestation of divine wrath. The latter is probably right. Adversaries discuss the psalmist's suffering and conclude that he is God-forsaken. In Israel's religious community, suffering always posed a question about the relation of the afflicted one to God, and the question became a major theological theme. When Psalm 71 is read during Holy Week the line "I have been like a portent to many" announces that the suffering of Jesus calls for understanding and response. A portent of what? Faith must say.[23]

Mays argued that the author's suffering had deeper meaning and that those who witnessed it deemed the condition to be something symbolic. The audience may have seen meaning in the suffering, but it does not appear that they knew the total purpose.[24] These passages demonstrate that authors used the word in reference to symbolic actions or conditions. Using the word in this manner did not require a miraculous undertone. Yet writers also used the word in reference to supernatural events.

THE USE OF מוֹפֵת FOR A MIRACULOUS EVENT

As noted, מוֹפֵת may have originated from an older verb form that authors used to describe something wonderful or beautiful. This will be an important fact moving forward in the development of this chapter. For example, one author wrote, "Analysis of the text shows that there can be no question of treating מוֹפֵת and אוֹת as synonyms. To be sure, a מוֹפֵת can serve as an אוֹת as in the case of the sun going backwards. But unlike the latter, מוֹפֵת always has to do with something out of the ordinary."[25] Both words had similar meanings, but they also had different nuances. The authors seemed to use מוֹפֵת more often to describe events that were abnormal. In fact, when Old Testament authors used מוֹפֵת to describe something miraculous, the event was consistently outside of the ordinary.

22. Gruber, *Psalms*, 469.
23. Mays, *Psalms*, 236.
24. Kraus, *Psalms*, 73.
25. *TDNT*, s.v. מוֹפֵת.

The Law

The books of the Law contain the majority of the occurrences of מוֹפֵת. The author of the book of Exodus used the word five times.[26] The author of the Book of Deuteronomy used it nine times.[27] Since the word only occurred thirty-six times in the entire Old Testament, these appearances in the Law account for almost half of all its usage.[28]

The first occurrence of the word in the Law is in Exod 4:21. In the context, God commanded Moses to perform wonders before Pharaoh.[29] In Exod 4:8–17, God told Moses that the miracles would be signs, but the author used a different word in Exod 4:21. It is not immediately clear why the author used a different word in reference to the same deeds. Douglas Stuart commented:

> But are these same three signs the ones that are indicated by the words "perform before Pharaoh all the wonders I have given you the power to do" in v. 21? Moses certainly did perform two of them before Pharaoh, that is, the first (changing his staff into a snake) and the third (changing water into blood), according to 7:8–24. But he did not perform the second miracle at all (changing his hand from healthy to leprous) before Pharaoh. This suggests that the three proof-of-calling signs are not coterminous with "all the wonders" that, as the narrative unfolds, turn out to be the ten plagues, the exodus itself, and the crossing of the Red Sea. The third of the proof signs, in other words, is only the first of many great signs of God's power.[30]

Stuart made a valid assertion that there is ambiguity concerning the miracles that Moses performed in front of Pharaoh.

According to Exod 7:8–13, the staff turned into a serpent in front of Pharaoh. The author wrote, "When Pharaoh says to you, 'prove yourself by working a miracle [מוֹפֵת],' then you shall say to Aaron, 'Take your staff and

---

26. *BDB*, s.v. מוֹפֵת.

27. Ibid.

28. Ibid.

29. Hyatt, *Exodus*, 86. Hyatt argued that the Hebrew concept of a miracle was undeveloped at this time, thus the word would be better translated "wonder" to avoid confusion. This author does not agree with Hyatt's claim that the concept of a miracle was undeveloped, however, he does affirm that a proper translation of the word would be "wonder." For more see Hyatt, *Exodus*, 86.

30. Stuart, *Exodus*, 145.

cast it down before Pharaoh, that it may become a serpent'" (Exod 7:9). The same event was a sign (אוֹת) to Moses in Exod 4:3–5. Therefore, it seems more likely that מוֹפֵת did not refer to a different event, as Stuart concluded; rather, it may have referred to the purpose of the event.

When the staff turned into a serpent for Moses, it served as a sign. It authenticated that God was capable of delivering the Israelites out of Egypt and that he had called Moses for this purpose. The same event performed before Pharaoh revealed that Moses and Aaron had direct access to a superior deity. The identical event had two distinct purposes based on the perspective of the viewer. For Moses, the event proved that God called him, but it had a different purpose for Pharaoh. James Bruckner observed:

> The three words God uses to describe the plagues are generally synonymous, but they have different referents. 'Miraculous signs' (*'ot*, lit. signs) is the most general term and does not necessarily imply the sense of 'miraculous' as the NIV adds ... The word 'wonders' (*mopet*) refers to a portent or symbol, often of a future event. In Exodus the term describes the staff-to-snake, the snow-white hand, and the plagues (4:21; 7:3, 9; 11:9, 10). The word indicates that these unusual sights are not the main event, but point to something in the future.[31]

Bruckner noted the different referents of the words; however, he is incorrect in his argument concerning the way the words function. For example, to what future event did the staff turning into a snake point? According to Exod 7:11, Pharaoh's response to the event was to summon his own magicians in order to reveal that Moses' God was not as powerful as he thought. It is more likely that the event struck Pharaoh with amazement but did not point to anything in the future.

The word functioned in a similar manner in Exod 11:9 and 10. In these verses, Moses had just confronted Pharaoh before the final plague. In verse 8, the author wrote that Moses left in "hot anger."[32] Moses was apparently flustered about the final confrontation with Pharaoh. In fact, all of Exod 10:29–11:8 is concerned with Moses' response to Pharaoh's death threat toward Moses in 10:28.[33]

---

31. Bruckner, *Exodus*, 74.

32. The language is a Hebrew idiom that essentially describes someone who is very angry. It literally reads, "burning nose" or "burning face."

33. See Spero, "Pharaoh's Three Offers," 93–96.

After Moses' departure, God spoke to him and reminded him that Pharaoh's determination was necessary.[34] The author wrote, "Pharaoh will not listen to you, that my wonders [מוֹפְתַי] may be multiplied in the land of Egypt" (Exod 11:9). Essentially, the author reused God's own words to Moses from Exod 7:3–4. In those verses, the writer recorded that God called the plagues his "wonders."[35] Thus, the final plague in Exod 12:29 was a part of God's wonders.[36] Overall, the way the author used the word in these contexts demonstrates that the word could refer to something miraculous.

The author of the book of Deuteronomy used מוֹפֵת nine times. The first occurrence is in Deut 4:34: "Or has any god ever attempted to go and take a nation for himself from the midst of another nation, by trials, by signs, by wonders [בְּמוֹפְתִים], and by war, by a mighty hand and an outstretched arm . . . all of which the Lord your God did for you in Egypt before your eyes." It is likely that here the author referred back to the plagues after the Israelites left Egypt. Gerhard von Rad stated, "Reference is made only to the miraculous, indeed specially to the spectacular nature of the individual events [the plagues] (God's voice was heard out of fire; God has come to choose a nation for himself). This and much else has brought Israel to know Yahweh as the true God."[37] Von Rad asserted that the nature of the events helped them remain at the forefront of Israel's history. The author of the text appeared to understand them as miraculous and labeled the events four different ways, one of which was "wonders."

The writer appealed to these past events as evidence that God would continue to provide for Israel and that God alone was worthy of their trust. Eugene Merrill argued, "Modern scholars might assert that the account at hand is also of the nature of myth or legend, but the canonical witness is that Moses, himself a historical figure, was appealing precisely to history and not myth or saga to make his theological point."[38] Thus, it appears these events, regardless of whether they were historical or miraculous, remained a focal point in Israelite history, and the author used מוֹפֵת to describe them.

---

34. Stuart, *Exodus*, 268. Stuart noted that this verse was in the pluperfect form, which designated it as retrospective.

35. For a good discussion on various interpretations of the plagues, see Van Seters, "Plagues," 31–39; Moss and Stackert, "Devastation," 362–72.

36. Roderick, "Exodus," 24.

37. Von Rad, *Deuteronomy*, 51.

38. Merrill, *Deuteronomy*, 131.

The Hebrew Word for 'Sign' and its Impact on Isaiah 7:14

The author of Deut 6:22 used מוֹפֵת in almost the exact same manner: "And the Lord showed signs and wonders [מֹפְתִים], great and grievous, against Egypt and against Pharaoh and all his household, before our eyes." Again, the writer used past events as a reminder of what God had done for Israel.[39] In this instance, however, the past events referred to the plagues. The author also labeled them using מוֹפֵת, which enforces the possibility that the word could refer to a miraculous event. This type of usage is common throughout the book of Deuteronomy.[40] In fact, the word appears in the same structure four more times.[41]

The writer of Deut 28:46 used מוֹפֵת in a unique way. In this context, the author recorded a number of curses that befell anyone who disobeyed God by breaking the covenant. At the end of this long list, the author wrote, "They shall be a sign and a wonder [מוֹפֵת] against you and your offspring forever" (Deut 28:46). Apparently, the curses acted as divine retribution from God because of a person's disobedience. Ronald Clements wrote:

> The commandments themselves will be the "sign and portent" of disaster for future generations. The wording is very significant since it carries a deliberate echo of the triumphant assurance with which Deuteronomy had recorded the story of how the Lord God had brought up Israel from Egypt "with signs and wonders."[42]

Clements identified the purpose of naming these curses a wonder. Their destructive nature caused a sense of disbelief or wonder in anyone who witnessed them.[43] It would be difficult to argue that these curses did not have a supernatural element in the mind of the writer. Thus, the text reinforced the idea that מוֹפֵת could refer to a miraculous event. Still, the word also appeared in this manner throughout the books of the Prophets.

The Prophets

The author of 1 Kgs 13:3 used מוֹפֵת in reference to a seemingly miraculous event. The context for the verse is the confrontation between a prophet of

---

39. Eakin, "Plagues," 474.

40. Von Rad, *Deuteronomy*, 50–51.

41. See Deut 7:19; 26:8; 29:2; 34:11. For the sake of brevity, this book cannot address each instance. Still, in each passage, the word clearly refers back to the plagues in some manner. See Deut 7:19; 26:8; 29:2; 34:11.

42. Clements, *Deuteronomy*, 503.

43. Ibid.

ETYMOLOGY AND USAGE OF מוֹפֵת

God and Jeroboam, King of Israel. The prophet declared that a son would be born to the house of David. Next, he provided the king with a sign that this would take place. The author of the text wrote, "And he gave a sign [מוֹפֵת] the same day, saying, 'This is the sign [מוֹפֵת] that the Lord has spoken: "Behold, the altar shall be torn down, and the ashes that are on it shall be poured out"'" (1 Kgs 13:3). Although the author used מוֹפֵת, translators commonly render the word as "sign."[44] The word obviously carried some of the same qualities as אוֹת. The context dictated how they functioned, but in this case, they were interchangeable. The word referred to the event that would take place in the future as confirmation of the predictive prophecy given in 1 Kgs 13:2.[45]

The sign appeared to be miraculous, and it occurred almost immediately. The event also seemed to carry a great deal of significance to the king. It authenticated what the prophet spoke about the coming of a future king named Josiah. Richard Nelson stated, "The withering of the king's hand bolsters the credibility of the oracle, though not directly connected to its content. The destruction of the altar likewise supports this prophetic word and also serves as a demonstration of the altar's future fate."[46] Nelson understood that the events appeared to be miraculous and they reinforced what the prophet said. Although מוֹפֵת typically referred to something that brought wonder or amazement, it also rarely functioned in the same manner as אוֹת.

The next occurrences of the word in the Prophets are found in Jer 32:20-21. The author of this text used מוֹפֵת similarly to the way the author of Deuteronomy made reference to the plagues. The writer of Jer 32:20 wrote, "You have shown signs and wonders [מֹפְתִים] in the land of Egypt, and to this day in Israel and among all mankind, and have made a name for yourself, as at this day."[47] The signs and wonders seemed to refer to the plagues, just as they did in the book of Deuteronomy.

---

44. See KJV, NKJV, NASB, NIV, RSV, NRSV, HCSB, and the NET Bible.

45. The nature of this event is often disputed based on disagreement between scholars concerning the prophecy given in 1 Kgs 13:2. The prophecy names Josiah as a coming king of Israel. It is not within the scope of this book to discuss the accuracy or historicity of this event, but for more on the nature of this text, see Dozeman, "Prophecy," 379–93; Walsh, "Kings," 355–70; Deboys, "Kings," 210–12.

46. Nelson, *Kings*, 83. Also see House, *Kings*, 188; Brueggemann, *Kings*, 167–68.

47. Also see Neh 9:10; Ps 105:5, 27; 135:9; 78:43. These passages all seem to refer to the plagues in the same way.

The Hebrew Word for 'Sign' and its Impact on Isaiah 7:14

The last use of this word in the Prophets (Joel 2:30) was in reference to supernatural activity. In the context of the prophecy of the Day of the Lord, the author of Joel described a time when God's supernatural activity would be widespread. In fact, the author described God's actions as the focal point of the entire prophecy. The author described restoration, destruction, and consummation for the nation of Israel, and God was the initiator of it all (Joel 2:1–29).

Towards the end of this specific prophecy, the author wrote, "And I will show wonders [מֹפְתִים] in the heavens and on the earth, blood and fire and columns of smoke" (Joel 2:30).[48] The author apparently included the celestial atmosphere in the oracle because it would be affected by the divine judgment. Ralph Klein noted, "These signs of theophany and cosmic changes are not isolated phenomena, but are part of the holy-war or divine-warrior ideology as it was transmitted by the royal cult."[49] The author of the text used מוֹפֵת as a way to describe how people would view these supernatural events. For instance, he did not say that the wonders would authenticate anything specific; he just stated that they would occur.[50] Those who witnessed them would be struck with wonder and awe, which would encourage them to call upon the name of the Lord in order to be saved (Joel 2:32).[51] Overall, it appears that the author understood these events to be supernatural, and he used מוֹפֵת as a way to describe how they functioned.

The Writings

The authors of the Writings used מוֹפֵת eight times.[52] As with אוֹת, this was less frequently than either the Prophets or the Law. The author of 1 Chron 16:12 used the word in the context of David's song of thanks. He wrote, "Remember the wonderful works he has done, his wonders [מֹפְתָיו], and the judgments he has pronounced" (1 Chron 16:12).[53] The text occurred at

---

48. There are numerous eschatological interpretations surrounding this passage, but it is not within the scope of this book to analyze them. For more information about the various positions, see Cole, "Joel," 33–55; Blaising, "Rapture," 259–70; Kline, "Resurrection," 757–70.

49. Klein, "Day," 517–25.

50. Bakon, "Day," 149–56.

51. Smith, *Joel*, Joel 2:30–31.

52. *BDB*, s.v. מוֹפֵת.

53. *The Holy Bible: Holman Christian Standard Version*, 1 Chron 16:12.

the heart of a hymn of praise that seemed to be a compilation of Ps 105:1–5 and 106:1, 47–48.⁵⁴ The author used מוֹפֵת in the parallelism of the verse.

In 1 Chron 16:12, מֹפְתָיו is parallel to נִפְלְאֹתָיו, which is translated as "wonderful works." The root of this word is פָּלָא, which, as noted, is closely related to יָפָה. The structure of the verse is even more significant when one recalls that יָפָה may be the original root of מוֹפֵת.⁵⁵ God provided the wonders, and there seemed to be a supernatural element to the verse. It appears that the "wonderful works" and "wonders" were synonymous, which implies a miraculous connotation for the word.

The writer of 2 Chron 32:24 and 31 also used מוֹפֵת. The author applied the word to the miracle of the sun moving backwards for Hezekiah. He wrote, "In those days Hezekiah became sick and was at the point of death, and he prayed to the Lord, and he answered him and gave him a sign [[מוֹפֵת 2) " Chron 32:24). This is the parallel account of Hezekiah's healing in 2 Kgs 20:1–11. The Chronicler used מוֹפֵת in reference to the sign, whereas the writer of the 2 Kgs passage used אוֹת. The major difference between the two accounts is that the writer of the Chronicles text did not mention the shadow moving back on the steps of Ahaz.⁵⁶

There may have been a reason that the Chronicler used מוֹפֵת instead of אוֹת. In the 2 Kings account, the focus was on the sun moving back on the steps, whereas the author of the Chronicles text emphasized Hezekiah's healing.⁵⁷ Geoffrey Bromiley stated, "The two Hebrew terms [אוֹת and מוֹפֵת] are not synonymous, but carry different accents, [this] may be seen from a comparison of 2 Kings. 20:1ff. and 2 Chr. 32:24, 31; the former stresses the sign and the latter the miracle."⁵⁸ Bromiley addressed an important difference between אוֹת and מוֹפֵת. Both accounts referred to a miracle, but the Chronicler may have understood the sign to be Hezekiah's healing.

The difference in the two words used to describe this miracle was what each author wanted to emphasize. Since the Chronicles writer never described the sun moving backwards, he may have only wanted to highlight the fact that God healed Hezekiah. The Kings writer seemed to focus more on the sign as an authentication of what God had said. This will be a

---

54. Hughes and Laney, "Chronicles," 153.
55. Gesenius, *Gesenius' Hebrew*, s.v. מוֹפֵת.
56. See Hughes and Laney, "Chronicles," 365.
57. Ibid.
58. *TDNTA*, s.v. τέρας.

key difference as this chapter continues. The Greek equivalent may provide more information about how writers viewed מוֹפֵת.

THE USE OF ΤΕΡΑΣ

Etymology

The Greek equivalent of מוֹפֵת is τέρας (*teras*). The word carried many of the same qualities as מוֹפֵת.[59] Rengstorf stated, "The word occurs in literature from Homer and is obviously part of the older Gk. vocabulary, since it is already widespread and fairly common in early times ... According to a common view τέρας is etymologically akin to πέλωρ, 'terrible miraculous sign,' then 'monster.'"[60] Based on Rengstorf's conclusions, it appears that מוֹפֵת and τέρας may have had similar meanings.

Thayer stated that the word was generally a descriptor of "something so strange as to cause it to be 'watched' or 'observed.'"[61] This is similar to the way authors used מוֹפֵת. Kenneth Wuest added that the word meant "a miracle whose purpose it is to awaken amazement in the beholder."[62] Again, the word was used to describe events that might bring astonishment, but not necessarily authentication. A good translation of the word would be something similar to "wonder," as is the case with מוֹפֵת.[63] In order to understand how the word compared to מוֹפֵת, it is necessary to trace its development beginning with its usage in the Greek Classical works.

---

59. *TDNT*, s.v. τέρας.

60. Ibid. Rengstorf claimed that the force of the word used in the context of the monster came from the fear that came at the confrontation of the creature. This example will be examined in greater detail below.

61. Thayer, *Lexicon*, s.v. τέρας.

62. Wuest, *Studies*, Mark 13:21.

63. Vincent, *Studies*, s.v. τέρας.

Development

Classical Usage[64]

HOMER

Homer used τέρας in the *Iliad* and the *Odyssey*. The way he used τέρας indicates that he understood how it was different from σῆμα.[65] Bromiley wrote, "In Homer the *téras* is only for human beings as in their search for the essence of things they experience their dependence on the gods and yet also their closeness to them. The *mántis* is needed to interpret the *téras*, but the *téras* itself may be given in answer to prayer."[66] Bromiley understood the word's connection to the miraculous, and he observed the presence of divine activity.

The author of the *Iliad* used the word in reference to the fear caused by a monster called the Gorgon: "[T]herein onset, that maketh the blood run cold, and therein is the head of the dread monster, the Gorgon, dread and awful, a portent [τέρας] of Zeus that beareth the aegis."[67] The author used τέρας to describe the way others viewed this creature. The monster created fear or terror, and it was from Zeus. The author used the word in the same manner Old Testament writers had used מוֹפֵת in reference to something supernatural.

Later in the *Odyssey*, the author used σῆμα to describe a sign Odysseus requested upon his return home. In that case, the sign was the word spoken by the girl at the mill, but the author also used τέρας in the same passage to describe the thunder:

> "Father Zeus, if of your good will ye gods have brought me over land and sea to my own country, when ye had afflicted me sore, let some one of those who are awaking utter a word of omen for me within, and without let a sign [τέρας] from Zeus be shown besides." So he spoke in prayer, and Zeus the counselor heard him. Straightway he thundered from gleaming Olympus, from high from out the clouds; and goodly Odysseus was glad. And a woman, grinding at the mill, uttered a word of omen from within

---

64. The author has chosen specific authors who make more prominent use of the word. This selection is by no means exhaustive regarding the classical works.

65. As noted, σῆμα is the earlier Greek word for σημεῖον.

66. *TDNTA*, s.v. τέρας.

67. Homer, *Iliad*, 249. Also see ibid., 559. In this context, the Trojans see a snake dropped by an eagle and claim that it was a τέρας from Zeus.

> the house hard by, where the mills of the shepherd of the people were set ... She now stopped her mill and spoke a word, a sign [σῆμα] for her master.⁶⁸

The sign that Odysseus sought did not occur until the girl spoke to him. The sound of the thunder caused awe or wonder in the girl, which may be the reason the author chose to use τέρας instead of σῆμα. Although the translator chose "sign" for both words, the original Greek had different purposes. Rengstorf summarized, "[T]he fact that τέρας can even serve in the classics as a t[erminus] t[echnicus] for fabled beings suggests that the origin of τέρας is to be sought in a world and a religion which are pre-homeric and are stamped by popular belief."⁶⁹ If Rengstorf is correct, then the word was popular before the Greeks used it in reference to their gods. The works of Philo may also shed light on the ancient use of this word.

Philo

Philo used τέρας, but only in special circumstances. For example, he only used the word in connection with the power of God, and he emphasized the miraculous nature of the word.⁷⁰ In one instance, Philo used the word in reference to the miracles God provided Moses at his commissioning. Evidently, Philo believed that Moses used those miracles to convince others that God had given him special authority. He wrote:

> Therefore the Jews had now to endure more terrible afflictions than before, and were indignant at Moses and his brother as deceivers, and accused them, sometimes secretly and sometimes openly, and charged them with impiety in appearing to have spoken falsely against God; and accordingly Moses began to exhibit the marvelous wonders [τέρατα] which he had been previously taught, thinking that thus he should be able to bring over those who saw them from their former incredulity to believe all that he said.⁷¹

It appears that Philo understood the meaning behind מוֹפֵת and used the Greek equivalent in its place.

---

68. Ibid., *Odyssey*, 281–83.
69. *TDNT*, s.v. τέρας.
70. Ibid.
71. Philo, *Works*, 467. Also see ibid., 515. Philo used the word in reference to the manna that God provided for the Israelites in the wilderness.

The author used the word again in reference to the quail God provided for the Israelites in the wilderness. Evidently, the writer believed that the quail came in large clouds each day for the people to collect. According to Philo, this daily occurrence created a degree of wonder in those who witnessed it. He stated, "It would have been natural therefore for them, being amazed at the marvelous nature of the prodigy [τέρας] which they beheld, to be satisfied with the sight, and being filled with piety to nourish their souls on that, and to abstain from eating flesh."[72] Again, Philo connected the word with the amazement the people felt, but the event did not authenticate anything to those who witnessed it.

Josephus

Flavius Josephus also used the word in his works. For example, he referred to strange things happening in Jerusalem as signs, and he used τέρας to describe them. He stated:

> Thus were the miserable people persuaded by these deceivers, and such as belied God himself; while they did not attend, nor give credit, to the signs [τέρατα] that were so evident and did so plainly foretell their future desolation . . . Thus there was a star resembling a sword, which stood over the city, and a comet, that continued a whole year. Thus also, before the Jews' rebellion, and before those commotions which preceded the war, when the people were come in great crowds to the feast of unleavened bread, on the eighth day of the month Xanthicus [Nisan], and at the ninth hour of the night, so great a light shone round the altar and the holy house, that it appeared to be bright day time; which light lasted for half an hour. This light seemed to be a good sign [τέρας] to the unskillful, but was so interpreted by the sacred scribes, as to portend those events that followed immediately upon it.[73]

Josephus seems to have understood these events to mean that the Romans were going to destroy Jerusalem.[74] Each time he used the word, it was always in reference to something out of the ordinary happening before the destruction of the temple in AD 70.[75] He believed that these supernatu-

---

72. Ibid., 629.
73. Josephus, *Wars*, 6.288–91.
74. See ibid., 6.296–98.
75. *TDNT*, s.v. τέρας.

ral events had a purpose, but nobody provided an interpretation of them.[76] Perhaps examining the Septuagint will reveal more about the early usage of τέρας.

The Septuagint

According to this author's research, the translators of the Septuagint faithfully used τέρας in place of מוֹפֵת throughout.[77] In fact, the translators used τέρας in thirty-four of the thirty-six different instances where מוֹפֵת occurred. Such a consistent translation provides strong evidence that the two words shared similar meanings. Rengstorf stated:

> In rendering מוֹפֵת the translators obviously paid careful attention to the fact that they must not obliterate the boundary between the specific senses of τέρας and σημεῖον. This may be seen from the fact that in Ex. 4:17, 21 אוֹת and מוֹפֵת are rendered acc[ording] to their varying senses by σημεῖον and τέρας even though in fact the ref[erence] is to the same thing.[78]

Rengstorf described why it was important for the translators of the Septuagint to use the two words differently. In fact, this also demonstrates that these translators understood the importance of how the two words operated. Therefore, it appears that τέρας carried the same linguistic qualities as מוֹפֵת.[79]

CONCLUSION

The investigation of this chapter demonstrated that the best translation of מוֹפֵת is "wonder." The evidence surrounding the etymology of the word suggests that the word might have come from an original root verb meaning "to be wonderful."[80] Furthermore, the chapter revealed that most authors used the word in reference to something that was out of the or-

---

76. Josephus, *Wars*, 6.295.
77. *TDNT*, s.v. τέρας.
78. Ibid. Also see Moule, *Miracles*, 236.
79. Interestingly, τέρας never occurred by itself in the entire New Testament or Apocrypha. Every time the word did appear, σημεῖον was parallel. Thus, the following chapter will examine how the two words function together and inspect their functional differences.
80. Gesenius, *Gesenius' Hebrew*, s.v. מוֹפֵת.

dinary. In many circumstances, the event so described caused a great deal of fear or wonder to those who witnessed it. The chapter also investigated circumstances in which authors used מוֹפֵת in reference to symbolic actions that did not have a supernatural element. These actions seemed to cause a degree of wonder in those who witnessed them, but these symbolic actions did not validate anything.

The chapter examined the function of the Greek word τέρας. Ancient authors used the word in the same manner as the Old Testament authors employed מוֹפֵת. The research demonstrated that the translators of the Septuagint replaced מוֹפֵת with τέρας consistently, which showed that the two words were apparently synonymous. Overall, the chapter demonstrated that authors of the Old Testament used מוֹפֵת in reference to the non-miraculous as well as the miraculous.

Like the usage of אוֹת, the statistical evidence suggests that when God provided the מוֹפֵת, it was considered miraculous. As mentioned, the authors of the books of the Old Testament used מוֹפֵת thirty-six times. Of those thirty-six occurrences, twenty-seven had God as the source of the מוֹפֵת. In each of the twenty-seven instances, there was a supernatural element to the מוֹפֵת.[81]

In addition, the section showed that מוֹפֵת and אוֹת had similar meanings but were not synonymous. The authors of the Old Testament evidently recognized their individuality and chose one of the two depending on the context. Nevertheless, the chapter also demonstrated that authors commonly used them together. Thus, a brief examination of how the two words operated together is necessary. It will also be necessary to further investigate how the two words differed in meaning.

---

81. See Appendix B.

4

Functional Differences between אוֹת and מוֹפֵת

Interpreters of the Old Testament have always had the difficult task of uncovering the meaning of Hebrew words in order to provide an accurate understanding of the text. When two Hebrew words occur nearly interchangeably, a degree of caution is required in uncovering the similarities and differences between the two words. This chapter attempts to determine the functional difference between two such words—אוֹת (*'ōt*) and מוֹפֵת (*môpēt*).

The authors of the books of the Old Testament used both words together in several important texts. The writer of Exodus used the two words almost interchangeably when referring to the plagues. For example, he used them both in Exod 7:3–4, where he quoted God as saying: "But I will harden Pharaoh's heart, and though I multiply my signs and wonders [-אֶת אֹתֹתַי וְאֶת-מוֹפְתַי] in the land of Egypt, Pharaoh will not listen to you. Then I will lay my hand on Egypt and bring my hosts, my people the children of Israel, out of the land of Egypt by great acts of judgment." The author used אוֹת and מוֹפֵת in reference to the events that God was going to bring upon Egypt. By doing so, he created a common phrase that other authors in the Old Testament used in their writings: "signs and wonders."

As noted, the writer used אוֹת and מוֹפֵת independently in reference to the same events (cf. Exod 8:23; 10:1, 2; 11:9).[1] Thus, it is difficult to

---

1. For a good discussion on this phrase, see McCasland, "Signs," 149–52.

determine why the author chose to use one word in a certain situation but used a different word in another. A clear distinction between the two words brings a better understanding of how the authors used them. Again, both words carried similar connotations but were also distinct in several ways. As a result, a great deal of misinterpretation exists surrounding their usage. This chapter seeks to resolve the confusion between the two words and to provide clarity on their usage in the Old Testament.

THE SIMULTANEOUS USAGE OF BOTH WORDS

Thus far, an individual analysis of each word was necessary in order to understand how authors used each word separately within the Old Testament. Still, in many texts, authors used both words in reference to the same events. Such usage adds a degree of difficulty for the interpreter. For instance, the question arises: "How could one event function as a sign *and* a wonder?" As examined in this chapter, the answer to this question is in the perspective of the event.[2]

The author of the book of Exodus used the two words simultaneously in Exod 7:3. This verse occurred in the context of Moses' preparation to go before Pharaoh. God promised deliverance, and he provided Moses and Aaron with a glimpse of how that deliverance would take place. God told Moses that he would "multiply my signs and wonders [אֶת-אֹתֹתַי וְאֶת-מוֹפְתַי] in the land of Egypt" (Exod 7:3).[3] Even though the two words were not synonymous, the "signs and wonders" seem to refer to the plagues. Joseph Haroutunian commented on John Calvin's stance: "What made a miracle a sign was the Word of God. A miracle without the Word was to Calvin a prodigy [wonder] which even the Pharaoh's magicians could perform (Ex. 7:12)."[4] From preliminary observations, this seems to be a possible explanation. F. J. Helfmeyer added that a wonder was different from a sign because of the purpose that it served.[5] He went on to say, "[T]he intention of a sign is not to terrify the onlooker, but to mediate an understanding or to moti-

---

2. *TWOT*, s.v. מוֹפֵת.

3. Authors use this phrase on numerous occasions in the Old Testament. In almost every instance, it appears that the author was referring back to the plagues narrative. Thus, the examination of this verse will also apply to all other passages where this phrase occurs. See Deut 6:22; 29:3; Neh 9:10; Jer 32:20, 21; Ps 78:43; 105:5, 27; 135:9.

4. Haroutunian, *Commentaries*, 40.

5. *TDOT*, s.v. אוֹת. Also *BDB*, s.v. מוֹפֵת.

vate a kind of behavior."[6] In Helmeyer's opinion, a wonder was unique from a sign based on the perspective of the viewer. If the event brought about a specific purpose, then it was a sign.

George Coats asserted, "[T]he signs function as weapons to convince the pharaoh that he should release Israel . . . the signs qualify the power of both Yahweh and Moses before the pharaoh."[7] Yet the same plagues also functioned as wonders, which reinforces the confusion of how the authors used both words. J. Alec Motyer elaborated on the functional distinction by stating:

> The first thing we can note, however, is that they [the plagues] are called signs (*'ot*) and wonders (*mopet*). These two words are often used together in the Old Testament. The distinction between them, as is so often the case with near synonyms, must not be over-pressed, but in a broad sense a "wonder" is something that halts people in their tracks, making them stop and stare, and a "sign" points beyond itself to something else. A "wonder" is meant to catch our attention, a "sign" is meant to engage our minds. A "wonder" astonishes, a "sign" instructs."[8]

Motyer identified vital distinctions between the two words. However, the author of Exodus used both words in reference to the same events; thus, it appears the distinction may have had something to do with the perspective of the person witnessing the event.

According to the author of the book of Exodus, God never designated specific plagues as either a sign or a wonder.[9] Yet the plagues may have functioned as both a sign and a wonder, depending on the perspective of the individual. For instance, the final plague may have been a sign (אוֹת) to those who feared God and obeyed his command to spread the blood on their doorposts and lintels. At the same time, it may have appeared as a wonder (מוֹפֵת) to those who remained unaware that judgment was coming. F. B. Meyer stated, "Up to this moment the signs (or plagues) had been illuminative. They were intended to answer Pharaoh's question, 'Who is the Lord?' and to convince Egyptians and Israelites that Jehovah was God of gods and Lord of lords. But the last plague was a stroke of awful judgment

---

6. Ibid.

7. Coats, *Exodus*, 68. Also Habershon, *Miracles*, 110; and Childs, *Exodus*, 78.

8. Motyer, *Exodus*, 76–77.

9. He did, however, quote God in designating certain events within the plagues as signs. Cf. Exod 8:22–23 and 10:1–2.

and punishment."[10] Thus, depending on one's perspective on a plague, it could either be a sign that God was faithful or an astonishing act that did not carry any specific purpose.[11] Perhaps an examination of how Greek authors used the equivalent will support this initial hypothesis.

THE GREEK EQUIVALENT ΣΗΜΕΙΑ ΚΑΙ ΤΕΡΑΤΑ

A preliminary analysis of how authors used the Hebrew phrase showed that both words referred to the same event. Greek authors used the phrase σημεῖα καὶ τέρατα similarly to the Hebrew writers.[12] Thus, an analysis of the Greek equivalent will help shed light on the way authors used the phrase in Scripture.

Upon close inspection, it appears that the Greek phrase carried the same linguistic qualities as its Hebrew equivalent. Marvin Vincent stated:

> The words [σημεῖα and τέρατα] do not denote different classes of supernatural manifestations, but these manifestations [sic] regarded from different points of view. The same miracle may be a mighty work, or a glorious work, regarded with reference to its power and grandeur; or a sign of the doer's supernatural power; or a wonder, as it appeals to the spectator.[13]

Vincent's conclusion concerning the differences in the two Greek words is almost identical to Motyer's analysis of the Hebrew phrase.[14] In addition, Kenneth Wuest stated:

> "Signs" is *sēmeion* (σημειον) a miracle whose purpose is that of attesting the claims of the one performing the miracle to be true. "Wonders" is *teras* (τερας) a miracle whose purpose it is to awaken amazement in the beholder. It is the same miracle regarded from different standpoints.[15]

Wuest's synopsis concluded that both words had their own definition. He also concluded that the perspective of the viewer might have determined which word the author chose to use.

10. Meyer, *Exodus*, 130.
11. Ibid.
12. *TWOT*, s.v. מוֹפֵת.
13. Vincent, *Studies*, 1:129.
14. Cf. Motyer, *Exodus*, 76–77.
15. Wuest, *Studies*, Mark 13:21.

Although both words had separate meanings, when combined, they carried both meanings in describing the same event. Geoffrey Bromiley wrote, "At first these terms come together to denote omens that the superstitious perceive in times of crisis. Two things that are not really the same combine in the formula because both are significant in times of human helplessness."[16] According to Bromiley, the Greek phrase had a similar meaning to the Hebrew phrase. Two individual words combined to create a phrase commonly used to describe the same event. As a result, it will be beneficial to analyze the Classical Greek works, the New Testament, and the Septuagint in order to determine whether this phrase is relevant to the discussion.

Development

The phrase was common in ancient writings. As noted, it appeared in several other Old Testament books in reference to the plagues. This trend continued through Greek writings as well. K. H. Rengstorf observed, "Thus in Greek-speaking Judaism in so far as this stands behind the literature comprised in the LXX the formula σημεῖα καὶ τέρατα based on the Deuteronomic model, seems to be reserved for God's wonders in the days of Moses."[17] Rengstorf argued that Greek culture developed its own equivalent because of familiarity with the Hebrew phrase.

Joseph Thayer noted that this phrase was popular in extrabiblical Greek literature. He ascribed its use to Philo, Polybius, Josephus, and Plutarch.[18] It seems most authors understood the meaning of the phrase and applied it to events with a supernatural element. The authors of the Greek Septuagint illustrated this fact well.

The Septuagint

According to Vernon McCasland, the authors of the Septuagint used σημεῖα καὶ τέρατα twenty-three different times.[19] The translators used the

16. *TDNTA*, s.v. σημεῖον.

17. Ibid.

18. Thayer, *Lexicon*, s.v. σημεῖον. This book cannot adequately address each of these classical authors, but it would be a worthy endeavor to examine how the phrase continued to develop through their works.

19. McCasland, "Signs," 150.

Greek phrase to replace the Hebrew in the translation of Exod 7:3. Every time the Hebrew phrase אֹתוֹת וּמֹפְתִים appeared, the writers faithfully rendered it as σημεῖα καὶ τέρατα.[20] Rengstorf added, "The Deuteronomic theologoumenon אֹתוֹת וּמוֹפְתִים becomes σημεῖα καὶ τέρατα in the LXX. This is always used where the expression occurs in the Mas[oretic] text ... it is almost always connected with recollection of the emancipation of Israel from Egypt."[21] According to Rengstorf, because the phrase originally occurred in reference to the plagues, writers kept that meaning in later times.

The evidence suggests that the Greek equivalent was synonymous with the Hebrew phrase. The connection implies that the connotations behind both Hebrew words carried over into the Greek language. The translators understood the function of both words and provided the closest possible translation. The New Testament authors also demonstrated this fact.

The Gospels

The New Testament writers used the phrase in a slightly different manner than the Old Testament writers. Instead of the plagues, the phrase seemed to reference other miraculous events. The author of Matthew's gospel used the phrase once in Matt 24:24.[22] In this context, Jesus spoke of a future time when false prophets would arise and work signs and wonders (cf. 2 Cor 12:12; 2 Thess 2:9). The writer used the phrase in analogously to how the Old Testament authors used the Hebrew equivalent. The plagues were both signs and wonders to all who witnessed them. According to Matt 24:24, these acts will be signs to some and wonders to others.[23]

The New Testament writers apparently understood the functional difference between the two words. For instance, Matthew used σημεῖον by itself ten different times. Most of these occurrences referred to the Jews asking Jesus for a sign. Matthew 12:39 reads, "But he answered them, 'An evil

---

20. *TDOT*, s.v. אוֹת.

21. *TDNTA*, s.v. σημεῖον.

22. The authors of the Synoptic Gospels do not use this phrase often. In fact, the author of Mark's gospel only used the phrase once in Mark 13:22. The author of Luke's gospel did not use the phrase at all. Thus, an examination of the occurrence in Matthew's gospel will suffice.

23. This book cannot address the complete meaning behind this verse. For more on the subject, see Blomberg, *Matthew*, 360–61; Long, *Matthew*, 270–72; Turner, *Matthew*, 578–80; Hauerwas, *Matthew*, 204–6; Osborne, *Matthew*, 887; Hobbs, *Matthew*, 338–42; Hare, *Matthew*, 279; Hendrickson, *Matthew*, 860–61.

and adulterous generation seeks for a sign [σημεῖον], but no sign [σημεῖον] will be given to it except the sign [σημεῖον] of the prophet Jonah'" (cf. Matt 16:1, 3, 4; Mark 8:11, 12; Luke 11:16, 29). As noted, the word in this context referred to a miracle the Jews wanted Jesus to perform in order to prove he was the Messiah. If Jesus had performed a miracle at their command, it would have functioned as a sign to the Jews because of their anticipation. The event would not have been a τέρας because the Jews wanted authentication, not oblivious amazement.

The author of the Gospel of John used the phrase once (John 4:48). The writer used the word in Jesus' response to the official's request to heal his son. Jesus' reply seems to be out of context, but upon further inspection, Jesus had a purpose for using the phrase.[24] As noted, the author of John's gospel often used σημεῖον in reference to Jesus' miracles.[25] Throughout these many occurrences, the writer employed the word to demonstrate that Jesus' miracles authenticated his divinity.[26] Gerald Borchert wrote, "In John a sign is more than just a wonder; it is a powerful act for the one who has eyes to see because it points to the reality of who Jesus is."[27] Thus, the author's use of σημεῖον alone reveals that he understood the functional difference between the two words.[28] Therefore, the "signs and wonders phrase" does not fit within John's typical use of the word.

The official's request is the important factor in this occurrence. Only Jesus knew the official's motivation for making this appeal. James Boice noted, "At first Jesus delivered a rebuke. He said, 'Except ye see signs and wonders, ye will not believe.' That was the equivalent of calling him a curiosity seeker and was perhaps directed as much towards the crowd that had gather as to the nobleman. It was a test of the man's faith or sincerity."[29] It seems that Jesus responded with the phrase "signs and wonders" to emphasize the fact that he was not performing miracles as a way to impress people.[30] Thus, he did not want to provide a wonder by simply healing the

---

24. Hughes, *John*, 139–40.

25. Cf. John 2:23; 3:2; 4:54; 6:2, 14, 26; 7:31; 9:16; 10:11; 11:47; 12:18; 12:37; 20:30.

26. Michaels, *John*, 79; Hailey, *John*, 105–13; Dennison, "Miracles as 'Signs,'" 192.

27. Borchert, *John*, 157.

28. In contrast, some authors take the position that there was a source known as "the signs source" that redactors used for the passages that mention signs in John. For a strong rebuttal to this claim, see Von Wahlde, *John*, 209–11.

29. Boice, *John*, 426.

30. Hailey, *John*, 105–7, 109–13.

Functional Differences between אוֹת and מוֹפֵת

official's son. When the official responded with sincerity, Jesus healed his son. The author of Acts also used the phrase in a similar manner.

Acts

Unlike the author of the Gospel of John, the writer of Acts used the phrase often. According to this author's research, the writer of Acts used σημεῖα καὶ τέρατα or some form of it eight times.[31] That number outweighs any other book in the New Testament. G. W. H. Lampe observed:

> Luke, however, has no hesitation in making *semia kai terata* a very prominent feature in Acts. When we read, for instance, that "through the hands of the apostles many signs and wonders took place among the people" and that "the people magnified them," we may well imagine that we are already on the way to the kind of "miracle-apologetic" which dominates the apocryphal Acts and so much else in later Christian literature.[32]

Lampe noted that the writer used the phrase in connection with the works of the apostles. This connection with the apostle's work is vital to understanding how the phrase functions in the book. For instance, the author designated many of the miracles that the apostles performed as signs and wonders.

The author of Acts first used the phrase in Peter's sermon on the Day of Pentecost. The author quoted Peter's allusion to Joel 2. Peter said, "And I will show wonders [τέρατα] in the heavens above and signs [σημείοις] on the earth below, blood, and fire, and vapor of smoke" (Acts 2:19). It is interesting to note that Peter added σημείοις to the original Septuagint rendering. Daniel Treier commented on the addition:

> Luke or Peter added "signs" (*sëmeia*) to the LXX rendering of Joel 2 in order to display the harmony between the text and the material that follows, both in the sermon (2:22) and the narrative (2:43). The miracles the crowd had seen during Jesus' ministry and would see in the future were signs of impending judgment, which called for repentance.[33]

---

31. *TDNT*, s.v. σημεῖον.
32. Lampe, "Miracles," 165–66.
33. Treier, "Joel," 21.

81

The Hebrew Word for 'Sign' and its Impact on Isaiah 7:14

It seems that Peter understood the nature of Jesus' miracles. The author of the Gospel of John used them as an attestation to Jesus' divinity, and it appears that Peter did so in this verse as well. The authors of the gospels and Acts did not view Jesus' miracles as simple tricks that he used to awe the crowds; instead, they saw them as verifications that he was the Messiah.[34]

The author of the book of Acts used the phrase again in 2:43, immediately after Peter's sermon. The apostles started performing miracles in the area, and as a result, "awe came upon every soul, and many wonders and signs [τέρατα καὶ σημεῖα] were being done through the apostles" (Acts 2:43). The question arises again: "Why did the apostles perform these miracles, and why did the author refer to them as signs and wonders?" The reason the author viewed the apostles' miracles as signs and wonders may be similar to why witnesses saw the plagues as signs and wonders. The crowds may have viewed the same miracle differently, depending on their perspective.

The writer of Acts used the phrase six additional times in the book, and all of these refer to miracles performed by the apostles.[35] Darrell Bock claimed that the miracles functioned as proof of the apostles' divine commissioning.[36] In contrast, Jaroslav Pelikan believed that the crowds recognized the significance of the miracles and that they instilled the people with fear (Acts 4:16).[37] Both positions seem likely, but a combination of the two is more logical. In one sense, the miracles functioned as signs—they authenticated the apostles' claims of divine commissioning. In another sense, the miracles functioned as wonders—they inspired awe or fear in those who witnessed them. Thus, the relationship of the two words was identical to that of the relationship between אוֹת and מוֹפֵת.[38]

---

34. Polhill, *Acts*, 112.

35. Cf. 4:30; 5:12; 6:8; 7:36; 14:3; 15:12. Each of these verses use the phrase in the same manner, thus for the sake of brevity, they have not been included. The writers of the Epistles also use the phrase occasionally, but again, each instance appears to be similar to the previously examined passages. See Rom 15:19; 2 Cor 12:12; 2 Thess 2:9; Heb 2:4.

36. Bock, *Acts*, 151–52. Also see Larkin, *Acts*, 52–54; Schnabel, *Acts*, 180–81.

37. Pelikan, *Acts*, 97–98.

38. Moule, *Miracles*, 237.

Functional Differences between אוֹת and מוֹפֵת

First-century AD Usage[39]

Philo

Philo of Alexandria did not use σημεῖα καὶ τέρατα often in his writings. According to this author's research, the phrase occurred on two different occasions. In both instances, it appears the author referenced the plagues of Egypt.[40] The first is found in Philo's discussion of the Israelites' attitude towards God in the wilderness: "And though God himself had declared his will to them by demonstrations clearer than any verbal commands, namely, by signs and wonders [σημεῖα καὶ τέρατα], still they required a yet more severe impression to be made upon them."[41] The author acknowledged that the plagues appeared to be an act of God, and he designated them as "signs and wonders."

The next reference occurred in Philo's writings on God's providence with reference to the Hebrew people. He stated, "Therefore he, who is merciful to all who are unjustly treated, having received their supplication, smote those who oppressed them with signs and wonders [σημεῖα καὶ τέρατα], and prodigies, and with all the marvelous works which he wrought at that time."[42] Again, it appears that the author referenced the plagues with this phrase.

Josephus

Flavius Josephus used the phrase occasionally in his writings. Unlike Philo, Josephus did not use the phrase in reference to the plagues. It appears that Josephus understood τέρας to possess a more magical connotation than σημεῖον. Thus, when he mentioned the plagues he avoided using τέρας. Josephus' motivation for doing so is not clear. Rengstorf commented on the issue:

> The reason is obviously that he does not want them to be seen in the light of apparent or actual magic. He thus protects Moses expressly against the suspicion of τερατουργίαι καὶ μαγεῖαι and

---

39. The author has chosen specific authors who use the word in a more prominent manner. This selection is by no means exhaustive regarding the post biblical works.

40. *TDNTA*, s.v. σημεῖον.

41. Philo, *Works*, 468. Also see ibid., 515. Philo used the word in reference to the manna that God provided for the Israelites in the wilderness.

42. Ibid., 588.

makes Moses no more than a θεατὴς τεράτων in Egypt. Σημεῖα are God's affair. They rest finally on his πρόνοια καὶ δύναμις. When God uses the σημεῖον He shows thereby that He is the εἷς θεὸς καὶ μέγιστος καὶ ἀληθὴς μόνος. When He works a τέρας, this is not important as such but as a σημεῖον it denotes God's presence and thus points to God.[43]

Rengstorf's conclusion is possible. Josephus may have avoided using the word because of the connotation τέρας carried. It appears that he did not apply the phrase to any event that involved God's activity and a human agent.[44]

The only time Josephus used the phrase was in reference to the actions of false prophets.[45] This usage may help determine why he never used it in reference to the plagues. The author wrote:

> And now these impostors and deceivers persuaded the multitude to follow them into the wilderness, and pretended that they would exhibit manifest wonders and signs [τέρατα καὶ σημεῖα], that should be performed by the providence of God. And many that were prevailed on by them suffered the punishments of their folly; for Felix brought them back, and then punished them.[46]

Evidently, the author understood these acts to be separate from the work of God and considered their miraculous works to be false. Overall, it appears that Josephus understood the difference between σημεῖον and τέρας. He used both in reference to miraculous acts from God, and he used σημεῖον as an authentication sign rather than in reference to a normal miracle. Finally, a brief examination of how the authors of select apocryphal works will conclude this section.

---

43. *TDNTA*, s.v. σημεῖον.

44. As noted, Josephus did use τέρας in reference to seemingly supernatural events in Jerusalem, but he implied that these events were the result of divine activity. The difference is that, in his eyes, God was the sole author of these abnormalities. Thus, it seems that Josephus did not use τέρας for an event if it involved God and a human agent.

45. MacRae, "Miracles," 143.

46. Josephus, *Ant.*, 20.167–68.

Functional Differences between אוֹת and מוֹפֵת

Apocryphal Works

Wisdom of Solomon

The author of the Wisdom of Solomon used σημεῖα καὶ τέρατα, but not in reference to the plagues. The author wrote, "If a man desire much experience, she [wisdom] knoweth things of old, and conjectureth aright what is to come: she knoweth the subtilties of speeches, and can expound dark sentences: she foreseeth signs and wonders [σημεῖα καὶ τέρατα], and the events of seasons and times."[47] The reference was vague, but it seemed to imply something miraculous. The context of the passage was the author's praise of wisdom. In this verse, the author apparently continued to illustrate the worth of wisdom, and he implied that having wisdom was more valuable than knowing signs and wonders. There is no way of knowing what, exactly, "signs and wonders" referred to, but the author evidently held them in high regard. Otherwise, he would not have used them to commend the value of wisdom.

Baruch

The author of Baruch used the phrase in reference to the plagues. He wrote, "And now, O Lord God of Israel, that hast brought thy people out of the land of Egypt with a mighty hand, and high arm, and with signs, and with wonders, and with great power, and hast gotten thyself a name, as appeareth this day" (Bar 2:11). The language referred to the plagues in the same manner as the previous texts. Thus, the phrase evidently continued to carry the same miraculous connotation in this period.

As noted, authors of different apocryphal works used each word individually as well; therefore, it appears that these authors understood the functional differences between the two words. When the author of Wisdom of Solomon and the author of Baruch used them together, they appeared to have knowledge of how previous authors had used the phrase. As a result, it can be assume that they understood how the two words could refer to the same event and still carry different meanings.

---

47. *The Cambridge Paragraph Bible*, Wis 8:8. Also see Wis 10:16.

The Hebrew Word for 'sign' and its Impact on Isaiah 7:14

CONCLUSION

This chapter revealed much about the functional differences between the two words. The evidence demonstrated that certain events took place that God designated as signs. These events functioned in a specific way. They revealed a truth about God or confirmed a promise that he had previously made. In this manner, these events served as a sign for those who witnessed them. The sign may or may not have been miraculous, but the phrase seemed to denote a miraculous event in most circumstances.

Other events took the designation of a wonder. These events did not hold a special meaning, but they inspired fear or reverence in the people who witnessed them. They were abnormal in nature and may have been symbolic of future events. Authors of Hebrew and Greek texts seem to have understood the differences between both words and used them accordingly.

The chapter also showed that authors used the phrase אֹתוֹת וּמֹפְתִים in reference to the plagues. Thus, the impact of the plagues differed based on the person witnessing them. Although both words may have referred to the same event, the functionality of each word differed.[48] For instance, a plague may have functioned as a sign to Pharaoh, but it may also have functioned as a wonder to an ordinary Egyptian who was unaware of the purpose behind it.

Examination of the Greek equivalents revealed that the authors of various Greek works understood this difference as well. The authors of the gospels never referred to Jesus' miracles strictly as wonders because they used the miracles for revealing his identity as the Messiah.[49] When the gospel writers used the Greek equivalent for "signs and wonders," they generally referred to the work of false prophets. In contrast, the author of the book of Acts used the phrase in reference to the works of the apostles. It appears that their miracles functioned as either a sign or a wonder, depending on who witnessed them.

Overall, it seems that when an author used אוֹת, the sign generally functioned to authenticate a promise or to reveal a greater truth. When an author used מוֹפֵת, the event inspired wonder or amazement in those who witnessed it. If an author used both words together, both words still carried their individual meanings based on the perspective of the viewer. This evidence is important for the discussion of Isa 7:14 because it demonstrates

---

48. Habershon, *Miracles*, 108.
49. Lampe, "Miracles," 166.

what the author of the text may have intended אות to mean. Thus, this research now focuses on the interpretation of Isa 7:14.

5

Historical Interpretations of Isaiah 7:14

A BASIC TRANSLATION OF Isa 7:14 is: "Therefore the Lord himself will give you a sign [אוֹת]. Behold, the virgin shall conceive and bear a son, and shall call his name Immanuel." It will be beneficial to cover some of the different interpretations of this verse. An analysis of the various approaches to the text will help show the strengths and weaknesses of each position. This overview will also demonstrate how scholars have interpreted the text throughout different periods of history. These different approaches will serve as a foundation for the final chapter of the book.

THE SEPTUAGINT TRANSLATION OF ISAIAH 7:14

The translators of the Septuagint (LXX) provided one of the earliest interpretations of Isa 7:14.[1] These seventy men interpreted the Hebrew text as they translated it into Greek. They had to choose Greek words that conveyed similar meanings to the Hebrew equivalents. As noted, there is disagreement about the translation of עַלְמָה.[2] When the translators came

---

1. It should be noted that the translators used σημεῖον in the translation of Isa 7:14. For more on this, see Troxel, "Isaiah 7, 14–16," 1–22; Coppens, "Isa 7:14–17," 670; Lobstein, *Birth*, 74–75; Miller, *Born*, 95.

2. This book does not intend to add to the numerous discussions surrounding the translation of עַלְמָה. However, for more on this subject, see Irwin, "'almah," 337–60; Reymond, "Isaiah 7:14," 1–15; Von Campenhausen, *Birth*, 25–27, 29, 34; Edwards, *Birth*, 40–41; Gromacki, *Birth*, 141–42; Knowling, *Virgin Birth*, 39; Lattey, "Almah," 89–95;

to this word in Hebrew, they chose παρθένος, which is commonly translated "virgin," as the Greek word to replace it. By doing so, they implied that they believed the woman would be a virgin when she conceived.[3]

Scholars disagree about the accuracy of such a translation, but the presence of παρθένος affords a significant glimpse into early Jewish thoughts on the text. Some scholars even argue that this translation affected early Christian interpretations. Frederick Bruner claimed that the author of Matthew's gospel only applied the verse to the birth of Jesus because παρθένος was present in the Septuagint. He stated:

> [W]hen Matthew read this text in his Greek Bible, where the Hebrew word "young woman" was translated "virgin," he was thrilled. Why? Because Matthew believed that Jesus, the promised and genealogical Son of David, was in fact born of a virgin... Matthew, a believer in the virgin birth, must have looked back at this Scripture and said to himself, "Isn't this perfect! Even the virgin birth was anticipated!" Isaiah didn't intend this reading.[4]

Bruner took the position that the author of Matthew was wrong when he applied Isa 7:14 to the birth of Jesus because of this mistranslation.

Regardless of the accuracy of the LXX translation, the fact remains that these early Jews were some of the first to provide their own interpretations. Craig Blomberg wrote, "Nevertheless, the LXX translation of *'almah* as *parthenos* ... shows that some Jews already two hundred years before Christ favored an interpretation in which this immediate fulfillment was not seen as exhausting Isaiah's prophecy."[5] In addition, Cyrus Gordon asserted:

Hayes, "Reconstruction," 5–9; Miguens, *Virgin Birth*, 119–20; Myers, "ʿalmah," 137–40; Niessen, "Virginity of the ʿalmah," 133–50; Owens, "Meaning of ʿalmah," 56–60; Sauer, "Almah Translation," 551–59.

3. de Sousa, "Parthenos," 232.

4. Bruner, *Matthew*, 35. George Riggan took a similar approach to the verse where he stated, "Parenthetically, the interpretation of this passage in Matt. 1:18–23 as a messianic oracle referring to a miraculous birth of Jesus is a mistaken reading. In the first place, Isaiah does not intend a miraculous birth. In the second, a birth seven hundred years later, even from a virgin, could hardly serve as a sign for Ahaz in his crisis" (Riggan, *Messianic*, 55). Also see Holladay, *Isaiah*, 74; Wegner, "Virgin Births," 481–83; Cf. Orr, *Virgin Birth*, 184–85; Miller, "Maidenhood," 242–46.

5. Blomberg, *Matthew*, 60. Also see Feinberg, "Virgin Birth and Isaiah 7:14," 13; Morris, *Nativity*, 41–42; Bourke, "Matthew," 160–75; Wilson, "Alma," 316–20.

The Hebrew Word for 'sign' and its Impact on Isaiah 7:14

> The commonly held view that "virgin" is Christian, whereas "young woman" is Jewish is not quite true. The fact is that the Septuagint, which is the Jewish translation made in pre-Christian Alexandria, takes *'almah* to mean "virgin" here. Accordingly, the New Testament follows Jewish interpretation in Isaiah 7:14.[6]

Finally, Theodoret of Cyrus, a bishop in the fifth century AD, also refuted the idea that the LXX translators were wrong. He said:

> I am astonished at the effrontery of Jews who do not accept the prophecy concerning the Virgin. Aquila and Theodotion and Symmachus translate the term not as "virgin" but as "young woman." They should realize that the testimony of the Seventy is more reliable than the witness of three, especially when this translation was unanimously accepted by all the translators. Moreover, the chronological facts give further support. The Seventy translated the Holy Scripture into Greek before the Incarnation of our Savior. They had no reason to falsify the passage.[7]

The translators of the LXX understood the text to refer to a virgin, whether or not that was Isaiah's original intention.

THE GOSPEL OF MATTHEW AND ISAIAH 7:14

The next area of interest is the interpretation of Isa 7:14. There have been numerous interpretations of this text throughout history.[8] After the translators of the LXX, one of the first to provide an interpretation was the author of the Gospel of Matthew.[9] As noted, he quoted Isa 7:14 in Matt 1:22–23, where he wrote, "All this took place to fulfill what the Lord had spoken by the prophet: 'Behold, the virgin shall conceive and bear a son, and they shall call his name Immanuel' (which means, 'God with us')." Scholars disagree about the reason the author included this verse as a reference to Jesus.[10]

---

6. Gordon, "*'Almah*," 106.

7. Wilken, *Isaiah*, 104.

8. McKane, "Isaiah 7:14–25," 208. For more on the authorship of this text, see Johnson, "Authorship," 218–27; McClain, "Isaiah," 33–46. The Isaiah Scroll found in Qumran also supports this position. For more on this subject, see Clark, "Dead Sea Scrolls," 122–30.

9. Brown, "Infancy Narrative," 468. Also see Conrad, "Annunciation," 656–63; Derrett, "Nativity," 81–108; Fitzmyer, "Conception," 541–75; Minear, "Birth Narratives," 1–22; Scott, "Intention," 68–82.

10. See Dennert, "Isa 7:14," 97–105; Nolan, *Christology*, 29–30; Durousseau, "Isaiah

Historical Interpretations of Isaiah 7:14

Stanley Hauerwas wrote, "Moreover, Matthew tells us all this was done so that the prophecy of Isa. 7:14 would be fulfilled."[11] Haurwas believed that the author of Matthew used Isa 7:14 correctly. In contrast, Thomas Long asserted, "To say that Jesus' birth 'fulfills' Isaiah 7:14 does not mean that the prophet Isaiah had Jesus in mind when these words were first produced. Indeed, Isaiah originally spoke this prophecy to a political and military crisis in his own time."[12] Long claimed that applying Isa 7:14 to the birth of Jesus destroyed the integrity of the author's original intent.

The result would be that the author of Matthew unknowingly applied the verse to the birth of Jesus even though that was never Isaiah's original intent. Regardless of whether the author of Matthew's gospel was correct, the fact remains that he interpreted Isa 7:14 in that way. He clearly understood Isaiah's verse to refer to the birth of Jesus and applied it accordingly.

EARLY JEWISH INTERPRETATIONS

The early Jewish rabbis commented on the Old Testament extensively. However, Jose Costa stated, "Ancient rabbinic literature says almost nothing about Isa. 7:14. Only one midrashic compilation explicitly interprets the verse, and it does not give it any messianic meaning."[13] Most early Jewish commentators argued that the promised child in Isa 7:14 was King Hezekiah.[14] Ancient Christian apologist Justin Martyr had a long discussion about this issue with a Jew named Trypho. Trypho suggested that the Christians incorrectly interpreted the verse as applying to Jesus and that

---

7:14b," 175–80; Bishop, "Nativity," 401–13; Cave, "Infancy Narrative," 382–91; Goodman, "Sources," 136–43; Guy, "Virgin Birth Tradition," 183; Menken, "Isaiah 7:14," 144–60.

11. Hauerwas, *Matthew*, 36. Also see Willis, "Matthew 1:23," 1–18; Hendrickson, *Matthew*, 146; Surburg, "Isaiah 7:14," 110–18; Sweeney, "Controversies," 142–58; Bourke, "Matthew," 160–75; Hobbs, *Matthew*, 16–18.

12. See Long, *Matthew*, 14–15; Turner, *Matthew*, 73; Wolf, "Immanuel," 449–56; Lincoln, "Matthew," 211–31.

13. Costa, "Ancient Rabbis," 117. Costa also argued that the author of Matthew provided an accurate midrashic interpretation of Isa 7:14. It should also be noted that the Isaiah Targum used עוּלֵימְתָא in place of עַלְמָה. Scholars disagree about the translation of this word as well. See Chilton, *Isaiah Targum*, 17. Cf. Pauli, *Isaiah*, 23.

14. See Greenstone, *Messiah*, 33–36; Riggan, *Messianic*, 55–56.

the correct identification of the child was Hezekiah.[15] According to I. W. Slotski, Ibn Ezra and David Kimchi also held this view.[16]

William Most argued that early evidence suggests some Jews believed Hezekiah was the promised Messiah. Most stated, "But there is newer evidence which has not been sufficiently noticed. According to the Babylonian Talmud (Sanhedrin 99a), Hillel, the great teacher of the time of Christ, said 'There will be no Messiah for Israel, because they already had him in the days of Hezekiah.'"[17] This connection is interesting because it may imply that early Jews believed Isa 7:14 was messianic.[18] Most went on to say:

> The implication is of great importance: The Jews at one time, as we saw from the words of the great Hillel, had considered Hezekiah as the Messiah, which meant that they did see Isaiah 7:14 as messianic, but later, to keep Christians from claiming that prophecy, they began to deny it was messianic, saying it did not mean Hezekiah.[19]

Most's argument is plausible, given the connection between Hezekiah and the messianic implications in the Talmud.

A later Jewish commentator, Rabbi Sholomo Yitzchaki (Rashi), argued that chronological issues prevented Hezekiah from being the promised child in Isa 7:14:

> Some interpret this as being said about Hezekiah, but it is impossible, because when you count his years, you find that Hezekiah was born nine years before his father's reign. And some interpret that this is the sign, that she was a young girl and incapable of giving birth.[20]

Rashi did not believe that the verse predicted the birth of a Messiah. He also disagreed with a common Jewish interpretation that the Immanuel child was King Hezekiah. As Brevard Childs commented, "Rashi had abandoned the earlier identification of the child with Hezekiah because of

---

15. Martyr, "Dialogue," 212. Early Jews had several different opinions on how the Messiah would be born. For more on their views see Patai, *Messiah*, 122–30; Higgins, "Messianic," 182–89; Frydland, *Messiah*, 88–90; McRay, "Virgin Birth," 61–71.

16. Slotski, *Isaiah*, 35.

17. Most, "Isaiah 7:14," 190.

18. See Neusner, *Messiah*, 240–43. Neusner argued that the interpretation intentionally avoided any messianic connection after Christians began using the verse as support for the virgin birth.

19. Most, "Isaiah 7:14," 193.

20. Yitzchaki, "Commentary," notes on "Immanuel" lines 5–9.

chronological inconsistency, and the child was seen rather as a later son of the prophet."[21] Most Jewish interpreters did not see a messianic connotation, and none seemed to believe the verse foretold the birth of Jesus.

INTERPRETATIONS BY THE EARLY CHURCH FATHERS[22]

The early church fathers also commented on this verse in numerous historical works. These men wrote on subjects that defended the core doctrines of the Christian faith. They consistently battled heresy, and their writings reflect that struggle. One of the doctrines most commonly debated was the incarnation of Christ.[23] As a result, the church fathers frequently discussed various passages in Scripture that addressed this subject. They also used these passages as evidence for their arguments, often citing Isa 7:14.

Tertullian

Tertullian was one of the first of the early church fathers to address the interpretation of Isa 7:14. In one instance, he wrote about the nature of the sign mentioned in Isa 7:14. Tertullian argued that it must have been something out of the ordinary:

> Well, but nature, says he, does not permit "a virgin to conceive," and still the prophet is believed. And indeed very properly; for he has paved the way for the incredible thing being believed, by giving a reason for its occurrence, in that it was to be for a sign. "Therefore," says he, "the Lord himself shall give you a sign; behold, a virgin shall conceive, and bear a son." Now a sign from God would not have been a sign, unless it had been some novel and prodigious thing.[24]

It appears that Tertullian believed Isa 7:14 referred to the birth of Jesus. He also appealed to the function of a sign as being more than an ordinary event. It seems he understood the sign to be the miraculous conception of Jesus.

---

21. Childs, *Isaiah*, 233.
22. The author has selected several early church fathers, but this list is not exhaustive.
23. Wilkinson, "Virgin Birth," 161.
24. Tertullian, *Latin Christianity*, 331. Also see Wilken, *Isaiah*, 98.

Irenaeus

Irenaeus wrote in defense of the faith against heresies that were often attacks upon the divinity of Christ. In one of his writings, he argued that Jesus was born fully God and fully human. In this instance, he quoted Isa 7:14 and stated: "He [Isaiah] both announced that He was to be born of a virgin, and points out beforehand that He is truly man, by the fact of His eating, and by calling Him a child, but also by setting Him a name."[25] Childs commented on Irenaeus' interpretation: "When dealing with the virgin birth in Isa. 7:14–16, Irenaeus pursues not only the miraculous elements but also the theological implications of Christ's being truly a man, who ate food, who was called a child, and given a name."[26] Childs confirmed that Irenaeus used Isa 7:14 to support that Jesus was not only born of a virgin, but also born fully man.

Justin Martyr

Justin Martyr, another early Christian writer, also defended different aspects of the Christian faith.[27] In his dialogue with Trypho, Martyr used Isa 7:14 in defending his argument that Jesus was prophesied to be born of a virgin.[28] He quoted Isa 7:10–16 and then stated:

> Now it is clear to all that no one of the race of Abraham was ever born, or even said to be born, of a virgin, except of our Christ. But, since you and your teachers venture to assert that the real words of Isaiah are not "Behold, a virgin shall conceive," but "Behold a young woman shall conceive, and bear a son," and since you refer this prophecy to your king Hezekiah, I will attempt to answer you and show that this prophecy applies to Him who we profess as our Christ.[29]

One of Justin's defenses in arguing that Jesus was the Christ was to use Isa 7:14 as support for his miraculous birth. Rachmiel Frydland also

---

25. Irenaeus, *Apostolic*, 82.
26. Childs, *Struggle*, 51.
27. Boslooper, *Virgin Birth*, 29–30.
28. Hall, *Fathers*, 135.
29. Martyr, "Dialogue," 213. Also see Knowling, *Virgin Birth*, 78–81; Willis, *Fathers*, 52. These authors also acknowledge that Justin Martyr defended the virgin birth by quoting Isa 7:14.

used Justin Martyr's text in defending that Jesus was the Messiah. Frydland stated, "He [Martyr] supports the supernatural birth of the Messiah with Isaiah 7:14. This leads to a lengthy discussion as to whether the Septuagint was correct in translating, 'Behold, the Virgin (*parthenos*)' or that it should be translated, 'Behold the young maiden' (*neanis*)."[30] Frydland understood that Justin interpreted the verse as referring to the birth of Jesus. Justin appears to have understood that this verse was a direct prophecy of Jesus' first coming.

Athanasius

Like Justin Martyr, Athanasius wrote against heresies about Jesus. Many of these heresies attacked the divine nature of Jesus, but others, like Gnosticism, denied Jesus' humanity. In one instance, Athanasius used Isa 7:14 to reinforce that Jesus was truly born of a virgin and was fully human. Athanasius wrote, "For prophets proclaimed beforehand concerning the wonder of the Virgin and the birth from her, saying: 'Lo, the virgin shall be with child, and shall bring forth a son, and they shall call his name Emmanuel, which is, being interpreted, God with us.'"[31] It would be difficult to argue that Athanasius did not believe Isa 7:14 applied to the birth of Jesus.

Ambrose

Saint Ambrose wrote many of his works as refutations of Gnosticism. Again, Gnosticism attacked the humanity of Jesus and sought to promote a more spiritual approach in its theology.[32] Like Athanasius, Ambrose argued that Jesus was completely human, and he used Isa 7:14 to support his stance. Ambrose stated:

> How, then, is the name of the council of Nicaea alleged and new statements introduced which our ancestors never thought, since surely the Scriptures say that Christ suffered according to the flesh, not according to the divinity; the Scriptures say that "a virgin shall receive in her womb and shall bring forth a son?" For she did

---

30. Frydland, *Messiah*, 89.
31. Athanasius, "Incarnation," 87.
32. Ottley, *Incarnation*, 344–60.

receive the power, and did bear a Son, whom she herself [sic] assumed from herself.³³

Ambrose referenced Isa 7:14 as "the Scriptures" and implied that Mary was the woman mentioned in the verse.³⁴

In another of Ambrose's writings, he discussed the angel's message to Mary in chapter 1 of Luke. Ambrose posed several questions about how Mary might have reacted and concluded that she would have expected some sort of miraculous birth. He stated, "Mary had read the word, you will receive a sign: Behold, a virgin shall conceive and bear a son. Therefore she believed that the prophecy would come true."³⁵ Again, it appears this ancient writer understood Isa 7:14 to be an early prophecy about the birth of Jesus.

Cyril of Alexandria

Saint Cyril of Alexandria also believed that the text was sacred, and he used it to defend the deity of Christ. He wrote, "We shall also find Emmanuel personally confirming faith in himself from the predictions of the prophets . . . and, by comparing the outcome of his achievements with the earlier prophecies, to have no doubts that he is the one who was proclaimed in advance in the Law and Prophets."³⁶ This text is not as clear, but Cyril referred to Emmanuel synonymously with Jesus. Considering that important fact, it is easy to see that Cyril drew from Isa 7:14 in calling Jesus by this name.

Gregory of Nyssa

Another early writer known as Gregory of Nyssa used Isa 7:14 in his writings. Gregory defended the virgin birth on several occasions, and in one instance, he wrote:

> Learn from the same prophet how the child is born, how the son is given. According to the law of nature? No, says the prophet. The Lord of nature is not a slave of the laws of nature. How then is the child born? Tell me. Behold, the prophet predicts, the virgin shall

---

33. Ambrose, "Incarnation," 239.
34. Ibid.
35. Wilken, *Isaiah*, 100.
36. Cyril of Alexandria, *Twelve Prophets*, 370–71.

be with child and bear a son, and they shall call him Emmanuel, which translated means, God with us.[37]

Gregory seemed to view the verse as a prophecy of Jesus' birth. He used Isa 7:14 to support his position. Many early writers defended doctrines relating to Christology, including Gregory. He valued the virgin birth, and he used Isa 7:14 to defend it.

Jerome

Modern history recognizes Jerome for his translation of the Latin Vulgate, but Jerome also provided an extensive commentary on several books of the Bible. One of those books is the Gospel of Matthew. In his commentary on Matt 1:22–23, Jerome addressed the issue of the Greek tense compared to the original Hebrew in Isa 7:14. He asserted:

> Matthew says: "She shall have in her womb," it was written in the prophet: "She shall receive in her womb." But because the prophet is predicting the future, he signifies what is going to happen and writes "she shall receive." The evangelist, because he is narrating the story not as a future event but as a past, has changed "she shall receive" and has written "she shall have." For one who has is by no means going to receive.[38]

Jerome was clear on his position regarding the interpretation of this verse. Childs added, "He [Jerome] is embarrassed that earlier Christian interpreters have been up to now incapable of refuting the Jewish objections to their Christological interpretation, and he sets out to remedy this situation."[39] Childs established that Jerome believed the verse predicted Jesus' birth.

John Chrysostom

John Chrysostom is another example of an early interpreter who used Isa 7:14 in reference to the birth of Jesus. He wrote, "You have heard, therefore, that the Father is called Lord. Come now, and let me show you that the Son is called God. 'Behold, the virgin shall be with child, and shall give birth to

---

37. Wilken, *Isaiah*, 101.
38. Jerome, *Matthew*, 63. Also see Wilken, *Isaiah*, 100–101.
39. Childs, *Struggle*, 95.

a son, and they shall call his name Immanuel; which means, 'God with us.'"[40] Chrysostom began by connecting Jesus to Isa 7:14. He seemed to believe that the name Immanuel reinforced the divinity of Jesus.

In another one of his writings, Chrysostom specifically addressed the nature of the sign in Isa 7:14, writing:

> The sign, he holds, was not given to Ahaz but to the Jewish people as a whole... In other words, he is speaking to the house of David. There the sign will break forth. What, then is the sign?... Now if she were not a virgin, it would hardly be a sign. A sign must be different from, indeed transcend, the ordinary workings of nature. It must be so strange and remarkable that those who see and hear it recognize its unique character. Sign means that it is significant. If it occurs in the ordinary course of things it could not be a sign. If he had said that a woman was to bear a child in the normal way, something that happens everyday, why would he call that a sign? This is why he did not say, "Look, a virgin," but "Look, the virgin." By using the definite article he indicates to us that this is something noteworthy and unique.[41]

Chrysostom provided a clear interpretation of the verse. He understood the significance of the sign, and he understood the verse to be a reference to the birth of Jesus.

Pope Leo the Great

Like many of the other church fathers, Pope Leo the Great was a remarkable apologist. He wrote against many of the same heresies as other fathers. In one instance, he wrote about the incarnation as a response to Flavian's attacks on the divinity of Jesus. He used Isa 7:14 as proof that Jesus was fully human and fully divine, stating, "He [Flavian] should have apprehended with his inward ear the declaration of Isaiah ... that the Christ who was brought forth from the Virgin's womb had the form of a man, but had not a body really derived from his mother's body."[42] He used the verse to support the idea that Jesus was born of a virgin and was still fully God.

---

40. Chrysostom, *Incomprehensible*, 143–44.
41. Wilken, *Isaiah*, 93–94.
42. Leo the Great, "Tome," 362.

HISTORICAL INTERPRETATIONS OF ISAIAH 7:14

INTERPRETATIONS BY THE REFORMERS[43]

While the church fathers battled heresy in almost all of their writings, by the time of the Reformation most of the councils had determined the essentials of Christian doctrine. As a result, many of the Reformers did not address the divinity of Jesus or the virgin birth. Nevertheless, several still used Isa 7:14 in their writings.

Philip Melanchthon

One example of such usage is Philip Melanchthon's writings. In one text, Melanchthon addressed the subject of signs in regards to faith. He dealt with the signs given to Hezekiah and Gideon before turning to the sign offered to Ahaz in Isa 7:11, explaining, "Isaiah rebuked Ahaz for despising the sign of the divine will toward him, for he did not believe the promise . . . Therefore, signs do not justify, but the faith of Hezekiah and Gideon had to be buoyed up, strengthened, and confirmed by such signs."[44] Apparently, Melanchthon believed the sign was a promise to Ahaz for the deliverance of Israel. He seems to have believed the sign acted as an authentication for Ahaz as well.

Martin Luther

Unlike Melanchthon, Martin Luther was unmistakably clear on his stance concerning the verse. Many of Luther's writings confronted individual issues, although he also lectured on various books of the Bible. In one instance, Luther lectured specifically on Isa 7:14. He stated:

> In Hebrew it is "has conceived," and that is the indication of a miracle; it is as if the prophet were already seeing it. Again, since he says that it is God's sign, it is necessary that that conception and birth be in a different manner than is commonly and naturally the

---

43. The author has selected specific Reformers who directly addressed Isa 7:14. Again, this list is not exhaustive. The author intentionally moved passed the Middle Ages because writers during this period had little to say about Isa 7:14. In one instance, Bernard of Clairvaux mentioned Isa 7:14 in his writings: "Isaiah says: Behold, a virgin shall conceive and bear a son. See you have a young woman, the Virgin. Do you also want to hear who the man is? He announces: And he will be called Emmanuel, that is, God with us" (Wilken, *Isaiah*, 107).

44. Melanchthon, *Melenchthon*, 134.

case, for it would not be a sign if one who today is a virgin would become pregnant after a half year. Therefore, she has to be both a virgin and with child. Matthew 1:21f. clearly explains this.[45]

Luther provided a clear interpretation of the verse. He also interpreted the sign to be the birth of the child and affirmed that Isa 7:14 applied to Jesus' birth in every way.

John Calvin

John Calvin, Luther's contemporary, also addressed the verse in his commentary on Isaiah. Calvin addressed the nature of the sign that Ahaz could have asked for in Isa 7:11, stating, "He [God] allows him an unrestricted choice of a miracle to demand either what belongs to earth or what belongs to heaven."[46] It appears that Calvin understood the sign God offered to Ahaz to be miraculous.

Calvin provided his interpretation of the event before he discussed any other aspects of Isa 7:14. He noted the controversy between Christians and Jews over the interpretation and claimed that the Jews had misconstrued the verse's true meaning. Calvin asserted that the Jews "are hard pressed by this passage for it contains an illustrious prediction concerning the Messiah."[47] Calvin examined the verse word by word and arrived at the translation of עַלְמָה. He claimed that "young woman" was a possible translation but argued it did not make sense in this context.

Calvin's reasoning for such a conclusion also focused on the nature of the sign: "For what wonderful thing did the Prophet say, if he spoke of a young woman who conceived through intercourse with a man? It would certainly have been absurd to hold out this as a sign or a miracle."[48] Calvin believed the verse prophesied the birth of Jesus based on his understanding of what a sign meant.

---

45. Luther, *Isaiah*, 84.
46. Calvin, *Isaiah*, 104.
47. Ibid., 107.
48. Ibid.

HISTORICAL INTERPRETATIONS OF ISAIAH 7:14

INTERPRETATIONS BY THE PURITANS[49]

John Owen

After Reformers like Calvin and Luther, another zealous group of writers known as the Puritans wrote on various doctrinal issues. One popular writer of the Puritan era was John Owen. Owen discussed a number of different doctrinal issues in his writings, and one of particular interest was the hypostatic union of Jesus. Owen addressed how Jesus was fully God yet still fully human and used Isaiah 7:14 as support for his argument:

> That which followeth hereon, is the union of the two natures in the same person, or the hypostatical union . . . Isa. vii. 14, "Behold, a virgin shall conceive, and bear a son, and shall call his name Immanuel," as Matt. i. 23. He who was conceived and born of the virgin was Immanuel, or God with us.[50]

Owen palpably believed that Isa 7:14 was biblical support for this theological doctrine.

Jonathan Edwards

One of the most well-known Puritans in history also addressed the verse. Jonathan Edwards discussed a number of different issues in his writings, including the interpretation of Isa 7:14. He stated:

> The thing here mentioned was a sign that God had mercy in store for them, and it was a sign that neither the nation nor the house of David could be destroyed inasmuch as this blessing was in them. That a child should be born of a virgin was a sign of God's power and ability to preserve them. That his name should be Immanuel, God with us, was a sign that [God] would be with them to preserve them. That this Immanuel was to be born of the house of David was a sign that they need not fear the cutting off of the crown of Israel in the house of David by setting up the son of Tabeal, or any other way.[51]

---

49. The author has selected specific Puritans in this section of the book. The list is not exhaustive.

50. Owen, *Christ*, 226.

51. Edwards, *Bible*, 637. Also see Beeke and Jones, *Puritan*, 405.

Again, Edwards was clear about his position on the verse. He argued that the verse was a reference to Jesus' birth. Furthermore, like Chrysostom, Edwards claimed that the sign was the birth of the child. The interpretation that Isa 7:14 predicted the birth of Jesus was one of the most prevalent in the history of this verse, but as scholarship developed, more interpretations arose.

A SELECTED ANALYSIS OF MODERN SCHOLARS[52]

In the modern era, biblical discussion reached new heights. Theories developed quickly and often. As noted, critical scholarship often drove the debate. Critical scholars presented more evidence against evangelical positions, and evangelical authors offered their rebuttals. This period of scholarship continues today. Several respected authors have offered their own interpretations of Isa 7:14.

There are three predominate views concerning the interpretation of this verse: future fulfillment, dual fulfillment, and contemporary fulfillment. Those who hold to a future fulfillment claim that only the birth of Jesus satisfied the prophecy. The dual fulfillment scholars argue that a child in Isaiah's day may have typified the birth of Jesus. The contemporary fulfillment claims that the prophecy was only in reference to an ordinary birth in Isaiah's day. Many scholars provide fresh evidence for the debate, which this chapter will now examine.

Future Fulfillment

J. Alec Motyer

J. Alec Motyer is a British biblical scholar widely recognized for his studies on Isaiah. In one commentary on Isa 7:14, Motyer addressed Isa 7:14 and analyzed each aspect of the verse.[53] He noted how the prophet presented the sign in the text, claiming that it represented a retrospective confirma-

---

52. The author has chosen specific modern scholars for their extensive work in the book of Isaiah, but this list is not exhaustive. For a complete list of authors, see Appendix C.

53. Motyer, *Isaiah*, 84.

tion of what God had already promised Ahaz.⁵⁴ Motyer then provided a thorough analysis of אוֹת and gave two possible explanations for the way writers used the word. He said, "Firstly, the sign is used in the sense of a 'present persuader,' it is designed to promote some action or reaction in the immediate present."⁵⁵ He went on to say, "The alternative understanding of 'sign' is that it is a 'future confirmation,' i.e., it is designed to follow a series of events, to confirm them as acts of God and to fix a stated interpretation upon them."⁵⁶ Motyer noted that it was incorrect to assume that Ahaz needed to witness the event in order for it to strengthen his faith. Motyer argued that Ahaz's faith was already determined, which is why he refused the original offer of a sign.⁵⁷ He also concluded that the sign was actually more of an attestation to the doom of Jerusalem instead of a sign of provision.⁵⁸

In the next section of his commentary, Motyer examined the translation of עַלְמָה. He noted that the word could mean "young woman" but argued that the context should be the determining factor. He cited several different passages for each possible translation and moved on to discuss the nature of a sign, arguing that "Even supposing that virgin is collective and that a rash of Immanuels appears in the land, such naming would be cynically dismissed in the palace as the product of female hysteria and not seen as a heaven-sent sign."⁵⁹ Motyer seemed to believe that the sign needed to be out of the ordinary for it to qualify as a sign.

Motyer next dealt with the identification of the Immanuel child. He wrote, "Finally, it is impossible to separate this Immanuel from the Davidic king whose birth delivers his people and whose complex name includes Mighty God."⁶⁰ He discussed the births of other children who could have fulfilled the prophecy. He noted that some scholars claimed Isaiah's son, Maher-Shalal-Hash-Baz, was the best candidate for the Immanuel child. He dismissed this possibility based on several different factors—the main one being that Isaiah's wife was not a virgin.⁶¹

---

54. Ibid. Also see Hanke, *Virgin Birth*, 23–29.
55. Motyer, "Isaiah 7:14," 120.
56. Ibid. For an excellent discussion on this, see Hindson, *Immanuel*, 34–46.
57. Motyer, "Isaiah 7:14," 120.
58. Ibid., 120–25.
59. Ibid., 85. Also see Evans, *Virgin Birth*, 97–104.
60. Ibid., 96.
61. Ibid.

Motyer argued that the birth of the child must have occurred sometime in the far future from when Isaiah gave the prophecy. He stated, "On the one hand, it seems Immanuel will be born within the immediate threat and on the other, that he will be born in the undated future, for before his birth Judah and Israel will be scattered and need regathering."[62] Motyer discussed how each child born in the line of David from that point forward served as "guardians" of the messianic line.[63] Eventually, Motyer concluded that the child would be born under Roman rule several hundred years after Isaiah gave the prophecy.

John Gresham Machen

John Gresham Machen was an American theologian during the twentieth century. He was the professor of New Testament at Princeton Seminary between 1906 and 1929 and was influential in the conservative movement during his lifetime. He also wrote extensively on the virgin birth of Jesus. In fact, he devoted entire books to the subject.

Machen discussed almost every issue surrounding the virgin birth from the narrative in Luke to the Jewish anticipation of a Messiah.[64] He spent a large amount of time discussing the possible translations of עַלְמָה, but concluded that although the word could mean "young woman" it was best translated as "virgin" in the context of Isaiah 7:14.[65] He then examined who the Immanuel child might have been. Machen agreed that Isaiah's son, Maher-Shalal-Hash-Baz, was a possible candidate, but concluded that Isaiah called his wife the "prophetess," thus "virgin" did not apply.[66] He also mentioned that the birth of Hezekiah did not satisfy the prophecy because he was born before Ahaz became king.[67] After rejecting all other interpretations he wrote: "Why should an ordinary birth be regarded as a 'sign?' That word naturally leads us to think of some event like the turning back of the sun on Hezekiah's dial, or the phenomena in connection with Gideon's fleece."[68]

62. Motyer, *Isaiah*, 87.
63. Ibid.
64. Machen, *Birth*, 288–89. Also see Vine, *Isaiah*, 35.
65. Machen, *Birth*, 289.
66. Ibid.
67. Ibid.
68. Ibid., 290–91.

Machen also presented evidence that the prophecy was a reference to the birth of Jesus.[69] He did not rule out the possibility that the verse may have had a dual fulfillment, but he favored a single fulfillment approach. He stated:

> So, in our passage, the prophet, when he placed before the rebellious Ahaz that strange picture of the mother and the child, was not merely promising deliverance to Judah in the period before a child then born should know how to refuse the evil and choose the good, but also, moved by the Spirit of God, was looking forward, as in a dim and mysterious vision, to the day when the true Immanuel, the mighty God and Prince of Peace, should lie as a little babe in a virgin's arms.[70]

Apparently, Machen interpreted the sign as the birth of the Immanuel child and saw the verse as a prophecy of Jesus' birth.[71]

Franz Delitzsch

Franz Delitzsch was a nineteenth-century theologian and Hebraist. He was a professor of theology at the University of Rostock, the University of Erlangen, and the University of Leipzig. He defended the Jews from anti-Semitic attacks and was a world-renowned scholar in the field of Old Testament studies. He also wrote a thorough commentary on the book of Isaiah.

The first detail Delitzsch examined in his discussion of the context of Isa 7:14 was the nature of the sign that God offered to Ahaz in Isa 7:11.[72] For Delitzsch, the crux of the interpretation of the passage relied on whether or not the sign was miraculous:

> A sign was something, some occurrence, or some action, which served as a pledge of the divine certainty of something else. This was secured sometimes by visible miracles performed at once . . . The thing to be confirmed on the present occasion was what the prophet had just predicted in so definite a manner, viz. the maintenance of Judah with its monarchy, and the failure of the wicked enterprise of the two allied kingdoms. If this was to be attested to

---

69. Ibid., 291.
70. Ibid., 293.
71. Ibid. Cf. Gray, *Isaiah*, 121.
72. Delitzsch, *Isaiah*, 215.

Ahaz in such a way as to demolish his unbelief, it could only be affected by a miraculous sign.[73]

Delitzsch declared that the event had to be miraculous in order for it to qualify as a sign.

Next, the author turned his attention to the woman who would bear the Immanuel child. He dismissed the possibility that it was Isaiah's wife by stating, "For if it were to her that he referred, he could hardly have expressed himself in a more ambiguous and unintelligible manner."[74] He supported this belief by arguing that עַלְמָה was the correct word for the description of this woman. Delitzsch claimed that the word implied a girl who was approaching the age of marriage but who remained a virgin.[75] He proceeded to examine the various interpretations of who the Immanuel child might have been.

Delitzsch scrutinized interpretations that argued the child was Hezekiah or some other contemporary baby boy.[76] Delitzsch proposed several reasons that these explanations did not satisfy the prophecy. One reason was Isaiah's use of הִנֵּה (*hinnēh*). Translators generally render the word as "behold" in English.[77] Delitzsch claimed the presence of this word was evidence that the prophecy would take place in the future, writing, "Moreover, the condition of pregnancy, which is here designated by the participial adjective הָרָה, was not an already existing one in this instance, but something future, as well as the act of bearing, since *hinnēh* is always used by Isaiah to introduce a future occurrence."[78] Based on this evidence, Delitzsch concluded that Jesus' birth fulfilled the prophecy. He stated, "But if the Messiah was to be Immanuel in this sense . . . His birth must also of necessity be a wonderful or miraculous one."[79] Thus, Delitzsch, like Motyer and Machen, argued for a single fulfillment view of the prophecy. Still, some scholars find evidence for a dual fulfillment approach to the text.

---

73. Ibid.
74. Delitzsch, 217. Also see Feinberg, "Isaiah 7:14," 253.
75. Delitzsch, 217.
76. Ibid.
77. Leupold, *Isaiah 1–9*, 153–58.
78. Delitzsch, *Isaiah*, 216. Also see Porúbčan, "Word 'ôt in Isaiah 7:14," 157; and Kissane, *Isaiah*, 87–90.
79. Ibid., 220.

Dual Fulfillment

Walter C. Kaiser

Walter Kaiser is a well-known scholar in the field of Old Testament studies whose article on the interpretation of Isa 7:14 took a different approach to the verse's interpretation than scholars like Motyer, Machen, and Delitzsch.[80]

Kaiser began the article by discussing the various hermeneutical methods one might use when examining a passage like Isa 7:14, explaining that the goal was to uncover what Isaiah and God intended "for Ahaz when they gave the declaration of Isaiah 7:14."[81] For Kaiser, this is the crux of the interpretive struggle. He concluded, "[I]t is improper to erect a dual meaning or a multi-tiered level of 'readings' to a prophetic text like Isaiah 7:14."[82] In essence, Kaiser was not willing to accept that Isaiah's prophecy mysteriously predicted the birth of Jesus if Isaiah never intended that meaning.

Kaiser went on to discuss his own interpretation of what the prophecy meant, beginning with the naming of Isaiah's three sons as signs. Kaiser stated, "Each of these three children are 'signs' and each child is born in fulfillment of the promise made to David that his seed should be eternal and that he would have an eternal dominion wielding a peaceful scepter."[83] For Kaiser, the issue was not the meaning of אות, but rather the promise that God gave to David. For instance, Kaiser spent the remainder of the article discussing the timeline for Hezekiah's birth. Hezekiah's birth was important because Kaiser believed he fulfilled the contemporary aspect of the prophecy in reference to the house of David.[84]

The author concluded that Hezekiah must have been the Immanuel child mentioned in the prophecy,[85] but Kaiser did not rule out that the prophecy also applied to the birth of Jesus. Kaiser claimed there would be another fulfillment in a later event, which he argued was Jesus' birth. In fact, he stated, "This is not to argue for a double sense or multiple meaning; instead, this definition seeks to represent the biblical facts which demand

---

80. For an alternative approach to the text that counteracts Kaiser's claims, see Johnson, "Authorship," 218–27.

81. Kaiser, "Isaiah 7:14," 55.

82. Ibid., 60.

83. Ibid., 61.

84. Ibid., 62.

85. This book cannot adequately address all of Kaiser's conclusions for this timeline. For more on the chronology of Hezekiah's birth and reign, see ibid., 62–66.

that the near and the distant were, in some real sense, linked in the prophetic revelatory vision from God."[86] In essence, Kaiser claimed that Isaiah meant for the verse to be applied to Hezekiah's and to Jesus' birth at the same time.

Kaiser maintained that the proper translation of עַלְמָה was "virgin."[87] This did not present a problem for Kaiser because he claimed that Hezekiah's birth did not have to be identical to the prophecy. He wrote:

> The only critical point is that both share enough distinctive common elements so that a single sense and meaning links them and thereby the one heeding Scripture will be unerringly pointed towards the final fulfillment. In this case, the most essential common feature shared is that both Hezekiah and Messiah were from "the House of David" which God had promised would never perish.[88]

Thus, Kaiser did not argue for an exclusively future fulfillment of the prophecy. He saw one intended meaning in the prophecy but claimed a dual fulfillment approach to be the most accurate interpretation of the verse.

John N. Oswalt

John Oswalt is a distinguished scholar in the field of Old Testament studies and has written multiple books on the subject. In his commentary on Isaiah, Oswalt addressed the nature of signs in Isa 7:14. Oswalt took a similar approach to Delitzsch, but he was not as conclusive in his argument. He stated, "In the Bible, signs may be miraculous, as in the deliverance from Egypt (Deut. 6:22) or the feeding of the five thousand (John 6:14), but they may also be a symbolic means whereby a prediction is made memorable."[89] Oswalt did not deny that signs could be miraculous, but he left room for the possibility that they could also be symbolic.[90]

Oswalt then turned his attention to the fulfillment of the prophecy. He did not discuss the translation of עַלְמָה until after he provided his evidence for what fulfilled the prophecy. Like Kaiser, Oswalt took a different approach to the fulfillment. He chose a dual fulfillment view, explaining,

---

86. Ibid., 62.
87. Ibid.
88. Ibid., 67.
89. Oswalt, *Isaiah*, 205.
90. Also see Ortland, *Isaiah*, 90–91.

"While maintaining that the primary reference was to Christ, they [scholars who hold to a dual fulfillment] have understood that the sign was fulfilled in a secondary way during Ahaz's lifetime."[91] Oswalt understood that the author of Matthew used the text as a reference to Jesus' birth, but he also argued that there must have been some sort of contemporary fulfillment.[92]

Oswalt went on to analyze what fulfilled the prophecy in the days of Ahaz. He admitted that "the enigmatic nature of the references" made it difficult to determine who the child of Ahaz's time may have been.[93] Nevertheless, Oswalt continued his examination by dismissing the possibility that the child was Hezekiah. He pointed out that Hezekiah was born in 741 BC, making him about six years old at the time of the prophecy. Oswalt concluded: "Immanuel and Maher-shalal-hash-baz were one and the same."[94] He claimed the birth of the child in Isa 8:3 and the reference to Immanuel in 8:10 proved they were synonymous. Based on this conclusion, Oswalt held to a dual fulfillment approach to the interpretation of Isa 7:14.

Herbert M. Wolf

Herbert Martin Wolf was a distinguished professor of Old Testament studies at Wheaton College. He served at this institution for over thirty years and was renowned as a conservative Old Testament scholar. Wolf contributed to a number of different Old Testament works, including a commentary on the book of Isaiah and a scholarly article concerning the interpretation of Isa 7:14.

In his commentary, Wolf began his examination of the passage by discussing Ahaz's difficult situation.[95] Wolf noted that God offered a sign as a way to "bolster Ahaz's faith."[96] He concluded that Ahaz refused the sign because he was already certain that appealing to Assyria was the best decision.[97] Because Ahaz rejected God's offer of a sign, Wolf stated, "Therefore

---

91. Oswalt, *Isaiah*, 208.
92. Ibid., 208–9.
93. Ibid., 212.
94. Ibid., 213.
95. Wolf, *Isaiah*, 90. Also see Wolf, "Immanuel," 449–56.
96. Ibid.
97. Ibid.

The Hebrew Word for 'Sign' and its Impact on Isaiah 7:14

God would give Ahaz a sign, and the king would have to listen to it."[98] Wolf quoted Isa 7:14 and discussed the various interpretations of the verse.

Wolf noted that most conservative scholars emphasize the messianic implications of the verse, but they fail to "fit the verse into its historical context."[99] He went on to say that critical scholars focus too closely on the contemporary fulfillment and ignore the possible messianic relationship to Jesus.[100] Wolf argued that the solution to this interpretive struggle might lie in the use of עַלְמָה in Ugaritic literature. He wrote:

> In Ugaritic literature there is a passage that says "a virgin will give birth" (*tld btlt* is parallel to *hl glmt tld bn*). In its context the phrase means that a particular virgin would soon be engaged and that after her marriage she would become the mother of a son. At the time the prediction was made, she was a virgin. This kind of announcement was a blessing on the upcoming marriage.[101]

Wolf believed that this piece of evidence was vital for understanding Isa 7:14, arguing that a similar announcement was taking place in the context of this verse.

Wolf went on to propose that Isaiah 7 and 8 showed Isaiah was about to be engaged to a prophetess.[102] He stated, "The first three verses of chapter 8 describe the engagement and marriage. After the wedding Isaiah's wife became pregnant and subsequently had a son named Maher-Shalal-Hash-Baz ... and he was to be a sign for Ahaz and his generation."[103] Wolf's approach solved the translation of עַלְמָה by allowing Isaiah to marry a new wife and showing how the sign would be relevant for the current generation. Wolf argued that a child must have been born within a period of three years of the prophecy, or it would not have qualified as a sign. He also concluded that Jesus' birth fulfilled Isa 7:14 in a fuller sense.[104] Like Oswalt and Kaiser, Wolf saw the verse fulfilled in a dual sense.

---

98. Ibid.
99. Ibid.
100. Ibid.
101. Ibid.
102. Ibid.
103. Ibid.
104. Wolf, *Isaiah*, 91.

Contemporary Fulfillment

Ronald E. Clements

Ronald Clements has contributed greatly to the discussion of this passage in his commentary on Isaiah. In that commentary, he first discussed the interpretation of the prophecy. He reviewed three possibilities for the woman's identity according to the contemporary approach. He stated that the woman may have been either any woman in the kingdom, a royal consort, or the prophet's wife.[105] Clements dismissed the first view because it robbed "the birth of the character of a sign."[106] He claimed, "[T]he removal of the threat had occurred before the birth took place."[107] Clements also dismissed the second view because the king would have become the giver of the prophetic message by naming the child. He concluded that the third view was correct because "it is not the birth which was to form the sign, but rather the name that was to be given to the child . . . Thus we have here the second in the series of three children, each bearing sign-names given by the prophet."[108] According to Clements, the names acted as a sign to Israel because of their symbolic nature. Each name contained a special meaning that applied to the future of Israel.[109]

Clements concluded that a sign "was not necessarily an event or object that was miraculous."[110] He went on to say, "This is evidently the case here, for it is to be the name which the child bears which constitutes the sign, rather than any circumstances surrounding the birth."[111] The name Immanuel represented the Lord's faithfulness to the nation, not the literal presence of God. For Clements, the verse had no messianic fulfillment, and he noted that those interpretations came in later Christian history.

---

105. Clements, *Isaiah*, 86.
106. Ibid.
107. Ibid. Also see Goulder, "Destiny," 203–65.
108. Clements, *Isaiah*, 86. Also see Brueggemann, *Isaiah*, 70. Brueggemann holds that the sign was the naming of the child as well.
109. Ibid.
110. Ibid., 87.
111. Ibid.

The Hebrew Word for 'sign' and its Impact on Isaiah 7:14

Otto Kaiser

Otto Kaiser is a renowned Old Testament scholar who taught at the University of Marburg. He has written several books on the Old Testament, including a commentary on the book of Isaiah. In his commentary, Kaiser took a similar approach to Clements.

First, Kaiser commented on the nature of the sign offered to Ahaz in Isa 7:11, explaining, "The sign guarantees that Yahweh's presence, power, promise, and threats will be realized."[112] Like many other commentators, Kaiser neither confirmed nor denied that the sign was to be miraculous. He noted that Ahaz could have asked for anything as confirmation but refused based on his own piety.[113] Kaiser then turned his attention to the interpretation of Isa 7:14. He noted the disagreement among scholars about what the verse meant and briefly discussed the translation of עַלְמָה. Kaiser dismissed any connection to a messianic prediction.

Kaiser's approach to this verse differed from most scholars before him. Kaiser stated that the Immanuel child was not Hezekiah for the chronological reasons already noted, but he also refuted the idea that the child was Isaiah's.[114] He stated, "[I]t is quite improbable that during the war with Syria and Ephraim yet another son should have been born to the prophet ... any speculation that he may have had a second wife is idle, since the texts say nothing of this."[115] Kaiser also dismissed the possibility that Immanuel was another name for Mahar-Shalal-Hash-Baz or Shear-Jashub,[116] claiming instead that there was a dual aspect to the sign.

Kaiser claimed that the nature of the sign depended on what God wanted to confirm to Ahaz. He wrote, "I cannot see that there is any doubt that the whole sense of the sign of God which Isaiah is proclaiming is that of a prophecy of doom."[117] The doom did not refer to Israel, but to the attacks of Syria and Ephraim. Next, Kaiser claimed that as a confirmation of that failure, women would name their sons Immanuel.[118] Kaiser asserted, "The danger will disappear so rapidly that women who are now with child

---

112. Kaiser, *Isaiah 1–12*, 98.
113. Ibid., 98–99.
114. Ibid.
115. Ibid.
116. Ibid.
117. Ibid., 103.
118. Ibid.

will name their sons, in thankfulness for being saved, 'Immanuel,' 'God with us.'"[119] Kaiser's approach is unique, but Kaiser still saw a contemporary fulfillment in the text.

Christopher R. Seitz

Another modern scholar who holds a contemporary fulfillment approach is Christopher Seitz. Seitz is professor of Old Testament at Yale Divinity School. He also has a commentary on the book of Isaiah. In his discussion on Isa 7:14, Seitz briefly addressed the nature of the sign:

> The provision of a sign that is meant to confirm the divine promise is a theme that appears in another later encounter between prophet and royal figure: on the occasion of Hezekiah's sickness unto death (37:7). There as here, the point of the sign is to underscore God's intention to do as he has promised.[120]

Seitz understood the sign represented a confirmation of God's promise to Ahaz and connected it with the sign provided to Hezekiah.

Seitz claimed that Ahaz's refusal of a sign meant that God would give a sign directly to the line of David; thus, the child must have been royalty. Seitz stated, "The prophet addresses a specific figure who is known by him and the kin, namely, 'the young woman' (*ha 'almah*). We take this specificity to mean that the young woman is one of the king's own consorts, who is known by him."[121] Seitz claimed that the woman in the king's harem had already conceived the child and eventually named him Immanuel. For Seitz, the significance of the child's name was the determining factor in the interpretation.[122] This child later became a part of the royal remnant after Assyria defeated Israel and proved God's faithfulness to the nation. This was the only interpretation Seitz entertained, and it was clearly a contemporary fulfillment approach.

---

119. Ibid.
120. Seitz, *Isaiah*, 78.
121. Ibid.
122. Ibid.

CONCLUSION

Scholars have clearly interpreted Isa 7:14 differently. Even some Jews disagreed with the LXX translation of עַלְמָה. The author of the Gospel of Matthew applied Isa 7:14 to the birth of Jesus. The church fathers consistently referred to Isa 7:14 to support the humanity and divinity of Jesus. Furthermore, scholars from the Reformation and Puritan eras also held to this interpretation. Substantial evidence demonstrates that such an interpretation was historically popular.

The rise of modern scholarship brought new interpretations to the discussion. Scholars generally took one of three positions: a future fulfillment, dual fulfillment, or contemporary fulfillment. Even these categories have their own subdivisions based on scholarly disagreement over the minutiae of what fulfilled the prophecy. Few of these scholars based their interpretations on the presence of אוֹת in the text. Some did not discuss it at all. Most argued that the existence of עַלְמָה or some other contextual evidence determined the interpretation of the prophecy.

In light of the evidence uncovered thus far, there is still no clear interpretation of the verse. Each view is reasonably supported by evidence. Thus, it is necessary to analyze how Isaiah used אוֹת throughout his book and determine whether its presence in 7:14 helps clarify this confusion.

6

Isaiah's Use of אוֹת

THE AUTHOR OF ISAIAH used אוֹת eleven times in his book, nine of which occurred outside of chapter 7.[1] An examination of how the prophet used the word elsewhere in his book will establish a foundation for how one should approach Isa 7:14. If the prophet used אוֹת in the same way as the other Old Testament writers, then one would expect its appearance in Isa 7:14 to follow the same pattern.

ISAIAH 8:18

After Isa 7:14, the first time the author used אוֹת was Isa 8:18: "Behold, I and the children whom the Lord has given me are signs [אֹתוֹת] and portents [מוֹפְתִים] in Israel from the Lord of hosts, who dwells on Mount Zion." The first part of the chapter reveals that God gave Isaiah another son with a symbolic name (Isa 8:1–3). Gary Smith noted, "Chapter 8 begins a new message (separate from chap. 7), though it is closely related to chap. 7, because both mention a child who will be a sign of God's plans for the future and both talk about the consequences of the Syro-Ephraimite war."[2] Smith observed that chapter 7 and 8 both mention children who functioned as signs.

---

1. *BDB*, s.v. אוֹת.
2. Smith, *Isaiah 1–39*, 219. Also see Irvine, *Isaiah*, 179–213.

The verb sequence of Isa 8:18 demonstrates that God gave Isaiah the children, and then the children were designated as signs.³ This is an important distinction to make, because God did not give the children directly as signs.⁴ Essentially, Isaiah referred to his sons' names in verse 18. Isaiah's name means, "YHWH will save."⁵ His first son's name, Shear-Jashub, means "A remnant shall return."⁶ The new son's name, Mahar-Shalal-Hash-Baz, means "hasten to the spoil, quick to the prey."⁷ Each name relayed a specific message to the people of Israel; thus, their names alone conveyed a message from God. Edward Kissane observed that the names all contained either a message of disaster or a promise of restoration.⁸

It appears that the writer used אוֹת and מוֹפֵת in the same way as other authors of Old Testament books. The names functioned symbolically as signs to anyone who heard the prophet's message because they authenticated God's words for the nation. In the same way, they were a wonder because they symbolized coming events, but they did so in an abnormal or marvelous way.

ISAIAH 19:20

The prophet did not use the word again until Isa 19:20: "It will be a sign [אוֹת] and a witness to the Lord of hosts in the land of Egypt. When they cry to the Lord because of oppressors, he will send them a savior and defender, and deliver them." The context for this verse is the oracle concerning Egypt. According to the oracle, there would be a time when an altar to the God of Israel would stand at the border of Egypt.⁹ The altar would act as a sign to those who saw it that God was for the nation (cf. Josh 22:9–12).¹⁰

---

3. Ibid.
4. Ibid.
5. Alexander, *Isaiah*, 184.
6. Ibid.
7. Ibid.
8. Kissane, *Isaiah*, 108. Also see Delitzsch, *Isaiah*, 238; Motyer, *Isaiah*, 96; and Goldingay, *Isaiah*, 69.
9. Delitzsch, *Isaiah*, 364–65. Scholars disagree about the time period for this prophecy. See Clements, *Isaiah*, 172; and Goldingay, *Isaiah*, 120. Cf. Motyer, *Isaiah*, 168–69.
10. Bultema, *Isaiah*, 200–201.

The author's use of אות in this text is almost identical to the way the author of Joshua used the word in Josh 4:6. In that verse, the Israelites built an altar as a memorial after crossing the Jordan River. Its purpose was to remind future generations of God's provision for the nation when they crossed into the promised land. The context of Isa 19:20 is similar to the Joshua passage, and the altar in Egypt appears to serve a similar purpose. It seems that God will designate the altar as a sign, and it will authenticate God's word to the nation that he is now the God of the land.[11] The usage does not appear to have a miraculous connotation.

ISAIAH 20:3

The prophet used the word again in Isa 20:3. According to the text, God commanded Isaiah to walk barefoot and naked for a period of three years. As in the case of the prophet Ezekiel, Isaiah's actions were a sign to those who saw him that God's judgment was about to occur in Egypt and Cush (Ezek 4:3).[12] John Oswalt commented, "The symbolic action here is the only one reported of Isaiah, but such activity was fairly frequent with Jeremiah and Ezekiel... Here Isaiah was acting out the fate of the captives."[13] As Oswalt noted, Isaiah's actions carried symbolic significance. The fourth verse reinforces Oswalt's observation: "So shall the king of Assyria lead away the Egyptian captives and the Cushite exiles" (Isa 20:4).

There is nothing strange about Isaiah's use of אות in this context. The word signified a symbolic action that authenticated a spoken word from God. There is nothing miraculous about its use, and it appears to function similarly to the previously examined symbolic actions in the Old Testament.

ISAIAH 37:30

Isaiah used אות again in Isa 37:20. The word appears after a long polemic against the nation of Assyria.[14] Hezekiah prayed to God and asked for protection from the invading nation. God responded that Assyria would not

---

11. Kissane, *Isaiah*, 220.
12. Young, *Isaiah*, 2:55–56. Also see Clements, *Prophecy*, 38–39.
13. Oswalt, *Isaiah*, 384.
14. Mauchline, *Isaiah*, 231.

conquer Jerusalem.[15] Isaiah 37:35 states that God would defend the city for his own sake and for the sake of David. At the end of the prophecy against Assyria, God designated certain events as a sign to confirm that his words would come true.[16] It is likely that the sign was for Hezekiah, since Assyria would not have heard the prophecy.[17]

The passage is difficult to interpret, but it seems that God declared the following years of harvest would serve as a sign to Israel. The focus is on the food production of the land over the next three years. According to Smith, the siege of Assyria would have cut off all of Israel's food supply.[18] Smith argued that Israel would not have had time to plant crops due to preoccupation with the defense against Assyria. The second year of harvest would also suffer because of the lack of grain, but the economy should have returned to normal by the end of the third year.[19] Young wrote, "In the third year, however, the people were to sow and harvest as usual, signifying that the period of calamity and danger would be over."[20] It appears that these events served as a sign to Israel and confirmed God's promise to deliver Jerusalem.[21]

The writer used אות in a common way in this passage. He prophesied an event that would take place at some point in the future and declared that the event would serve as a sign to the people. The sign authenticated God's promise. Alexander noted that scholars disagree about whether or not this event was miraculous based on the presence of אות:

> Some take it in its strongest sense of miracle, and refer it, either to the usual divine interposition for the subsistence of the people during the sabbatical years, or to the miraculous provision promised in this particular case. Others understand it here as simply meaning an event inseparable from another, either as an antecedent or a consequent, so that the promise of the one is really a pledge of the other.[22]

---

15. Brueggemann, *Isaiah*, 294.
16. Widyapranawa, *Isaiah*, 247.
17. Smith, *Isaiah 1–39*, 628.
18. Ibid., 629.
19. Oswalt, *Isaiah*, 664–65. Also see Isa 55:13. The word occurs in similar fashion there.
20. Young, *Isaiah*, 498.
21. Leupold, *Isaiah 1–39*, 572–37.
22. Alexander, *Isaiah*, 71.

It appears that the latter interpretation fits the context. Alexander's observation substantiates the idea that these events did not have a miraculous nature. They occurred through the course of natural circumstances and carried the distinction of a sign. Note that God did not directly give the sign to Hezekiah; instead, he designated future events that would serve as a sign. This distinction seems to be the best way to differentiate between a miraculous or non-miraculous event. It does not appear that there was anything miraculous about the sign.

ISAIAH 38:7

The prophet used אוֹת twice in Isa 38:7 in the context of Hezekiah's healing. The author of 2 Kings recorded the parallel account and used the word in the same way. Isaiah wrote, "'This shall be the sign [אוֹת] to you from the Lord, that the Lord will do this thing that he has promised: Behold, I will make the shadow cast by the declining sun on the dial of Ahaz turn back ten steps.' So the sun turned back on the dial the ten steps by which it had declined" (Isa 38:7–8). Most scholars agree that the event certainly appeared to be miraculous. Otto Kaiser stated, "To attempt to give a scientific explanation of this legend is simply to destroy it. An eclipse of the sun, moreover, would not have brought about the event which is described."[23]

Hezekiah's healing appeared to be miraculous, and the sun moving backwards seems miraculous as well. The difference between the sign in Isa 37:30 and this passage is not the event itself. The true difference lies in who gave the sign. The Hebrew text reads that the sign would come מֵאֵת יהוה וְזֶה-לְךָ הָאוֹת . A basic translation would be: "And this will be the sign to you from the Lord." Motyer stated that the source of the sign was "from the very presence of the Lord."[24] This type of construction was absent from the previously examined passages in Isaiah. God gave the sign to Hezekiah because he asked for one. It appears that Hezekiah understood the significance of a sign and needed the authentication to confirm God's promise (cf. Judg 6:17). God was the author of the sign, and it was miraculous (cf. Gen 4:15; Num 14:22; 17:10; Judg 6:17; 2 Kgs 20:8). If the sign is only a

---

23. Kaiser, *Isaiah 13–39*, 402. This author does not agree with Kaiser that the event was only a legend, but does agree that an attempt at a scientific explanation is not necessary.

24. Motyer, *Isaiah*, 292.

designated event or object, then it does not appear to be miraculous (cf. Gen 17:11; Num 2:3; Josh 4:6; 1 Sam 2:34).

ISAIAH 66:19

Isaiah did not use the word again until Isa 66:19. The context for this passage is the declaration of God's glory among the nations. Isaiah used a phrase that included אוֹת: "And I will set a sign [אוֹת] among them. And from them I will send survivors to the nations, to Tarshish, Pul, and Lud, who draw the bow, to Tubal and Javan, to the coastlands far away, that have not heard my fame or seen my glory. And they shall declare my glory among the nations" (Isa 66:19).[25] Isaiah never described the sign, which has led to disagreement among scholars.

Shalom Paul argued that it was a reference to the Lord's ownership of his people.[26] Paul believed that the sign would be similar to the mark that God set on Cain in Gen 4:15 or the mark given to believers in Ezek 9:4.[27] Paul could be correct in noting the similarity to the mark on Cain, but the author of the Ezekiel passage did not use אוֹת when he described that mark.[28] Based on such evidence, this does not appear to have been the author's intent in Isa 66:19. The sign seems to be an event, which would coincide with the word's usage elsewhere in similar contexts (cf. Exod 3:12).

The sign also appears to carry a miraculous connotation because God would be the one providing it. Alexander stated, "[T]he clause before us would appear to mean, I will work a miracle among them or before them."[29] Smith commented, "It might be the miraculous defeat of Gog and Magog (Ezek. 38:18–23; Joel 3:9–16), God's personal appearance on the Mount of Olives to save his people with a great earthquake or some completely new divine act unparalleled in previous history."[30] Furthermore, Young stated, "[I]t is probably that we are to understand this particular sign as partaking of the nature of the miraculous . . . In the light of the context we

---

25. Also see Isa 44:13. The word occurs in the same manner in that passage.
26. Paul, *Isaiah*, 626. Also see Jefferson, "Isaiah," 225–30; Bucksbazen, *Isaiah*, 67.
27. Ibid.
28. The Hebrew word used in that passage was תָּו, and it appears in other passages that denote a physical mark on an object or person (cf. 1 Sam. 21:13).
29. Alexander, *Isaiah*, 475.
30. Smith, *Isaiah 40–66*, 749. Also see Motyer, *Isaiah*, 541. Motyer argued that it was the cross.

must interpret this as the whole wondrous series of events that occurred when the ancient Jewish nation was cast off and the Church of Jesus Christ founded."[31] Any of these interpretations are possible, but regardless of the event, it appears that because God would provide the sign, something miraculous would take place.

ISAIAH 7:11 AND 14

The evidence demonstrates that Isaiah used אות in a normal manner throughout his book. He used it in the same way as other Old Testament writers. He also used it twice in the confrontation with Ahaz in Isa 7:11 and 14. According to the text, Ahaz was in distress because Rezin, the king of Syria, and Pekah, the king of Israel, had formed a coalition against Judah (Isa 7:1).[32] In fact, Isaiah wrote, "When the house of David was told, 'Syria is in league with Ephraim,' the heart of Ahaz and the heart of his people shook as the trees of the forest shake before the wind" (Isa 7:2).

God commanded Isaiah to meet Ahaz "at the end of a conduit of the upper pool on the highway to the Washer's Field" (Isa 7:3). There does not seem to be a clear reason why Isaiah met Ahaz at this location. Some speculate that Ahaz may have feared an oncoming battle; thus, he was checking the water supply.[33] Regardless of the reason for the meeting location, Isaiah met Ahaz in a time of crisis.

The Syro-Ephraimite War forced Ahaz to decide which military alliance Judah would join.[34] Israel and Syria chose to fight against the Assyrian Empire, and upon discovering Ahaz's indecision, chose to attack Judah as well. Ahaz had several options, but all of them involved some sort of war. He was undoubtedly concerned about the future of Judah.[35] According to the text, God commanded Isaiah to tell Ahaz not to fear the coalition (Isa 7:4-6). He told Ahaz that the two nations would not stand and that within sixty-five years Israel would be "shattered from being a people" (Isa 7:7-8). That concern was the foundation for Isaiah's use of אות in this passage.

---

31. Young, *Isaiah*, 3:532.

32. Brueggemann, *Isaiah*, 64-65. Also see Brown, "Isaiah XII," 128-31; Kraeling and Heinrich, "Immanuel," 277-97.

33. For an overview of the various possibilities for this location, see Young, *Isaiah*, 1:271-72; Smith, *Isaiah 1-39*, 207-8.

34. Wildberger, *Isaiah*, 292-300.

35. Stacey, *Isaiah*, 50.

The Hebrew Word for 'Sign' and its Impact on Isaiah 7:14

A Sign for Ahaz

Isaiah declared that Ahaz might ask any sign from God that he wished. He stated, "Ask a sign [אות] of the Lord your God; let it be as deep as Sheol or high as heaven" (Isa 7:11). Ahaz's opportunity to choose any sign was similar to Hezekiah's offer in 2 Kgs 20:8–11, but even Hezekiah was only given two options.[36] The phrase "as deep as Sheol or high as heaven" (Isa 7:11) implies that Ahaz could ask for anything he wanted to authenticate God's promise of deliverance.[37]

The sign did not have to be miraculous. Oswalt wrote, "It is commonly assumed among commentators that the references to the depth and the heights necessarily mean that Isaiah was calling on Ahaz to ask for a miraculous sign . . . All the prophet is saying is that there is no limit on what Ahaz may ask."[38] In contrast, Paul Wegner stated, "In Isaiah 7:12, the sign could have been anything from the miraculous to Ahaz' mere whim, but the emphasis would clearly have been on the miraculous (since it was intended to convince Ahaz of God's protection)."[39] A miraculous or non-miraculous event would have sufficed, based on the evidence of this chapter. God could have designated an ordinary event as a sign, and it would have still authenticated his promise to Ahaz.

Ahaz refused to ask for a sign because he did not wish to put God to the test (Isa 7:12). Many scholars interpret this response as an arrogant rejection of God's offer for provision.[40] Otto Kaiser stated:

> His answer appears outwardly a pious one: it is not man's part to tempt God, but God's part to try men. But there are situations in which outward piety and inward belief are identical, and where man in his egotism hides from the call of the living God, uttered here and now, behind his piety, apparently sanctified by tradition . . . His plan is made. He is no longer prepared to submit to discussion, not even for God. Consequently he will not have anything to do with the offer of a sign . . . Clearly Ahaz had at least in the back

---

36. Motyer, "Isaiah 7:14," 120.

37. Ibid. Also see Payne, "Accession," 40–52; Moriarty, "Emmanuel," 226–33; Mørk, "Isaiah 7.14," 152–68.

38. Oswalt, *Isaiah*, 205.

39. Wegner, "Virgin Births," 471. Wegner's comments here indicate that he believes the sign given to Ahaz was miraculous, but his interpretation of the passage signifies otherwise. Also see Bostock, "Virgin Birth," 260–63.

40. See Ortland, *Isaiah*, 90; Wildberger, *Isaiah*, 305; Young, *Isaiah*, 1:280–81, 1:283.

of his mind the feeling that God might give a sign and thereby bring his plans to nothing.[41]

Because of this rejection, God declared that he would provide a sign of his own choosing (Isa 7:14). In fact, Ahaz's rejection of the sign was a foundational point in the conversation.[42]

Scholars disagree about what Isaiah meant when he said, "Hear then, O house of David!" (Isa 7:13). Some claim that the phrase was another way of speaking directly to Ahaz and the royal court.[43] This option is appealing because Isaiah used the plural form of "you" when he addressed the house of David.[44] Some scholars argue that "house of David" implied more than just those present to hear Isaiah.[45] Kissane asserted, "The plural indicates that the prophecy is of import to the whole dynasty of David and not to Ahaz alone."[46] Gerard Van Groningen took a different approach, stating, "First, the Davidic house is addressed, and through it the entire nation of Judah under its rule ... Ahaz, a son of the Davidic house, has the privilege and responsibility to serve as Yahweh's covenantal agent during a difficult time in Judah's political history."[47] Groningen's interpretation seems to be accurate. Ahaz was the current representative of the Davidic line. Thus, when Isaiah addressed the house of David, he was speaking to Ahaz and the future lineage of David.[48]

A Sign for the House of David

After Ahaz refused the sign, the house of David became the focal point of Isaiah's confrontation with Ahaz. Isaiah told Ahaz, "Therefore the Lord himself will give you a sign [אוֹת]. Behold, the virgin shall conceive and bear a son, and shall call his name Immanuel" (Isa 7:14). The controversy of this verse often revolves around the interpretation of עַלְמָה, as scholars debate

---

41. Kaiser, *Isaiah*, 98–99.

42. Ibid.

43. See Clements, *Isaiah*, 87; Stacey, *Isaiah*, 55; Surburg, "Isaiah 7:14," 110–18; Delitzsch, *Isaiah*, 216; Young, *Isaiah*, 1:282; Alexander, *Isaiah*, 166.

44. Young, *Isaiah*, 1:282.

45. See Smith, *Isaiah*, 212; Oswalt, *Isaiah*, 206; Bultema, *Isaiah*, 107; Motyer, *Isaiah*, 84; Wildberger, *Isaiah*, 306.

46. Kissane, *Isaiah*, 87.

47. Van Groningen, *Messianic*, 523. Cf. Zimmermann, "Immanuel," 154–59.

48. Ibid.

whether it should be translated "virgin" or "young woman." The focus here is on the sign.

Ahaz refused to ask for a sign, but God provided one anyway. Isaiah wrote that אֲדֹנָי הוּא (*ā dôn hû'*) would give the sign. The construction is emphatic; thus it literally reads, "The (sovereign) *Lord himself* will give you a sign."[49] It would have been acceptable for Isaiah to have said אֲדֹנָי would give the sign, but he reinforced the subject by adding the pronoun הוּא, therefore leaving no doubt about who would provide the sign.[50] Young noted:

> Possibly Isaiah deliberately uses this designation instead of the covenant name Yahweh. He wants to bring to the fore the might and omnipotence of the One who will give the sign. He who alone can give a sign, whether it be in heaven above or on the earth beneath, will now exercise his prerogative. *'adon* has control over all things, and Isaiah may have used this word by way of rebuke to the king. It is *'adon*, even He, who will give you the sign.[51]

Young observed a possible reason for Isaiah's use of אֲדֹנָי. The use of both words provides conclusive evidence that God was the giver of the sign. These words in conjunction with הִנֵּה (*hinnēh*), bring attention to the prophecy.[52] All of this evidence affects the interpretation of the sign.

Interpretations of the Sign

One's understanding of אוֹת in this verse may dictate the interpretation of sign. For instance, Robert Miller asserted that there was never any intention for the birth to be miraculous.[53] According to scholars who accept this view, if Isaiah never intended the sign to be miraculous, then there would be nothing significant about the birth of the Immanuel child.

Critical and evangelical scholars hold various opinions about what the sign was. Peter Miscall asserted, "The sign itself is ambiguous as it may consist of one element, for example, the child or the name, or of the entire process."[54] Miscall observed that there is not a clear designation of what

---

49. Italics added.
50. Also see Hindson, *Immanuel*, 32–33.
51. Young, *Isaiah*, 1:284.
52. Delitzsch, *Isaiah*, 217.
53. Miller, *Born*, 95. For more on the various interpretations, see Lattey, "Interpretations of Is. 7:14," 147–54.
54. Miscall, *Isaiah*, 37–38.

the sign was intended to be. As noted, there are three primary approaches to the fulfillment of the sign: a contemporary fulfillment, a dual fulfillment, and a future fulfillment.[55]

Contemporary Fulfillment

Those who see a contemporary fulfillment see the sign fulfilled in two possible ways: the naming of a child already born or the birth of a new child. Clements argued, "More importantly than this, it is not the birth which was to form the sign, but rather the name that was to be given to the child ... Thus we have here the second in the series of three children, each bearing sign-names given by the prophet."[56] Scholars who hold this view claim that the woman could have been Isaiah's wife,[57] a woman in Ahaz's consort,[58] or any woman in the nation.[59]

Scholars who hold a version of the contemporary position have proposed that the child's name was a sign.[60] Anyone who saw the child remembered that God was with Israel and that he promised to deliver the nation.[61] Brian Dennert asserted, "There is nothing overtly miraculous about the birth of this child. While a sign (אוֹת) can be miraculous, it does not require a miracle, only something that prompts belief in God."[62] Peter Miscall added, "In this reading the sign concerns not a miraculous birth

---

55. Ibid.

56. Clements, *Isaiah*, 86. Also see Brueggemann, *Isaiah*, 70; Stacey, *Isaiah*, 55; Ludemann, *Virgin Birth*, 70–71; Palmer, *Virgin Birth*, 4–5; Widyapranawa, *Isaiah*, 42–43; Parrinder, *Parentage*, 12–15; Miguens, *Virgin Birth*, 156–57; Lobstein, *Birth*, 75–76.

57. Youngblood, *Isaiah*, 47–48. The problem with this view is that Isaiah uses the word וְיֹלֶדֶת, which comes from יָלַד (*yālad*). There is debate about the translation of the word, but regardless of one's interpretation, the only way for Youngblood's position to be true is to make the word mean "has born." Given the construction of the word, there is no way for this to be possible.

58. Scholars who hold this position sometimes conclude that the royal son was Hezekiah. The chronological difficulty is a major weakness for this position. Furthermore, the Old Testament writers never refer to Hezekiah as "Immanuel." It does not make sense that he could fulfill this prophecy. For a thorough interpretation of this view, see Mauchline, *Isaiah*, 98; and Wildberger, *Isaiah*, 311–13.

59. Muckle, *Isaiah*, 30–31; Wildberger, *Isaiah*, 312–13; and Jensen, "Immanuel," 220–39.

60. Dennert, "Isa 7:14," 98. Also see Kelley, "Isaiah," 75; Seitz, *Isaiah*, 79.

61. Dennert, "Isa 7:14," 79.

62. Ibid.

of a unique child in the distant future but a birth in the immediate future and then deliverance from the attack shortly after the birth."[63] In addition, George Gray stated:

> It has been repeatedly argued by Christian scholars from Justin Martyr downwards that the sign which Yahweh is Himself to choose and give must be a miracle ... but the argument rests on a misconception of what the term אות, *sign*, necessarily implies, and of the purpose of the particular sign here contemplated; Yahweh had been willing to do a miracle to convince Ahaz, but a very ordinary event may serve to remind him, when the time comes, that what His prophet predicted has come true. The miracle here, so far as there is a miracle, may lie solely in the prediction. Neither the term אות, *sign*, nor the circumstances compel us to seek a miracle in the event predicted.[64]

Gray concluded that after Ahaz rejected God's proposal to provide a miracle, God determined to give Ahaz an ordinary event—the birth of a child named Immanuel.

The strength of this view relies on the reality that Ahaz would have witnessed the sign. Yeoman Muckle added, "And we are bound to believe that what is mentioned here is intended for Ahaz and his contemporaries ... Isaiah was concerned with the immediate future of his own time."[65] Thus, the sign reminded Ahaz of God's control every time he saw the Immanuel child, but the sign was not miraculous.

Dual Fulfillment

Scholars who hold to the second interpretation have suggested that the sign was the birth of a child in Isaiah's day and a prophecy foretelling the birth of Jesus. Therefore, there was a dual fulfillment.[66] A woman of Isaiah's day bore a child and named him Immanuel. This child served as a reminder that God would deliver Israel regardless of the faithlessness of Ahaz. Wegner wrote:

---

63. Miscall, *Isaiah*, 177. Also see Barton, *Isaiah*, 80. Also see Kamesar, "Isaiah 7:14," 51–75.

64. Gray, *Isaiah*, 123–24. Also see Slotski, *Isaiah*, 35.

65. Muckle, *Isaiah*, 30. Also see Brown, *Resurrection*, 64–65.

66. See Kaiser, "Isaiah 7:14," 66; Morris, *Nativity*, 41;Van Groningen, *Messianic*, 526; Oswalt, *Isaiah*, 208; LaSor, *Isaiah 7:14*, 8–9.

The child would have been born about 734 BC when the Syro-Ephraimite army had left to defend Damascus. At one point then, the people of Jerusalem faced almost certain doom, yet shortly afterwards the armies were gone. This would be convincing evidence that God had indeed delivered them. We believe that the woman had good reason to name her child "Immanuel" based upon the historical situation.[67]

According to Wegner, the birth of this child and his symbolic name provided the immediate fulfillment of the promised sign. Van Groningen added, "Mary's giving birth to Jesus Christ gave full realization to what the virgin's giving birth and naming her son did in an incomplete, but nevertheless, in a real manner."[68] Again, the strength of this interpretation is that Ahaz and his contemporaries would have witnessed the sign.

Those who take this approach argue that the birth of the Immanuel child fulfilled the sign in Isaiah's day but that the birth of Jesus gave it fuller meaning.[69] Wegner went on to say, "The dilemma with this passage is readily apparent—the sign is entirely fulfilled in its context; Matthew, however picks it up and says that it is fulfilled in Christ. First, it is important to remember this is not a prophecy, but a sign."[70] Wegner concluded that the verse was only a sign, not a prophecy, which affects its interpretation. He stated:

> I believe that the key to how Matthew reuses OT passages can be found within the text itself. Matthew employs the Greek word πληρόω meaning "to make full, fill, fill up, complete," to indicate that he believes the OT passage is being "filled up" by Jesus . . . This is not to say that OT passages are prophesying Jesus, since they can be completely understood within their OT content.[71]

Wegner concluded that Jesus' birth gave more meaning to the sign in Isaiah's day because Matthew used it in his gospel, but that purpose was not Isaiah's intent.

---

67. Wegner, "Virgin Births," 477. Wegner's interpretation is not representative of the typical mainstream dual fulfillment approach. While Wegner eventually concluded that the sign could apply to the birth of Jesus, he does not seem to believe that was the author's original intent.

68. Van Groningen, *Messianic*, 536.

69. See Wolf, "Immanuel," 449–56.

70. Wegner, "Virgin Births," 478. Also see Lattey, "Isaias 7:14," 69–76.

71. Ibid., 481. Also Van Groningen, *Messianic*, 536.

The Hebrew Word for 'sign' and its Impact on Isaiah 7:14

Future Fulfillment

Scholars who accept the future fulfillment view argue that only the birth of Jesus fulfilled the sign.[72] These scholars typically argue that Isaiah intended the sign to be miraculous; thus, an ordinary birth would not suffice. The woman would be a virgin when she conceived a child, the child would literally be "God with us" due to his divine nature, and Isaiah predicted that it would happen.[73] Alexander asserted:

> Ahaz had been offered the privilege of choosing any sign whatever, in heaven or on earth. Had he actually chosen one it would not doubt have been something out of the ordinary course of nature, as in the case of Gideon and Hezekiah. On his refusal to choose, a sign is given him unasked, and although it does not necessarily follow that it was precisely such as he would have selected... yet it seems very improbable that after such an offer, the sign bestowed would be merely a thing of every day occurrence, or at most the application of a symbolical name. This presumption is strengthened by the solemnity with which the Prophet speaks of the predicted birth, not as a usual and natural event, but as something which excites his own astonishment, as he beholds it in prophetic vision... the prophecy relates to something more than a natural and ordinary birth.[74]

Moishe Rosen added, "[R]emember that Isaiah 7:14 promised a 'sign.' An ordinary birth does not seem especially significant as a sign. The evidence points to the fact that what Isaiah is actually talking about, as incredible as it may seem, is a virgin birth."[75]

The argument focuses on the nature of אות in the context of Isa 7:14. These scholars interpret the word to mean something miraculous in this

---

72. Alexander, *Isaiah*, 170–72; Bultema, *Isaiah*, 107–8; Delitzsch, *Isaiah*, 216–20; Kissane, *Isaiah*, 89–90; Orr, *Virgin Birth*, 127–36; Motyer, *Isaiah*, 86; Hanke, *Virgin Birth*, 23–24; Lockyer, *Prophecies*, 60–61; Machen, *Birth*, 293; Gromacki, *Birth*, 140–49; Leupold, *Isaiah*, 158–60; Enslin, "Nativity," 317–38; Smith, *Isaiah*, 213–16; Vine, *Isaiah*, 35; Brown, *When Jesus Came*, 99–100; Young, *Isaiah*, 1:291; Reymond, *Messiah*, 104–5; Crannell, "Birth," 347–62.

73. Scotland, "Virgin," 27–32.

74. Alexander, *Isaiah*, 167.

75. Rosen, *Y'Shua*, 17.

passage; thus, a virgin birth would constitute something supernatural.[76] The birth authenticated God's promise that Judah would not fall.[77]

The difficulty with this approach is finding the relevance for Ahaz. Opponents of this interpretation often point to the fact that a baby's birth seven hundred years later would hardly be a comfort to Ahaz in his circumstance.[78] For instance, Oswalt argued, "But the traditional understanding is not without problems either, for it has tended to ignore the bearing of the sign upon Ahaz's own situation."[79] Oswalt correctly observed that many proponents of this view often fail to address this connection.

Scholars have provided several different answers to this problem. Robert Vasholz suggested that Isa 7:16 described a different child than 7:14–15.[80] Charles Feinberg claimed that the sign concerned Ahaz because the Messiah would be born in Judah, which implied that the kingdom would stand.[81] J. Barton Payne argued that because the sign was a prophecy, Ahaz would not have questioned the time of its fulfillment.[82] Payne explained, "Even as the Lord's second coming should motivate our faithful conduct, no matter how distant it may be . . . so Isaiah 7:14, on his miraculous first coming, was equally valid for motivating Ahaz, 730 years before Jesus' birth."[83]

John Machen, Edward Young, and Robert Reymond offered a different solution to the problem. They proposed the answer lies within Isa 7:15–22. The description of the child eating "curds and honey" is significant because only the remnant would eat this fare after Assyria had defeated much of the land.[84] They claim that this aspect of the sign carried a degree of doom for Ahaz and that the Immanuel child would identify himself with the remnant by eating the same thing.[85] The relevance for Ahaz was the time it would take this child to discern good and evil (Isa 7:16).

Isaiah 7:16 reads, "For before the boy knows how to refuse the evil and choose the good, the land whose two kings you dread will be deserted."

---

76. Müller, "Conceive," 203–7.
77. Sloyan, "Virgin," 81–84. Also see Alexander, *Isaiah*, 167.
78. Wildberger, *Isaiah*, 312.
79. Oswalt, *Isaiah*, 208.
80. Vasholz, "Isaiah 7 and 8," 82–83. Also see Calvin, *Isaiah*, 104–5.
81. Feinberg, "Isaiah 7:14," 258.
82. Payne, *Prophecy*, 292.
83. Ibid.
84. Reymond, *Messiah*, 103.
85. Ibid.

These scholars argue that the time period mentioned in this verse could have one of two different meanings. The first possible explanation is that this period was about two years, which would coincide with the time it normally takes a child to reach an age of discernment.[86] Reymond concluded that "within a couple of years or so, the threat from the northern alliance would have been removed."[87] Assyria destroyed Damascus around 732 BC, which allowed the Assyrians to carry many people from the northern kingdom into exile.

The second possible interpretation of this time period could be about thirteen years, which represented the child's age of legal accountability.[88] This period of time would have been from 734 BC to 721 BC, during which both Damascus and Samaria were overthrown.[89] Reymond summarized, "[I]t is not the time between the giving of the sign and its fulfillment that should be made the basis of relevance for Ahaz's day; rather, it is the time between the birth of the miraculous child and his coming to the age of discernment that makes the prophecy relevant to Ahaz's day."[90] Machen paraphrased the verse this way: "I see a wonderful child ... whose birth shall bring salvation to his people; and before such a period of time shall elapse as would lie between the conception of the child in his mother's womb and his coming to years of discretion, the land of Israel and Syria shall be forsaken."[91] This interpretation seems logical. It sees the birth of the child as the sign, yet still applies the sign to Ahaz and his contemporaries.

One more possible solution exists. Kirk Kilpatrick argued that the presence of Isaiah's son, Shear-jashub (Isa 7:3) is important to consider in the interpretation of Isa 7:15–16.[92] Kilpatrick suggested that after Isaiah provided Ahaz with the prophecy of the Immanuel child in Isa 7:14, he turned his attention to Shear-jashub.[93] Kilpatrick claimed that there can be a confusion of the antecedent in Hebrew.[94] He claimed that Isaiah was

---

86. Young, *Isaiah*, 1:292–93.
87. Reymond, *Messiah*, 103.
88. Ibid., 104.
89. Young, *Isaiah*, 1:293.
90. Reymond, *Messiah*, 104. Also see Wolverton, "Isaiah 8:5–15 and 7:14," 284–91.
91. Machen, *Birth*, 292.
92. Also see Blenkinsopp, *Isaiah*, 227. Blenkinsopp does not hold Kilpatrick's position, but he does argue that the presence of the child is significant in the narrative.
93. Kilpatrick, "Views of the 'Immanuel' Sign," unpublished lecture notes.
94. Ibid. For another example of this problem, see Isaiah 37:36.

referring to Shear-jashub when he stated that the child would eat curds and honey.⁹⁵ The child was still young, and by the time he was of moral decision-making, the threat would subside.⁹⁶ As with Machen, Young, and Raymond's view, this consideration is what would have been relevant to Ahaz.

CONCLUSION

Overall, Isaiah used אוֹת in the same way as other Old Testament authors. He applied the word to symbolic actions or names in Isa 8:18, 19:20, 20:3, and 37:30. Isaiah also used the word in reference to miraculous events in Isa 38:7 and 66:19. In the passages that refer to seemingly miraculous events, God was the author of the sign. This characteristic has been a determining factor in whether or not the sign was miraculous. It appears that a distinct pattern in the Old Testament shows that a God-given sign is always miraculous.

According to the data, the authors of the books of the Old Testament used אוֹת seventy-nine times. In forty-four of those instances, God designated a sign or an author used אוֹת to describe an ordinary object.⁹⁷ In all of these forty-four occurrences, the sign did not have a supernatural element. The evidence suggests that the authors of these passages understood this principle.

In the remaining thirty-five instances, God specifically provided the sign, and the sign had a miraculous connotation (Gen 4:15; Exod 4:8, 9, 17; Num 17:10; Judg 6:17).⁹⁸ In Isa 7:14, the Hebrew construction emphatically showed that God provided the sign. Not only does Isaiah declare that God would be the provider of the sign, he emphatically stated that אֲדֹנָי הוּא (the sovereign Lord himself) would give the sign (Isa 7:14). Furthermore, according to this author's research, Isa 7:14 is the only time in the Old Testament that the emphatic אֲדֹנָי הוּא appears in connection with אוֹת. The combination of this evidence suggests that Isaiah intended the sign to be miraculous.

---

95. Kilpatrick, "Views of the 'Immanuel' Sign."
96. Ibid.
97. See Appendix A.
98. Many of these occurrences refer to the plagues. While God did not specifically provide a sign in those particular contexts, he did give the plagues as signs.

If Isaiah intended the sign to be miraculous, then only an abnormal birth would suffice. The logical conclusion is that the woman Isaiah prophesied would give birth was a virgin at the time of conception. She later gave birth to a child symbolically named Immanuel. The birth of the child confirmed that Assyria would not destroy the Davidic line and that Judah would survive. Within a period of no more than twelve years, both nations that endangered Judah's existence would no longer be a threat. Thus, a future fulfillment of the prophecy seems to be the best approach to the text.

7

Conclusion

THIS BOOK BEGAN WITH an examination of the treatment of miracles by the writers of the Old Testament in order to investigate whether these authors saw God's divine intervention in certain events. Evidence showed such events served a specific purpose: at times, some events proved God's power over nature and revealed his wrath. For instance, the flood and the destruction of Sodom and Gomorrah were a result of God's judgment.

In other instances, certain events demonstrated God's providence for his people. Some authors recorded these events with the belief that God miraculously intervened in order to sustain life. God provided food for the Israelites in the wilderness, and he brought food for Elijah in a time of need. The authors attributed these events to God's intervention.

Finally, the author also provided an analysis of how some events fulfilled covenants. These events contained a supernatural element and fulfilled covenant promises from God. The birth of Isaac and the plagues on Egypt were fulfillments of previous covenants. The writer concluded that miraculous events were common in the Old Testament, and they served specific purposes. The author determined that miracles were a common part of Old Testament culture. The writers of the Old Testament believed that God intervened in the laws of nature to cause events that were outside of the ordinary.

In chapter 2, the author analyzed the way the Old Testament writers used אוֹת. The writer examined the etymology of the word and how the authors of the Old Testament used it in their writings. The author

The Hebrew Word for 'Sign' and its Impact on Isaiah 7:14

demonstrated that the word functioned in two common ways. In the first way, writers used the word in reference to ordinary objects or symbolic events. In these scenarios, an item or an action was designated as a sign, but there was no evidence that the sign was intended to be miraculous.

The second way the word appeared in the Old Testament was in reference to miraculous events. In these texts, God provided the sign. The sign was an event that God determined, and it authenticated his spoken word. These events always involved a supernatural element and served a distinct purpose. God deemed the plagues on Egypt to be signs, and he provided a miraculous sign to Gideon and Hezekiah. The chapter also examined the various cognates of אוֹת and demonstrated that these cognates functioned in the same manner. The Akkadian cognate was distinct from the Hebrew word, but authors still used it in reference to divine actions from the gods. The Aramaic cognate functioned in a synonymous way as the Hebrew word. In fact, if the cognate appeared in a passage with divine activity, the sign was usually miraculous.

The author also analyzed the way classical authors used σημεῖον in their works. The writer demonstrated that these writers understood the word could carry a supernatural connotation and applied it to signs from the gods. The New Testament writers used σημεῖον in reference to some of Jesus' miracles or a miraculous event meant to authenticate something. The author of the Gospel of John used σημεῖον to denote some of Jesus' miracles, which demonstrates the word's ability to confirm an event. The writer concluded that אוֹת could signal a miraculous event if it involved divine activity.

In chapter 3, the author addressed the usage of מוֹפֵת in the Old Testament. The writer examined the origin of the word and discussed how the writers of the Old Testament used it. The author discovered that a common translation of the word was "wonder." Like אוֹת, authors used the word for miraculous and non-miraculous events. An example of non-miraculous usage is found in writers' use of the word to describe symbolic actions. These actions were out of the ordinary and normally caused wonder or astonishment in those who witnessed them.

The writer also revealed that authors used מוֹפֵת in reference to miraculous events (Exod 4:21; 7:9; 1 Chron 16:12). These events did not authenticate anything; rather, they brought amazement to anyone who observed them. Unlike אוֹת, this word brought attention to the miracle but did not

CONCLUSION

confirm a previously spoken word. The author also examined the Greek cognate for מוֹפֵת.

The third chapter also demonstrated that τέρας carried the same definition as מוֹפֵת in Greek works. The author examined Classical Greek works and determined that the writers used τέρας in reference to a miracle that did not authenticate anything but instead caused wonder or amazement. The translators of the LXX faithfully used τέρας in place of מוֹפֵת throughout. Furthermore, the writers of the New Testament did not use τέρας by itself in reference to any miracle, which enforced the idea that a σημεῖον was needed to authenticate something.

In chapter 4, the researcher analyzed the functional differences between אוֹת and מוֹפֵת. The writer showed that authors used both words to describe certain events. The simultaneous usage of both words created a common phrase: "signs and wonders." The author of Exodus applied this phrase to the plagues, which carried into other works of the Old Testament. This usage forced the author to examine how an event could be both a sign and a wonder. The answer was in the perspective of the viewer. A sign authenticated something to the viewer who anticipated it, but to the viewer who expected nothing, the event brought wonder. In this way, authors used אוֹת and מוֹפֵת together intentionally.

The author also examined the Greek phrase σημεῖα καὶ τέρατα and found it functioned in the same manner. The writers of the New Testament did not use this phrase in reference to Jesus' miracles because those miracles were only intended to substantiate Jesus' authority. The authors more commonly applied this phrase to the miracles of the apostles. Those events authenticated their apostleship but also caused astonishment in others. It appears that the writers understood the key differences between both words and only applied the phrase to a miracle if they wanted to convey both meanings.

In chapter 5, the author reviewed the historical interpretations of Isa 7:14. The research began with the Septuagint's translation of Isa 7:14. The researcher discovered that these early Jews were among the first to provide an interpretation of the verse. By translating the Hebrew word as παρθένος, the Septuagint's translator implied the woman would be a virgin when she conceived. The author also examined how the writer of the Gospel of Matthew used the verse. The writer of Matthew's gospel clearly understood the verse to be a reference to the birth of Jesus.

Next, the writer examined early Jewish interpretations of the passage. There was some evidence that a small number of early Jews may have seen messianic significance in the verse. Still, most of the rabbis did not see a future fulfillment for the text. Many claimed that the child was Hezekiah and did not apply the verse to Jesus' birth. In contrast, the early church fathers consistently used Isa 7:14 as support for Jesus' humanity and divinity. They quoted the verse on numerous occasions as evidence that Jesus was predicted to be born of a virgin and that he was both fully God and fully human. The Reformers and Puritans were not as vocal on the subject, but scholars from both periods interpreted Isa 7:14 as a prophecy of the birth of Jesus.

Finally, the researcher analyzed the interpretations of select modern scholars. The writer's data revealed that there were three prominent interpretations of the verse: a future fulfillment, dual fulfillment, and a contemporary fulfillment. Numerous scholars provided credible evidence to support their claims.

The author determined that scholars who hold to a future fulfillment saw the sign as miraculous. They interpreted the verse to be a prophecy of Jesus' birth. Scholars who took the dual fulfillment view argued that the birth of Jesus did not satisfy the requirement for Ahaz to see the promised sign. They argued that a child born in Isaiah's day partially satisfied the prophecy, but Jesus' birth completely fulfilled the sign. These scholars did not see the birth of the contemporary child as a miraculous sign but would claim the fulfillment in the birth of Jesus was miraculous. Finally, research showed that a number of scholars understood that the birth of a child in Isaiah's day fulfilled the prophecy. They claimed a woman of that time gave birth to a son and symbolically named him Immanuel. Many of these scholars based their argument on the fact that Ahaz needed to see the promised sign and that Isaiah did not intend it to be miraculous.

In the final chapter of the book, the author examined Isaiah's use of אות. The writer analyzed each instance in which Isaiah used the word and compared its usage to previously examined Old Testament passages. The author concluded that Isaiah used אות in the exact same manner as other Old Testament authors. The evidence demonstrated that Isaiah used אות normally in Isa 7:11 and 14. The researcher showed that the word referred to a sign offered to Ahaz as confirmation that God would not allow the invading forces to destroy Judah. Ahaz rejected God's offer. As a result, God affirmed that he himself would provide a sign of his own choosing.

Conclusion

The author presented evidence that the grammatical construction confirmed God was the sole author of the sign. Based on the objective pattern that God-given signs were miraculous, the author concluded that Isaiah intended the sign of Isa 7:14 to be miraculous as well. Only a virgin birth would have been abnormal enough to be considered miraculous, because all other births would have occurred within the laws of nature. Isaiah used אוֹת because the event authenticated God's spoken word to Ahaz and to the Davidic line. He understood that the event would be miraculous but did not use מוֹפֵת because the future event substantiated a previous promise. The writer also showed the prophecy had relevance for Ahaz because of the span of time mentioned in Isa 7:15–17. Within an undetermined number of years, the threat of destruction from these invaders would be gone.

Based on this evidence, the only birth that satisfies such a miraculous event was the birth of Jesus. According to the author of the Gospel of Matthew, Mary was a virgin when she conceived and gave birth to her firstborn son (Matt 1:18–25). Jesus' birth fulfilled the requirements of the miraculous sign and authenticated God's faithfulness.

The author has provided objective evidence that demonstrates Isaiah seems to have intended others to see the upcoming sign as miraculous. If the birth was to be miraculous, then the best translation of עַלְמָה would be "virgin." As a result, the author of the Gospel of Matthew correctly applied Isa 7:14 to the birth of Jesus. The author believes this is a helpful contribution to the study of this important Old Testament passage.

Appendix A
Occurrences of אוֹת in the Old Testament with Miraculous or Non-Miraculous Results

אוֹת Designated or Given by God	Reference	Event	Result
Designated	Gen 1:14	Sun, moon, and stars	Non-miraculous
Given	Gen 4:14	Mark on Cain	Miraculous
Designated	Gen 9:12	Rainbow	Non-miraculous
Designated	Gen 9:13	Rainbow	Non-miraculous
Designated	Gen 9:17	Rainbow	Non-miraculous
Designated	Gen 17:11	Circumcision	Non-miraculous
Designated	Exod 3:12	Worship at Sinai	Non-miraculous
Given	Exod 4:8 (2)	Sign given to Moses	Miraculous
Given	Exod 4:9	Sign given to Moses	Miraculous
Given	Exod 4:17	Signs given to Moses	Miraculous
Given	Exod 4:28	Signs before Pharaoh	Miraculous
Given	Exod 4:30	Signs before Pharaoh	Miraculous
Given	Exod 7:3	Plagues	Miraculous
Given	Exod 8:23	Division of land	Miraculous
Given	Exod 10:1	Plagues	Miraculous
Given	Exod 10:2	Plagues	Miraculous
Designated	Exod 12:13	Sign of blood	Non-miraculous
Designated	Exod 13:9	Sign of memorial	Non-miraculous
Designated	Exod 13:16	Sign of memorial	Non-miraculous
Designated	Exod 31:13	Sign of the Sabbath	Non-miraculous

Appendix A

אוֹת Designated or Given by God	Reference	Event	Result
Designated	Exod 31:17	Sign of the Sabbath	Non-miraculous
Designated	Num 2:2	Tribal markers	Non-miraculous
Given	Num 14:11	Plagues	Miraculous
Given	Num 14:22	Plagues	Miraculous
Designated	Num 16:38	Censers of priests	Non-miraculous
Given	Num 17:10	Aaron's budding rod	Miraculous
Given	Deut 4:34	Plagues	Miraculous
Designated	Deut 6:8	Sign of memorial	Non-miraculous
Given	Deut 6:22	Plagues	Miraculous
Given	Deut 7:19	Plagues	Miraculous
Given	Deut 11:3	Plagues	Miraculous
Designated	Deut 11:18	Sign of memorial	Non-miraculous
Given	Deut 13:1	Miracles of prophets	Miraculous
Given	Deut 13:2	Miracles of prophets	Miraculous
Given	Deut 26:8	Plagues	Miraculous
Designated	Deut 28:46	Sign of memorial	Non-miraculous
Given	Deut 29:2	Plagues	Miraculous
Given	Deut 34:11	Plagues	Miraculous
Designated	Josh 2:12	Sign of scarlet thread	Non-miraculous
Designated	Josh 4:6	Sign of memorial	Non-miraculous
Designated	Josh 24:17	Plagues	Miraculous
Given	Judg 6:17	Fire consuming food	Miraculous
Designated	1 Sam 2:34	Death of Eli's sons	Non-miraculous
Designated	1 Sam 10:7	Saul meets prophets	Non-miraculous
Designated	1 Sam 10:9	Saul meets prophets	Non-miraculous
Designated	1 Sam 14:10	Philistine actions	Non-miraculous
Designated	2 Kgs 19:29	Fruitful harvest	Non-miraculous
Given	2 Kgs 20:8	Sign for Hezekiah	Miraculous
Given	2 Kgs 20:9	Sun moved backward	Miraculous
Given	Neh 9:10	Plagues	Miraculous
Designated	Job 21:29	Testimony of men	Non-miraculous
Designated	Ps 65:8	Creation	Non-miraculous
Designated	Ps 74:4 (2)	Military symbols	Non-miraculous

Occurrences of אות in the Old Testament

אות Designated or Given by God	Reference	Event	Result
Designated	Ps 74:9	Military symbols	Non-miraculous
Given	Ps 78:43	Plagues	Miraculous
Given	Ps 86:17	Sign of favor	Miraculous
Given	Ps 105:27	Plagues	Miraculous
Given	Ps 135:9	Plagues	Miraculous
Given	Isa 7:11	Sign for Ahaz	Miraculous
Given	Isa 7:14	Sign of Immanuel	Miraculous
Designated	Isa 8:18	Symbolic actions	Non-miraculous
Designated	Isa 19:20	Sign of memorial	Non-miraculous
Designated	Isa 20:3	Symbolic actions	Non-miraculous
Designated	Isa 30:7	Fruitful harvest	Non-miraculous
Given	Isa 38:7	Sun moved backward	Miraculous
Given	Isa 38:22	Sign for Hezekiah	Miraculous
Designated	Isa 44:25	Testimony of men	Non-miraculous
Designated	Isa 55:13	Sign of memorial	Non-miraculous
Given	Isa 66:19	Sign of division	Miraculous
Designated	Jer 10:2	Sun, moon, and stars	Non-miraculous
Given	Jer 32:20	Plagues	Miraculous
Given	Jer 32:21	Plagues	Miraculous
Designated	Jer 44:29	Symbolic event	Non-miraculous
Designated	Ezek 4:3	Symbolic actions	Non-miraculous
Designated	Ezek 14:8	Symbolic event	Non-miraculous
Designated	Ezek 20:12	Sign of Sabbath	Non-miraculous
Designated	Ezek 20:20	Sign of Sabbath	Non-miraculous

Appendix B

Occurrences of מוֹפֵת in the Old Testament with Miraculous or Non-Miraculous Results

אוֹת Designated or Given by God	Reference	Event	Result
Given	Exod 4:21	Miracles for Pharaoh	Miraculous
Given	Exod 7:3	Plagues	Miraculous
Given	Exod 7:9	Miracles for Pharaoh	Miraculous
Given	Exod 11:9	Plagues	Miraculous
Given	Exod 11:10	Plagues	Miraculous
Given	Deut 4:34	Plagues	Miraculous
Given	Deut 6:22	Plagues	Miraculous
Given	Deut 7:19	Plagues	Miraculous
Given	Deut 13:1	Miracle of prophet	Miraculous
Given	Deut 13:2	Miracle of prophet	Miraculous
Given	Deut 26:8	Plagues	Miraculous
Designated	Deut 28:46	Sign of memorial	Non-miraculous
Given	Deut 29:2	Plagues	Miraculous
Given	Deut 34:11	Plagues	Miraculous
Given	1 Kgs 13:3 (2)	Destruction of altar	Miraculous
Given	1 Kgs 13:5	Destruction of altar	Miraculous
Given	1 Chr 16:12	Unknown miracles	Miraculous
Given	2 Chr 32:24	Healing of Hezekiah	Miraculous
Given	2 Chr 32:31	Healing of Hezekiah	Miraculous

Occurrences of מוֹפֵת in the Old Testament

אוֹת Designated or Given by God	Reference	Event	Result
Given	Neh 9:10	Plagues	Miraculous
Designated	Ps 71:7	Symbolic actions	Non-miraculous
Given	Ps 78:43	Plagues	Miraculous
Given	Ps 105:5	Unknown miracles	Miraculous
Given	Ps 105:27	Plagues	Miraculous
Given	Ps 135:9	Plagues	Miraculous
Designated	Isa 8:18	Symbolic action	Non-miraculous
Designated	Isa 20:3	Symbolic actions	Non-miraculous
Given	Jer 32:20	Plagues	Miraculous
Given	Jer 32:21	Plagues	Miraculous
Designated	Ezek 12:6	Symbolic action	Non-miraculous
Designated	Ezek 12:11	Symbolic action	Non-miraculous
Designated	Ezek 24:24	Symbolic action	Non-miraculous
Designated	Ezek 24:27	Symbolic action	Non-miraculous
Given	Joel 2:30	Miracles of judgment	Miraculous
Designated	Zech 3:8	Symbolic action	Non-miraculous

Appendix C
Interpretations of Isa 7:14 by Modern Scholars

Contemporary Fulfillment	Dual Fulfillment	Future Fulfillment
J. Edward Barrett	Gleason L. Archer	Joseph A. Alexander
Robert Bratcher	Joseph P. Brennan	Oswald T. Allis
John Bright	Robert D. Culver	James L. Boyer
Walter Brueggemann	Andrew R. Fausset	James M. Bulman
R. E. Clements	Scott Golike	Harry Bultema
John Goldingay	Walter C. Kaiser	James O. Buswell
Norman Gottwald	William S. LaSor	D. A. Carson
George B. Gray	H. C. Leupold	Tan Wai Choon
E. Hammershaimb	P. Douglas McIntosh	John J. Davis
Otto Kaiser	Clyde M. Miller	Franz Delitzsch
Emil Kraeling	Dale Moody	Charles Feinberg
Antti Laato	Walter Mueller	Hobart Freeman
John Lindblom	Carl Naegelsbach	Robert G. Gromacki
J. Lust	Raymond Ortland	Robert H. Gundry
John Mauchline	John N. Oswalt	Howard A. Hanke
Peter D. Miscall	John J. Owens	R. Laird Harris
J. Yeoman Muckle	Gene Rice	William Hendriksen
Christopher R. Seitz	Alfred Sauer	Edward E. Hindson
K. Stendahl	Milton S. Terry	Elliot E. Johnson
David Sweets	Charles C. Torrey	Homer A. Kent Jr.
I. W. Slotki	Gerard Van Groningen	Edward J. Kissane
David Stacey	John H. Walton	Herbert Lockyer
S. H. Widyapranawa	John D. W. Watts	John G. Machen

Interpretations of Isa 7:14 by Modern Scholars

Contemporary Fulfillment	Dual Fulfillment	Future Fulfillment
Hans Wildberger	Paul D. Wegner	Alva J. McClain
	John T. Willis	Stephen R. Miller
	Herbert M. Wolf	J. Alec Motyer
	Hing Hoong Wong	Richard Niessen
		James Orr
		J. Barton Payne
		Stefan Porubcan
		George Prabhu
		Robert L. Reymond
		Gary V. Smith
		James E. Smith
		Paul L. Tan
		Timothy Tow
		R. Dick Wilson
		Ronald F. Youngblood
		Edward J. Young

Bibliography

Achtemeier, Paul J. *Harper's Bible Dictionary.* San Francisco: Harper & Row, 1985.
Alden, Robert L. *Job.* Edited by E. Ray Clendenin, Kenneth A. Matthews, and David S. Dockery. New American Commentary 11. Nashville: Broadman & Holman, 1993.
———. *Theological Wordbook of the Old Testament.* Edited by R. Laird Harris, Gleason L. Archer Jr., and Bruce K. Waltke. Chicago: Moody, 1980.
Alexander, Joseph A. *Commentary on the Prophecies of Isaiah.* 1953. Reprint, Grand Rapids: Zondervan, 1971.
Alexander, T. Desmond. *Exodus.* Edited by D. Guthrie, J. A. Motyer, et al. New Bible Commentary: 21st Century Edition. Downers Grove, IL: InterVarsity, 1994.
Ambrose, Saint. "The Sacrament of the Incarnation of Our Lord." In *Saint Ambrose: Theological and Dogmatic Works,* translated by Roy J. Deferrari and edited by Roy J. Deferrari, James A. Magner, Bernard M. Peebles, et al., 154–264. The Fathers of the Church: A New Translation 44. Washington, DC: Catholic University of America, 1963.
Amorim, Allan P. "An Analysis of the Background and Purposes of Selected Miracles in the Gospels Applied to Issues of Faith and Healing in Brazil." PhD diss., Mid-America Baptist Theological Seminary, 2009.
Anderson, Robert A. *Signs and Wonders: A Commentary on the Book of Daniel.* Grand Rapids: Eerdmans, 1984.
Arndt, William F., and F. Wilbur Gingrich. *A Greek-English Lexicon of the New Testament and Other Early Christian Literature.* 1957. Reprint, Chicago: University of Chicago, 1973.
Ashby, Godfrey. *Exodus: Go out and Meet God.* Edited by Frederick Carlson Holmgren and George A. F. Knight. International Theological Commentary. Grand Rapids: Eerdmans, 1998.
Athanasius, Saint of Alexandria. "On the Incarnation." In *Christology of the Later Fathers,* edited by Edward R. Hardy. Library of Christian Classics 3. Philadelphia: Westminster, 1954.
Austin, Steven A., and Kurt P. Wise. "The Pre-Flood/Flood Boundary: As Defined in Grand Canyon, Arizona, and Eastern Mojave Desert, California." In *Proceedings of the Third International Conference on Creationism Held July 18–23, 1994,* edited by Robert E. Walsh, 38–39. Pittsburgh, PA: Creation Science Fellowship, 1994.
Baars, W. "Little-known Latin Fragment of the Wisdom of Solomon." *Vetus Testamentum* 20 (1970) 230–33.

Bibliography

Barrick, William D. "Noah's Flood and Its Geological Implications." In *Coming to Grips with Genesis: Biblical Authority and the Age of the Earth*, edited by Terry Mortenson and Thane H. Ury, 251–81. Green Forest, AR: Master, 2012.

Bailey, Randall C. "'And They Shall Know That I Am YHWH!': The P Recasting of the Plague Narratives in Exodus 7–11." *Journal of the International Theological Center* 22 (1994) 7–17.

Bakon, Shimon. "The Day of the Lord." *Jewish Bible Quarterly* 38 (2010) 149–56.

———. "On a Latin Fragment of Sirach." *Vetus Testamentum* 15 (1965) 280–81.

Barton, J. *Isaiah 1–39*. Old Testament Guides 19. Sheffield, UK: Sheffield Academic, 1995.

Beeke, Joel R., and Mark Jones. *A Puritan Theology: Doctrine for Life*. Grand Rapids: Reformation Heritage, 2012.

Benjamin, Tammi, and Marc Mangel. "The Ten Plagues and Statistical Science as a Way of Knowing." *Judaism* 48 (1999) 17–34.

Bergen, Robert D. *1, 2 Samuel*. Edited by E. Ray Clendenen, Kenneth A. Mathews, and David S. Dockery. New American Commentary 7. Nashville: Broadman & Holman, 1996.

Bishop, E. F. F. "Bethlehem and the Nativity: Some Travesties of Christ." *Anglican Theological Review* 46 (1964) 401–13.

Blaising, Craig A. "The Day of the Lord and the Rapture." *Bibliotheca Sacra* 169 (2012) 259–70.

Blenkinsopp, Joseph. *Opening the Sealed Book: Interpretations of the Book of Isaiah in Late Antiquity*. Grand Rapids: Eerdmans, 2006.

Block, Daniel I. *Judges, Ruth*. Edited by E. Ray Clendenen, Kenneth A. Matthews, and David S. Dockery. New American Commentary 6. Nashville: Broadman & Holman, 1999.

Block, Joel. "Ten Plagues of Egypt." *Religious Education* 71 (1976) 519–26.

Blomberg, Craig L. *Matthew*. Edited by E. Ray Clendenen, Kenneth A. Matthews, and David S. Dockery. New American Commentary 22. Nashville: Broadman & Holman, 1992.

Bock, Darrell L. *Acts*. Edited by Robert W. Yarbrough and Robert H. Stein. Baker Exegetical Commentary on the New Testament. Grand Rapids: Baker, 2007.

Boice, James M. *The Gospel of John: An Expositional Commentary*. Coming of the Light Series 1. Grand Rapids: Zondervan, 1975.

Borchert, Gerald L. *John*. Edited by E. Ray Clendenen, Kenneth A. Matthews, and David S. Dockery. New American Commentary 25A. Nashville: Broadman & Holman, 1996.

Boslooper, Thomas D. *The Virgin Birth*. Philadelphia: Westminster, 1962.

Bostock, Gerald. "Virgin Birth or Human Conception." *Expository Times* 97 (1986) 260–63.

Botterweck, G. Johannes, and Helmer Ringgren, eds. *Theological Dictionary of the Old Testament*. Vol. 1. Translated by John T. Willis. Grand Rapids: Eerdmans, 1980.

Bourke, M. "The Literary Genus of Matthew 1–2." *Catholic Biblical Quarterly* 22 (1960) 160–75.

Box, George H. *The Book of Isaiah: Translated from a Text Revised in Accordance with the Results of Recent Criticism, with Introductions, Critical Notes, and Explanations, and Two Maps*. 1908. Reprint, London: Pitman & Sons, 1974.

Brensinger, Terry L. *Judges*. Edited by Elmer Martens and Willard M. Swartley. Believer's Church Bible Commentary. Scottdale, PA: Herald, 1999.

Bromiley, Geoffrey W. *Theological Dictionary of the New Testament: Abridged in One Volume*. Edited by Gerhard Kittel, Gerhard Friedrich, and Geoffrey W. Bromiley. Grand Rapids: Eerdmans, 1995.

Brooks, James A. *Mark*. Edited by E. Ray Clendenen, Kenneth A. Matthews, and David S. Dockery. New American Commentary 23. Nashville: Broadman & Holman, 1991.

Brown, Francis. "The Date of Isaiah XII." *Journal of Biblical Literature* 9 (1890) 128–31.

Brown, Francis, S. R. Driver, and Charles A. Briggs. *The Brown-Driver-Briggs Hebrew and English Lexicon*. Peabody, MA: Hendrickson, 2000.

Brown, Handel H. *When Jesus Came*. Grand Rapids: Eerdmans, 1963.

Brown, Raymond E. *The Birth of the Messiah: A Commentary on the Infancy Narratives in Matthew and Luke*. Garden City, NY: Doubleday, 1977.

———. "The Gospel Infancy Narrative Research from 1976–1986: Part I (Matthew)." *Catholic Biblical Quarterly* 48 (1986) 468–83.

———. *The Virginal Conception and the Bodily Resurrection of Jesus*. New York: Chapman, 1974.

Broyles, Craig C. *Psalms*. Edited by Robert L. Hubbard Jr. and Robert K. Johnston. New International Biblical Commentary 11. Peabody, MA: Hendrickson, 1999.

Bruckner, James K. *Exodus*. Edited by W. Ward Gasque, Robert L. Hubbard Jr., and Robert K. Johnston. Understanding the Bible Commentary Series. Grand Rapids: Baker, 2008.

Brueggemann, Walter. *1 and 2 Kings*. Edited by R. Scott Nash, Samuel E. Balentine, et al. Smyth & Helwys Bible Commentary. Macon, GA: Smyth & Helwys, 2000.

———. *Exodus*. Vol. 1 of *The New Interpreter's Bible*, edited by Leander E. Keck, Thomas G. Long, Bruce C. Birch, et al. Nashville: Abingdon, 1994.

———. *First and Second Samuel*. Edited by James Luther Mays, Patrick D. Miller, and Paul J. Achtemeier. Interpretation: A Bible Commentary for Teaching and Preaching. Louisville: Westminster John Knox, 1990.

———. *Isaiah 1–39*. Louisville: Westminster John Knox, 1998.

Bruner, Frederick D. *Matthew: A Commentary*. Grand Rapids: Eerdmans, 2004.

Bucksbazen, Victor. *The Prophet Isaiah*. Collingswood, NJ: Spearhead, 1971.

Bultema, Harry. *Commentary on Isaiah*. Translated by Cornelius Lambregtse. Grand Rapids: Kregel, 1981.

Burney, Charles Fox. *The Book of Judges, with Introduction and Note, and Notes on the Hebrew Text of the Books of Kings, with an Introduction and Appendix*. Library of Biblical Studies. New York: Ktav, 1970.

Calvin, John. *Calvin: Institutes of the Christian Religion*. Edited by John T. McNeill, John Baillie, and Henry P. Van Dusen. Library of Christian Classics 20. Philadelphia: Westminster, 1960.

———. *Isaiah*. Vol. 3 of *Calvin's Commentaries*. Puritan Commentary Series. Grand Rapids: Associated Publishers & Authors, [1971?].

The Cambridge Paragraph Bible of the Authorized English Version. Bellingham, WA: Logos, 2006.

Cave, C. H. "St. Matthew's Infancy Narrative." *New Testament Studies* 9 (1963) 382–91.

Charlier, J. P. "La Notion du Signe (Sêmeion) dans le IVe évangile." *Revue des Sciences Philosophiques et Théologiques* 43 (1959) 434–48.

Childs, Brevard S. *The Book of Exodus: A Critical, Theological Commentary*. Edited by G. Ernest Wright, John Bright, James Barr, et al. Old Testament Library. Philadelphia: Westminster, 1974.

Bibliography

———. *The Struggle to Understand Isaiah as Christian Scripture*. Grand Rapids: Eerdmans, 2004.

Chilton, Bruce D., trans. *The Isaiah Targum*. With introduction, apparatus, and notes by Bruce D. Chilton. Vol. 2 of The Aramaic Bible. Wilmington, DE: Glazier, 1987.

Christensen, Duane L., and N. Narucki. "The Mosaic Authorship of the Pentateuch." *Journal of the Evangelical Society* 32 (1989) 465–71.

Chrysostom, Saint John. *On the Incomprehensible Nature of God*. Translated by Paul W. Harkins and edited by Roy J. Deferrari, James A. Magner, Bernard M. Peebles, et al. The Fathers of the Church: A New Translation 72. 1984. Reprint, Washington, DC: Catholic University of America, 1988.

Ciampa, Roy E., and Brian S. Rosner. *The First Letter to the Corinthians*. Pillar New Testament Commentary. Grand Rapids: Eerdmans, 2010.

Clark, David J. "The Influence of the Dead Sea Scrolls on Modern Translations of Isaiah." *Bible Translator (Ja, Jl Technical Papers)* 35 (1984) 122–30.

Clark, Douglas K. "Signs in Wisdom and John." *Catholic Biblical Quarterly* 45 (1983) 201–9.

Clements, Ronald E. *Deuteronomy*. Vol. 2 of *The New Interpreter's Bible*, edited by Leander E. Keck, Thomas G. Long, Bruce C. Birch, et al. Nashville: Abingdon, 1998.

Exodus. Edited by P. R. Ackroyd, A. R. C. Leaney, and J. W. Packer. The Cambridge Bible Commentary. London: Cambridge University, 1972.

———. *Isaiah 1–39*. Edited by R. E. Clements and Matthew Black. The New Century Bible Commentary. Grand Rapids: Eerdmans, 1980.

———. *Isaiah and the Deliverance of Jerusalem: A Study of the Interpretation of Prophecy in the Old Testament*. Sheffield, UK: Sheffield Academic, 1980.

Clines, David J. A., ed. *The Dictionary of Classical Hebrew*. Vol. 1. Sheffield: Sheffield Academic, 1993.

Coats, George W. *Exodus 1–18*. Edited by Rolf P. Knierim and Gene M. Tucker. The Forms of the Old Testament Literature Commentary 2A. Grand Rapids: Eerdmans, 1999.

Cohn, Robert L. *2 Kings*. Berit Olam: Studies in Hebrew Narrative and Poetry Commentary. Collegeville, MN: Liturgical, 2000.

Cole, Alan D. "A Critique of the Prewrath Interpretation of the Day of the Lord in Joel 2–3." *Detroit Baptist Seminary Journal* 9 (2004) 33–55.

Cole, R. Dennis. *Numbers*. Edited by E. Ray Clendenen, Kenneth A. Mathews, and David S. Dockery. New American Commentary 3B. Nashville: Broadman & Holman, 2000.

Conrad, Edgar W. "The Annunciation of Birth and the Birth of the Messiah." *Catholic Biblical Quarterly* 47 (1985) 656–63.

Cooper, Lamar E., Sr. *Ezekiel*. Edited by E. Ray Clendenen, Kenneth A. Mathews, and David S. Dockery. New American Commentary 17. Nashville: Broadman & Holman, 1994.

Coppens, D. "La Prophétie de la 'almah: Isa 7:14–17." *Ephemerides Theologicae Lovanienses* 28 (1952) 648–78.

Costa, Jose. "The Matthean Reading of Isaiah 7:14 and the Midrash of Ancient Rabbis." In *Infancy Gospels: Stories and Identities*, edited by Claire Clivaz, Andreas Dettwiler, Luc Devillers, et al., 116–36. Tübingen, Germany: Mohr Siebeck, 2011.

Cyril, Saint of Alexandria. *Commentary on the Twelve Prophets*. Vol. 2. Edited by Thomas P. Halton, Elizabeth Clark, Robert D. Sider, et al., and translated by Robert C. Hill. The Fathers of the Church: A New Translation 116. Washington, DC: Catholic University of America, 2008.

Bibliography

Crannell, Phillip W. "The Supernatural Birth of Christ." *Review and Expositor* 29 (1932) 347–62.

Davies, Benjamin. *A Compendious and Complete Hebrew and Chaldee Lexicon to the Old Testament with an English-Hebrew Index.* Grand Rapids: Zondervan, 1960.

Davis, Dale R. *2 Kings: The Power and Fury.* Reprint ed. Ross-Shire, UK: Christian Focus, 2009.

Davis, John J. *Moses and the Gods of Egypt: Studies in Exodus.* Grand Rapids: Baker, 1986.

Deboys, David G. "1 Kings 13—a 'New Criterion' Reconsidered." *Vetus Testamentum* 41 (1991) 210–12.

Dennert, Brian C. "A Note on Use of Isa 7:14 in Matt 1:23 through the Interpretation of the Septuagint." *Trinity Journal* 30 (2009) 97–105.

Dennison, William D. "Miracles as 'Signs': Their Significance for Apologetics." *Biblical Theology Bulletin* 6 (1976) 190–202.

Derrett, J. Duncan M. "Further Light on the Narrative of the Nativity." *Novum Testamentum* 17 (1975) 81–108.

DeWolfe, L. Harold. *The Case for Theology in Liberal Perspectives.* Philadelphia: Westminster, 1959.

Douglas, George C. M. *Isaiah One and His Book One: An Essay and An Exposition.* 1895. Reprint, London: Nisbet, 1965.

Dozeman, Thomas B. "The Way of the Man of God from Judah: True and False Prophecy in the Pre-Deuteronomic Legend of 1 Kings 13." *Catholic Biblical Quarterly* 44 (1982) 379–93.

Driver, Godfrey R. "The Aramaic of the Book of Daniel." *Journal of Biblical Literature* 45 (1926) 110–19.

Durousseau, Clifford Hubart. "Isaiah 7:14b in New Major Christian Bible Translations." *Jewish Bible Quarterly* 41 (2013) 175–80.

Duhm, Bernhard. *Das Buch Jesaja, Hand Kommentar Zum Alten Testament.* Göttingen, Germany: Vandenhoeck & Ruprecht, 1892.

Eakin, Frank E. "Plagues and the Crossing of the Sea." *Review and Expositor* 74 (1977) 473–82.

Easton, M. G. *Easton's Bible Dictionary.* Oak Harbor, WA: Logos Research Systems, 1996.

Edwards, Jonathan. *The Blank Bible.* Edited by Harry S. Stout, John E. Smith, Jon Butler, et al. The Works of Jonathan Edwards Series 24. New Haven: Yale University Press, 2006.

Edwards, Douglas. *The Virgin Birth in the History and Faith.* London: Faber & Faber, 1943.

Elwell, Walter A., and Philip Wesley Comfort. *Tyndale Bible Dictionary.* Wheaton: Tyndale, 2001.

Emerton, John A. "An Examination of Some Attempts to Defend the Unity of the Flood Narrative in Genesis, pt 1." *Vetus Testamentum* 37 (1987) 401–20.

———. "An Examination of Some Attempts to Defend the Unity of the Flood Narrative in Genesis, pt 2." *Vetus Testamentum* 38 (1988) 1–21.

Enns, Paul P. *Judges.* Bible Study Commentary. Grand Rapids: Zondervan, 1982.

Enns, Peter. "William Henry Green and the Authorship of the Pentateuch." *Journal of the Evangelical Society* 45 (2002) 385–403.

Enslin, M. S. "The Christian Stories of the Nativity." *Journal of Biblical Literature* 59 (1940) 317–38.

Evans, William. *Why I Believe the Virgin Birth of Jesus Christ.* Los Angeles: Bible Institute of Los Angeles, 1924.

Bibliography

Feinberg, Charles L. "The Virgin Birth and Isaiah 7:14." *Master's Seminary Journal* 22 (2011) 11–17.

———. "The Virgin Birth in the Old Testament and Isaiah 7:14." *Bibliotheca Sacra* 119 (1962) 251–58.

Fields, Wilbur. *Exploring Exodus.* Bible Study Textbook Series. Joplin, MO: College, 1986.

Fitzmyer, Joseph A. "The Virginal Conception in the New Testament." *Theological Studies* 34 (1973) 541–75.

Ford, J. Massyngberde. *Revelation* in *The Anchor Bible Commentary.* Edited by William F. Albright, Frank M. Cross, Raymond, E. Brown, et al. Garden City, NY: Doubleday, 1975.

Fox, Douglas A. "The Ninth Plague: An Exegetical Note." *Journal of the American Academy of Religion* 45 (1977) 219.

Frankel, Hermann. *Early Greek Poetry and Philosophy: A History of Greek, Epic, Lyric, and Prose to the Middle of the Fifth Century.* Translated by Moses Hadas and James Willis. New York: Blackwell, 1973.

Fretheim, Terence E. *Exodus.* Edited by James L. Mays, Patrick D. Miller, and Paul J. Achtemeier. Interpretation: A Bible Commentary for Teaching and Preaching. Louisville: Westminster John Knox, 1991.

———. *Genesis.* Vol. 1 of *The New Interpreter's Bible*, edited by Leander E. Keck, Thomas G. Long, Bruce C. Birch, et al. Nashville: Abingdon, 1994.

———. *First and Second Kings.* Louisville: Westminster, 1999.

———. "The Plagues as Ecological Signs of Historical Disaster." *Journal of Biblical Literature* 110 (1991) 385–96.

Freytag, Ralferd C. "The Hebrew Prophets and Sodom and Gomorrah." *Consensus* 32 (2008) 55–69.

Froede, Carl R., Jr. "The Global Stratigraphic Record." *Creation Ex Nihilo Technical Journal* 11 (1997) 40–43.

Frydland, Rachmiel. *What the Rabbis Know about the Messiah: A Study of Genealogy and Prophecy.* Edited by Elliot Klayman. Cincinnati, OH: Messianic, 1993.

Garstang, John, and J. B. E. Garstang. *The Story of Jericho.* London: Marshall, Morgan, & Scott, 1940.

———. "The Date of the Destruction of Jericho." *Palestine Exploration Fund Quarterly Statement* (1927) 96–100.

Gesenius, H. W. F. *Gesenius' Hebrew and Chaldee Lexicon to the Old Testament Scriptures.* Translated by Samuel P. Tregelles. 1836. Reprint, Grand Rapids: Baker, 1979.

Godley, A. D. *Herodotus.* Vol. 1. Cambridge, MA: Harvard University, 1940.

Goldingay, John. *Isaiah.* Edited by Robert L. Hubbard Jr. and Robert K. Johnston. New International Biblical Commentary 13. Peabody, MA: Hendrickson, 2001.

Goodman, F. W. "Sources of the First Two Chapters in Matthew and Luke." *Church Quarterly Review* 162 (1961) 136–43.

Gordon, Cyrus H., "*'Almah* in Isaiah 7:14." *Journal of Bible and Religion* 21 (1953) 106.

Goulder, M. D. *Incarnation and Myth: The Debate Continued.* Grand Rapids: Eerdmans, 1979.

———. "Jesus, the Man of University Destiny." In *The Myth of God Incarnate*, edited by John Hicks, 203–65. Philadelphia: Westminster, 1977.

———. *Midrash and Lection in Matthew.* London: SPCK, 1974.

Gray, George B. *A Critical and Exegetical Commentary on the Book of Isaiah: I-XXVII.* International Critical Commentary on the Holy Scriptures of the Old and New Testaments. Edinburgh: T. & T. Clark, 1975.
Gray, John. *Joshua, Judges, Ruth.* Edited by R. E. Clements and Matthew Black. The New Century Bible Commentary. Grand Rapids: Eerdmans, 1986.
Greenstone, Julius H. *The Messiah Idea in Jewish History.* 1906. Reprint, Philadelphia: Jewish Publication Society of America, 1948.
Grogan, Geoffrey W. *Psalms.* Edited by J. Gordan McConville and Craig Bartholomew. The Two Horizons Old Testament Commentary. Grand Rapids: Eerdmans, 2008.
Gromacki, Robert G. *The Virgin Birth: Doctrine of Deity.* Nashville: Nelson, 1974.
Gruber, Mayer I. *Rashi's Commentary on Psalms.* Edited by J. Neusner, H. Basser, A. J. Avery-Peck, et al. Brill Reference Library of Judaism 18. Boston: Brill, 2004.
Gunn, David M. *Judges.* Edited by John Sawyer, Christopher Rowland, and Judith Kovacs Blackwell Bible Commentaries. Malden, MA: Blackwell, 2005.
Guy, Herold A. "The Origin of the Virgin Birth Tradition." *Expository Times* 79 (1968) 183.
Habershon, Ada R. *The Study of the Miracles.* 1911. Reprint, London: Morgan & Scott, 1980.
Hailey, Homer. *That You May Believe: Studies in the Gospel of John.* Grand Rapids: Baker, 1973.
Hall, Christopher A. *Reading Scripture with the Church Fathers.* Downers Grove: InterVarsity, 1998.
Hamlin, E. John. *At Risk in the Promised Land: A Commentary of the Book of Judges.* Grand Rapids: Eerdmans, 1990.
Hanke, Howard A. *The Validity of the Virgin Birth.* Grand Rapids: Zondervan, 1963.
Hare, Douglas R. A. *Matthew.* Edited by James Luther Mays, Patrick D. Miller, and Paul J. Achtemeier. Interpretation: A Bible Commentary for Teaching and Preaching. Louisville: Westminster John Knox, 1993.
Harland, James P. "Sodom and Gomorrah: The Location of the Cities of the Plain." *Biblical Archaeologist* 5 (1942) 17–32.
Haroutunian, Joseph. Introduction to *Calvin: Commentaries,* by John Calvin. Edited by Joseph Haroutunian and Louise P. Smith. The New Library of Christian Classics 23. Philadelphia: Westminster, 1958.
Harrison, R. K. *Numbers.* Edited by Kenneth L. Barker. Wycliffe Exegetical Commentary. Chicago: Moody, 1990.
Hartley, John E. *The Book of Job.* Edited by R. K. Harrison. The New International Commentary on the Old Testament. Grand Rapids: Eerdmans, 1988.
———. *Genesis.* Edited by W. Ward Gasque, Robert L. Hubbard Jr., and Robert K. Johnston. Understanding the Bible Commentary Series. Grand Rapids: Baker, 2000.
Hartman, Louis F. "Sirach in Hebrew and in Greek." *Catholic Biblical Quarterly* 23 (1961) 443–51.
Hauerwas, Stanley. *Matthew.* Edited by R. R. Reno, Robert W. Jenson, Robert Louis Wilken, et al. Brazos Theological Commentary on the Bible. Grand Rapids: Brazos, 2006.
Hayes, John Haralson. "Historical Reconstruction, Textual Emendation, and Biblical Translation: Some Examples From the RSV." *Perspectives in Religious Studies* 14 (1987) 5–9.

Bibliography

Hendrickson, William. *Matthew: Exposition of the Gospel According to Matthew.* New Testament Commentary. Grand Rapids: Baker, 1979.

Higgins, A. J. B. "Jewish Messianic Belief in Justin Martyr's Dialogue with Trypho." In *Messainism in the Talmudic Era*, edited by Leo Landman, 182–89. New York: KTAV, 1979.

Hindson, Edward E. "The Immanuel Prophecy." *Mid-America Theological Journal* 15 (1991) 79–86.

———. *Isaiah's Immanuel: A Sign of His Times or the Sign of the Ages?* Phillipsburg, NJ: Presbyterian & Reformed, 1979.

Hobbs, Herschel H. *An Exposition of the Gospel of Matthew.* Grand Rapids: Baker, 1965.

Hodge, Charles. *Systematic Theology.* Electronic version. Oak Harbor, WA: Logos Research Systems, 1997.

Hoffmeier, James K. "The Arm of God Versus the Arm of Pharaoh in the Exodus Narratives." *Biblical* 67 (1986) 378–87.

Holladay, William L. *A Concise Hebrew and Aramaic Lexicon of the Old Testament.* Grand Rapids: Eerdmans, 1971.

———. *Isaiah: Scroll of a Prophetic Heritage.* Grand Rapids: Eerdmans, 1978.

The Holy Bible, English Standard Version. Wheaton: Standard Bible Society, 2001.

The Holy Bible: Holman Christian Standard Bible. Nashville: Holman Bible Publishers, 2003.

The Holy Bible: King James Version. Electronic ed. of the 1769 edition of the 1611 Authorized Version. Bellingham WA: Logos Research Systems, 1995.

Homer. *The Iliad.* Translated by A. T. Murray. Cambridge, MA: Harvard University, 1928.

———. *The Odyssey.* Translated by A. T. Murray. Cambridge, MA: Harvard University, 1930.

Howard, David M., Jr. *Joshua.* Edited by E. Ray Clendenen, Kenneth A. Mathews, and David S. Dockery. New American Commentary 5. Nashville: Broadman & Holman, 1998.

Hubbard, David A. "Hope in the Old Testament." *Tyndale Bulletin* 34 (1983) 33–59.

Huey, F. B. *Jeremiah, Lamentations.* Edited by E. Ray Clendenen, Kenneth A. Mathews, and David S. Dockery. New American Commentary 16. Nashville: Broadman & Holman, 1993.

Hughes, R. Kent. *Genesis: Beginning and Blessing.* Preaching the Word Series. Wheaton: Crossway, 1999.

———. *John: That You May Believe.* Preaching the Word Series. Wheaton: Crossway, 1999.

Hughes, Robert B., and J. Carl Laney. "1 and 2 Chronicles." In *Tyndale Concise Bible Commentary*, 145–61. Tyndale Reference Library. Wheaton: Tyndale, 2001.

Hyatt, James Philip. *Exodus.* Edited by Ronald E. Clements and Matthew Black. New Century Bible Commentary. Grand Rapids: Eerdmans, 1971.

Irenaeus. *Proof of the Apostolic Preaching.* Translated by Joseph P. Smith. Edited by Johannes Quasten and Joseph C. Plumbe. Ancient Christian Writers: The Works of the Fathers in Translation 16. New York: Newman, 1952.

Irvine, Stuart A. *Isaiah, Ahaz, and the Syro-Ephraimatic Crisis.* Atlanta: Scholars, 1990.

Irwin, William A. "That Troublesome 'almah and Other Matters." *Review and Expositor* 50 (1953) 337–60.

Jacob, Benno. *The Second Book of the Bible: Exodus.* Translated by Walter Jacob and Yaakov Elman. Hoboken, NJ: KTAV, 1992.

Janzen, J. Gerald. *Exodus*. Louisville: Westminster John Knox, 1997.
Jefferson, Helen G. "Notes on the Authorship of Isaiah 65 and 66." *Journal of Biblical Literature* 68 (1949) 225–30.
Jensen, Joseph. "The Age of Immanuel." *Catholic Biblical Quarterly* 41 (1979) 220–39.
Jerome, Saint. *Commentary on Matthew*. Edited by Thomas P. Halton, Elizabeth Clark, Robert D. Sider, et al., and translated by Thomas P. Scheck. The Fathers of the Church: A New Translation 117. Washington, DC: Catholic University of America, 2008.
Johnson, Elliott E. "Dual Authorship and the Single Intended Meaning of Scripture." *Bibliotheca Sacra* 143 (1986) 218–27.
Josephus, Flavius. *The Works of Josephus: Complete and Unabridged*. Translated by William Whiston. Peabody, MA: Hendrickson, 1996.
Kaiser, Otto. *Isaiah 1–12: A Commentary*. Edited by G. Ernest Wright, John Bright, James Barr, et al. Old Testament Library. Philadelphia: Westminster, 1972.
———. *Isaiah 13–39: A Commentary* in the *Old Testament Library*. Edited by G. Ernest Wright, John Bright, James Barr, et al. Philadelphia: Westminster, 1974.
Kaiser, Walter C., Jr. "The Promise of Isaiah 7:14 and the Single-Meaning Hermeneutic." *Evangelical Journal* 6 (1988) 55–70.
———. *Toward and Exegetical Theology*. Grand Rapids: Baker, 1981.
Kamesar, Adam. "The Virgin of Isaiah 7:14: The Philological Argument from the Second to the Fifth Century." *Journal of Theological Studies* 41 (1990) 51–75.
Keener, Craig S. *A Commentary on the Gospel of Matthew*. Grand Rapids: Eerdmans, 1999.
Keil, C. F., and Franz Delitzsch. *The Pentateuch*. Vol 1 of *Commentary on the Old Testament in Ten Volumes*. Translated by James Martin. Grand Rapids: Eerdmans, 1975.
Kelley, Page. "Isaiah." In vol. 12 of *The Broadman Bible Commentary*, 149–374. Nashville: Broadman, 1971.
Kenyon, Kathleen. *Digging up Jericho*. New York: Praeger, 1957.
Khoo, Jeffery E. "The Sign of the Virgin Birth: The Exegetical Validity of a Strictly Messianic Fulfillment of Isaiah 7:14." MDiv thesis, Grace Theological Seminary, 1991.
Kilpatrick, R. Kirk. "Against the Gods of Egypt: An Examination of the Narrative of the Ten Plagues in Light of Exodus 12:12." PhD diss., Mid-America Baptist Theological Seminary, 1995.
———. "Views of the 'Immanuel' Sign: Isaiah 7:14." Lecture presented at the Mid-America Baptist Theological Seminary, Cordova, TN, March 2009.
Kissane, Edward J. *The Book of Isaiah*. Dublin: Browne & Nolan, 1943.
Kitchen, Kenneth A. "The Aramaic of Daniel." In *Notes on Some Problems in the Book of Daniel*, edited by D. J. Wiseman, 31–79. London: Tyndale, 1996.
Klein, Ernst. *A Comprehensive Etymological Dictionary of the Hebrew Language for Readers of English*. New York: Macmillan, 1987.
Klein, Ralph W. "Day of the Lord." *Concordia Theological Monthly* 39 (1968) 517–25.
Kline, J. Bergman. "The Day of the Lord in the Death and Resurrection of Christ." *Journal of the Evangelical Theological Society* 48 (2005) 757–70.
Knight, Harold. "Old Testament Conception of Miracle." *Scottish Journal of Theology* 5 (1952) 355–61.
Knowling, R. J. *Our Lord's Virgin Birth and the Criticism of Today*. London: SPCK, 1904.
Koehler, Ludwig, and Walter Baumgartner. *The Hebrew and Aramaic Lexicon of the Old Testament*. Revised by Walter Baumgartner and Johann Jakob Stamm with assistance from Benedikt Hartmann, Zeʿev Ben-Hayyim, Eduard Yechezkel Kutscher, and Philippe Reymond. 4 vols. Leiden: Brill, 1994.

Bibliography

Kraeling, Emil, and Gottlieb Heinrich. "The Immanuel Prophecy." *Journal of Biblical Literature* 50 (1931) 277–97.
Kraus, Hans-Joachim. *Psalms 60–150: A Commentary*. Translated by Hilton C. Oswald. Minneapolis: Augsburg, 1989.
Lampe, G. W. H. "Miracles in the Acts of the Apostles." In *Miracles: Cambridge Studies in Their Philosophy and History*, edited by Charles F. D. Moule, 165–66. London: Mowbray, 1965.
Landrum, George. "What a Miracle Really Is." *Religious Studies* 12 (1976) 49–57.
Larkin, William J., Jr. *Acts*. Edited by Grant R. Osborne, D. Stuart Briscoe, and Haddon Robinson. IVP New Testament Commentary Series. Downers Grove: InterVarsity, 1995.
LaSor, William S. *Isaiah 7:14—"Young Woman" or "Virgin?"* Pasadena: privately printed, 1952.
Lattey, Cuthbert. "The Emmanuel Prophecy: Isaias 7:14." *Catholic Biblical Quarterly* 8 (1946) 369–76.
———. "The Term *Almah* in Is. 7:14." *Catholic Biblical Quarterly* 9 (1947) 89–95.
———. "Various Interpretations of Is. 7:14." *Catholic Biblical Quarterly* 9 (1947) 14–54.
Leithart, Peter J. *1 and 2 Kings*. Edited by R. R. Reno, et al. Brazos Theological Commentary on the Bible. Grand Rapids: Brazos, 2006.
Leo the Great. "The Tome of Leo." In *Christology of the Later Fathers*, edited by Edward R. Hardy and translated by William Bright, 359–70. Library of Christian Classics 3. Philadelphia: Westminster, 1954.
Leupold, H. C. *Exposition of Isaiah 1–39*. Vol. 1. Grand Rapids: Baker, 1968.
———. *Exposition of Isaiah 40–56*. Vol. 2. Grand Rapids: Baker, 1971.
Lewis, C. S. *Miracles: A Preliminary Study*. New York: Macmillan, 1947.
Liddell, H. G. *A Lexicon: Abridged from Liddell and Scott's Greek-English Lexicon*. Oak Harbor, WA: Logos Research Systems, 1996.
Lincoln, Andrew T. "Contested Paternity and Contested Readings: Jesus' Conception in Matthew 1.18–25." *Journal for the Study of the New Testament* 34 (2012) 211–31.
Lobstein, Paul. *The Virgin Birth of Christ: An Historical and Critical Essay*. Translated by Victor Leuliette. New York: Putnam, 1903.
Lockyer, Herbert. *All the Messianic Prophecies of the Bible*. Grand Rapids: Zondervan, 1973.
———. *All the Miracles of the Bible: The Supernatural in Scripture, Its Scope, and Significance*. Grand Rapids: Zondervan, 1961.
Long, Thomas G. *Matthew*. Edited by Patrick D. Miller and David L. Batrlett. Westminster Bible Companion. Louisville: Westminster John Knox, 1997.
Longman, Tremper, III. *How to Read Exodus*. Downers Grove: InterVarsity, 2009.
Ludemann, Gerd. *Virgin Birth? The Real Story of Mary and Her Son Jesus*. Harrisburg, PA: Trinity, 1997.
Luther, Martin. *Lectures on Isaiah Chapters 1–39*. Vol. 16 of *Luther's Works*. Edited by Jaroslav Pelikan and Hilton C. Oswald and translated by Herbert J. A. Bouman. St. Louis: Concordia, 1969.
Luyster, Robert. "Myth and History in the Book of Exodus." *Religion* 8 (1978) 155–70.
Lytton, Timothy D. "'Shall Not the Judge of the Earth Deal Justly?': Accountability, Compassion, and Judicial Authority in the Biblical Story of Sodom and Gomorrah." *Journal of Law and Religion* 18 (2002) 31–55.
Machen, J. Gresham. *The Virgin Birth of Christ*. 1930. Reprint, Grand Rapids: Baker, 1974.

Bibliography

MacRae, George. "Miracles in the Antiquities of Josephus." In *Miracles: Cambridge Studies in Their Philosophy and History*, edited by Charles F. D. Moule, 143. London: Mowbray, 1965.

Margulis, B. "Plagues Tradition in Ps 105." *Biblica* 50 (1969) 491–96.

Martin, James D. *Judges*. Edited by P. R. Ackroyd, R. C. Leaney, and J. W. Packer. Cambridge Bible Commentary. London: Cambridge University Press, 1975.

Martyr, Justin. "Dialogue with Trypho." In the *Writings of Justin Martyr*, edited by Ludwig Schopp, Rudolph Arbesmann, Roy J. Deferrari et al., and translated by Thomas B. Falls, 33–111. The Fathers of the Church: A New Translation 6. New York: Christian Heritage, 1948.

Matthews, Kenneth A. *Genesis 1–11:26*. Edited by E. Ray Clendenen, Kenneth A. Mathews, and David S. Dockery. New American Commentary 1A. Nashville: Broadman & Holman, 1996.

———. *Genesis 11:27–50:26*. Edited by E. Ray Clendenen, Kenneth A. Mathews, and David S. Dockery. New American Commentary 1B. Nashville: Broadman & Holman, 1996.

Mauchline, John. *Isaiah 1–39*. 1962. Reprint, London: SCM, 1972.

Mays, James L. *Psalms*. Edited by James L. Mays, Patrick D. Miller, and Paul J. Achtemeier. Interpretation: A Bible Commentary for Teaching and Preaching. Louisville: Westminster John Knox, 1994.

Mavrodes, George I. "Miracles and the Laws of Nature." *Faith and Philosophy* 2 (1985) 333–46.

McCann, J. Clinton. *Judges*. Edited by James Luther Mays, Patrick D. Miller, and Paul J. Achtemeier. Interpretation: A Bible Commentary for Teaching and Preaching. Louisville: Westminster John Knox, 2002.

McCasland, S. Vernon. "Portents in Josephus and in the Gospels." *Journal of Biblical Literature* 51 (1932) 323–35.

———. "Signs and Wonders." *Journal of Biblical Literature* 76 (1957) 149–52.

McClain, T. Van. "Introduction to the Book of Isaiah." *Mid-America Theological Journal* 15 (1991) 33–46.

McKane, William. "Interpretation of Isaiah 7:14–25." *Vetus Testamentum* 17 (1967) 208–19.

McKeown, James. *Genesis*. Edited by J. Gordon McConville and Craig Bartholomew. Two Horizons Old Testament Commentary. Grand Rapids: Eerdmans, 2008.

McRay, John. "The Virgin Birth of Christ." *Restoration Quarterly* 3 (1959) 61–71.

Melanchthon, Philip. *Melenchthon and Bucer*. Library of Christian Classics 19. Edited by Wilhelm Pauck. London: SCM, 1969.

Menken, Martinus J. J. "The Textual Form of the Quotation from Isaiah 7:14 in Matthew 1:23." *Novum Testamentum* 43 (2001) 144–60.

Merrill, Eugene H. *Deuteronomy*. Edited by E. Ray Clendenen, Kenneth A. Mathews, and David S. Dockery. New American Commentary 4. Nashville: Broadman & Holman, 1994.

———. *Kingdom of Priests: A History of Old Testament Israel*. 2nd ed. Grand Rapids: Baker, 2008.

———. "The Sign of Jonah." *Journal of The Evangelical Theological Society* 23 (1980) 23–30.

Meyer, F. B. *Exodus Chapters I–XX*. London: Marshall, Morgan, & Scott, 1952.

Michaels, J. Ramsey. *John*. Edited by W. Ward Gasque. New International Biblical Commentary. Peabody, MA: Hendrickson, 1989.

Miguens, Manuel. *The Virgin Birth: An Evaluation of Scriptural Evidence*. Westminster, MD: Christian Classics, 1975.

Miller, Clyde M. "Maidenhood and Virginity in Ancient Israel." *Restoration Quarterly* 22 (1979) 242–46.

Miller, Robert J. *Born Divine: The Births of Jesus and Other Sons of God*. Santa Rosa, CA: Polebridge, 2003.

Miller, Stephen R. *Daniel*. Edited by E. Ray Clendenen, Kenneth A. Matthews, and David S. Dockery. The New American Commentary 18. Nashville: Broadman & Holman, 1995.

———. "The Literary Style of the Book of Isaiah and the Unity Question." PhD. diss., Mid-America Baptist Theological Seminary, 1982.

Minear, P. S. "The Interpreter and the Birth Narratives." *Symbolae Biblicae Uppsalienses* 13 (1950) 1–22.

Miscall, Peter D. *Isaiah*. Sheffield: Sheffield, 1993.

Mollat, D. "Le Semeion Johannique." *Bibliotheca Ephemeridum Theologicarum Lovanensium*, 13 (1959) 209–18.

Moloney, Francis J. *Signs and Shadows: Reading John 5–12*. Minneapolis: Fortress, 1996.

———. *The Gospel of Mark: A Commentary*. Grand Rapids: Baker, 2002.

Moriarty, Frederick L. "The Emmanuel Prophecies." *Catholic Biblical Quarterly* 19 (1957) 226–33.

Mørk, Hans-Olav. "Hearing the Voice of the Other: Engaging Poets and Writers as Bible Translators, with a Case Study on Isaiah 7.14." *Bible Translator* 63 (2012) 152–68.

Morris, Henry M. *The Genesis Record: A Scientific and Devotional Commentary on the Book of Beginnings*. Grand Rapids: Baker, 1976.

Morris, Henry M., and John C. Whitcomb, Jr. "The Genesis Flood: Its Nature and Significance," *Bibliotheca Sacra* 117 (1960) 204–13.

Morris, Leon. *The Story of the Christ Child: A Devotional Study of the Nativity Stories in St. Luke and St. Matthew*. Grand Rapids: Eerdmans, 1960.

Moss, Candida R., and Jeffrey Stackert. "The Devastation of Darkness: Disability in Exodus 10:21–23, 27, and Intensification in the Plagues." *Journal of Religion* 92 (2012) 362–72.

Most, William G. "The Problem of Isaiah 7:14." *Faith & Reason* 18 (1992) 181–99.

Motyer, J. Alec. "Context and Content in the Interpretation of Isaiah 7:14." *Tyndale Bulletin* 21 (1970) 118–25.

———. *The Message of the Exodus: The Days of Our Pilgrimage*. Edited by J. Alec Motyer, John Stott, and Derek Tidball. The Bible Speaks Today: Old Testament Series. Downers Grove: InterVarsity, 2005.

———. *The Prophecy of Isaiah: An Introduction and Commentary*. Downers Grove: InterVarsity, 1993.

Moule, Charles F. D. *Miracles: Cambridge Studies in their Philosophy and History*. London: Mowbray, 1965.

Muckle, J. Yeoman. *Isaiah 1–39*. London: Epworth, 1960.

Müller, Walter W. "Virgin Shall Conceive." *Evangelical Quarterly* 32 (1960) 203–7.

Myers, Albert E. "Use of 'almah in the Old Testament." *Lutheran Quarterly* 7 (1955) 137–40.

BIBLIOGRAPHY

Naylor, Peter J. *Numbers*. Edited by D. Guthrie, J. A. Motyer, et al. New Bible Commentary: 21st Century Edition. Downers Grove: InterVarsity, 1994.

Nelson, Richard. *First and Second Kings*. Edited by James Luther, Patrick D. Miller Jr., and Paul J. Acthemeier. Interpretation: A Bible Commentary for Teaching and Preaching. Atlanta: John Knox, 1987.

Neusner, Jacob. *Messiah in Context*. Philadelphia: Fortress, 1984.

New American Standard Bible: 1995 Update. LaHabra, CA: Lockman Foundation, 1995.

Newman, Robert C. "On Fulfilled Prophecy as Miracle." *Philosophia Christi* 3 (2001) 63–67.

Niessen, Richard. "The Virginity of the 'almah in Isaiah 7:14." *Bibliotheca Sacra* 137 (1980) 133–50.

Nolan, Brian M. *The Royal Son of God: The Christology of Matthew 1-2 in the Setting of the Gospel*. Göttingen, Germany: Vandenhoeck & Ruprecht, 1979.

Northrup, Bernard E. "Identifying the Noahic Flood in Historical Geology: Part One," in *Proceedings of the Second International Conference on Creationism Held July 30-August 4, 1990*, ed. Robert E Walsh, 173–79. Pittsburgh, PA: Creation Science Fellowship, 1990.

———. "Identifying the Noahic Flood in Historical Geology: Part Two," in *Proceedings of the Second International Conference on Creationism Held July 30-August 4, 1990*, ed. Robert E Walsh, 181–85. Pittsburgh, PA: Creation Science Fellowship, 1990.

Oakley, William P. *An Exegesis of the Revelation*. Memphis, TN: Master Design, 1999.

Oppenheim, A. Leo. *I and J*. Vol. 7 of *The Assyrian Dictionary*, edited by Erica Reiner, William L. Moran, and Elizabeth Bowman. Chicago: Oriental Institute and J. J. Augustine, 1960.

———. *The Interpretation of Dreams in the Ancient Near East*. Philadelphia: American Philosophical Society, 1956.

Orr, James. *The Virgin Birth of Christ*. London: Hodder & Stoughton, 1908.

Ortland, Raymond C. *Isaiah: God Saves Sinners*. Wheaton: Crossway, 2005.

Osborne, Grant R. *Matthew*. Edited by Clinton E. Arnold, George H Guthrie, William D. Mounce, et al. Zondervan Exegetical Commentary on the New Testament. Grand Rapids: Zondervan, 2010.

Oswalt, John N. *The Book of Isaiah*. The New International Commentary on the Old Testament. 1986. Reprint, Grand Rapids: Eerdmans, 1988.

Ottley, Robert L. *The Doctrine of the Incarnation*. 5th ed. London: Methuen, 1911.

Owen, John. *On the Person of Christ*. Vol. 1 of *The Works of John Owen*. Edited by William H. Goold. 1850–53. Reprint, Carlisle, PA: The Banner of Truth Trust, 1977.

Owens, John J. "The Meaning of 'almah in the Old Testament." *Review & Expositor* 50 (1953) 56–60.

Palmer, Frederic. *The Virgin Birth*. New York: Macmillan, 1924.

Pannenberg, Wolfhart. "The Concept of Miracle." *Zygon: Journal of Religion & Science* 37 (2002) 759–62.

Parrinder, Geoffrey. *Son of Joseph: The Parentage of Jesus*. Edinburgh: T. & T. Clarke, 1992.

Patai, Raphael. *The Messiah Texts*. Detroit: Wayne State University, 1979.

Paul, Shalom. *Isaiah 40-66: Translation and Commentary*. Edited by David N. Freedman and Astrid B. Beck. Eerdmans Critical Commentary. Grand Rapids: Eerdmans, 2012.

Pauli, C. W. H. *The Chaldee Paraphrase on the Prophet Isaiah*. London: London's Society's House, 1871.

Bibliography

Payne, David F. *1 and 2 Samuel*. Edited by D. Guthrie, J. A. Motyer, et al. New Bible Commentary: 21st Century Edition. Downers Grove: InterVarsity, 1994.

Payne, J. Barton. *Encyclopedia of Biblical Prophecy*. New York: Harper & Row, 1973.

———. "The Unity of Isaiah: Evidence from Chapters 36–39." *Bulletin of the Evangelical Theological Society* 6 (1963) 50–56.

———. "The Relationship of the Reign of Ahaz to the Accession of Hezekiah." *Bibliotheca Sacra* 126 (1969) 40–52.

Pelikan, Jaroslav. *Acts*. Edited by R. R. Reno, Robert W. Jenson, Robert L. Wilken, et al. Brazos Theological Commentary on the Bible. Grand Rapids: Brazos, 2005.

Peters, John P. "Notes on Some Difficult Passages in the Old Testament." *Journal of Biblical Literature* 11 (1892) 38–52.

Pfeiffer, Charles F. *The Biblical World: A Dictionary of Biblical Archaeology*. 1966. Reprint, Nashville: Broadman, 1976.

Philo of Alexandria. *The Works of Philo: Complete and Unabridged*. Translated by Charles D. Yonge. Peabody: Hendrickson, 1996.

Pixley, George V. *On Exodus: A Liberation Perspective*. Translated Robert R. Barr. Maryknoll, NY: Orbis, 1987.

Polhill, John B. *Acts*. Edited by E. Ray Clendenen, Kenneth A. Matthews, and David S. Dockery. The New American Commentary 26. Nashville: Broadman & Holman, 1992.

Porúbčan, Štefan. "Word ‹ôt in Isaia 7:14." *Catholic Biblical Quarterly* 22 (1960) 144–59.

Pritchard, James B., ed. *The Ancient Near East: A New Anthology of Texts and Pictures, Volume II*. Princeton: Princeton University Press, 1975.

———. "Motifs in Old Testament Miracles." *Crozer Quarterly* 27 (1950) 97–109.

Purinton, Carl E. "Translation Greek in the Wisdom of Solomon." *Journal of Biblical Literature* 47 (1928) 276–304.

Putter, Ad. "Sources and Backgrounds for Descriptions of the Flood." *Studies in Philology* 94 (1997) 137.

Remus, Harold. "'Magic or Miracle:' Some Second-Century Instances." *Second Century: A Journal of Early Christian Studies* 2 (1982) 127–56.

Rengstorf, K. H. *Theological Dictionary of the New Testament*, Vol. 7. Edited by Geoffrey William Bromiley and Gerhard Friedrich. Grand Rapids: Eerdmans, 1971.

Reymond, Eric D. "The Poetry of the Wisdom of Solomon Reconsidered." *Vetus Testamentum* 52 (2002) 385–99.

Reymond, Robert L. *Jesus, Divine Messiah*. Rosshire, Scottland: Mentor, 2003.

———. "Who is the 'LMH of Isaiah 7:14." *Presbyterion* 15 (1989) 1–15.

Robinson, Gnana. *Let Us Be Like the Nations: A Commentary on the Books of 1 and 2 Samuel*. Edited by Frederick Carlson Holmgren and George A. F. Knight. International Theological Commentary. Grand Rapids: Eerdmans, 1993.

Roderick, Bradley P. "God's Mission to Egypt in the Exodus." *Theological Educator* 52 (1995) 21–26.

Rosen, Moishe. *Y'Shua*. Chicago: Moody, 1982.

Ross, Allen P. *A Commentary on Psalms: Volume 2 (42–89)*. Kregel Exegetical Library Series. Grand Rapids: Kregel, 2011.

Riggan, George A. *Messianic Theology and Christian Faith*. Philadelphia: Westminster, 1967.

Rushdoony, Rousas John. *Genesis*. Vol. 1 of *Commentaries on the Pentateuch*. Vallecito, CA: Ross, 2002.

Sabourin, Léopold. "Old Testament Miracles." *Biblical Theology Bulletin* 1 (1971) 227–61.
Sauer, Alfred von Rohr. "The Almah Translation in Isa 7:14." *Concordia Theological Monthly* 24 (1953) 551–59.
Schaaffs, Werner. *Theology, Physics, and Miracles*. Translated by Richard L. Renfield. Washington, DC: Canon, 1973.
Schiermeier, Quirin. "Oceanography: Noah's Flood." *Nature* 430 (2004) 718–19.
Schnabel, Eckhard J. *Acts*. Edited by Clinton J. Arnold, George H. Guthrie, William D. Mounce, et al. Zondervan Exegetical Commentary on the New Testament. Grand Rapids: Zondervan, 2012.
Schneider, Tammie J. *Judges*. Berit Olam: Studies in Hebrew Narrative and Poetry Commentary. 13 vols. Collegeville, MN: Liturgical, 2000.
Scotland, N. A. D. "Conceived by the Holy Spirit, Born of the Virgin Mary." *Evangelical Review of Theology* 10 (1986) 27–32.
Scott, J. W. "Matthew's Intention to Write History." *Westminster Theological Journal* 47 (1985) 68–82.
Seitz, Christopher R. *Isaiah 1–39*. Edited by Patrick D. Miller Jr. and Paul J. Achtemeier. Interpretation: A Bible Commentary for Teaching and Preaching. Louisville: Westminster John Knox, 1993.
Shea, William H. and Ed Christian, "The Chiastic Structure of Revelation 12:1–15:4: The Great Controversy Vision." *Andrews University Seminary Studies* 38 (2000) 269–92.
Simpson, Cuthbert A. *Composition of the Book of Judges*. Oxford: Alden, 1957.
Slotski, I. W. *Isaiah: Hebrew Text and Hebrew Translation with an Introduction and Commentary*. London: Soncino, 1961.
Sloyan, Gerard S. "Conceived by the Holy Ghost, Born of the Virgin Mary." *Interpretation* 33 (1979) 81–84.
Smith, Gary V. *Isaiah 1–39*. Edited by E. Ray Clendenen, Kenneth A. Mathews, and David S. Dockery. The New American Commentary 15A. Nashville: Broadman & Holman, 2007.
———. *Isaiah 40–66*. Edited by E. Ray Clendenen, Kenneth A. Mathews, and David S. Dockery. The New American Commentary 15B. Nashville: Broadman & Holman, 2007.
———. *Joel*. In vol. 1 of *The Minor Prophets*, edited by Thomas Edward McComiskey, Joel 2:30–31. Electronic version. Joplin, MO: College, 1992).
Smith, James E. *The Books of History*. Electronic version. Joplin, MO: College, 1995.
———. *The Minor Prophets*. Electronic version. Joplin, MO: College, 1992.
———. *The Pentateuch*. 2nd ed., electronic version. Joplin, MO: College, 1993.
———. *The Wisdom Literature and Psalms*. Electronic version. Joplin, MO: College, 1996.
Soggin, J. Alberto. *Joshua: A Commentary*. Old Testament Library. Philadelphia: Westminster, 1972.
———. *Judges: A Commentary*. Translated by John Bowden. London: SCM, 1981.
de Sousa, Rodrigo. "Is the Choice of Parthenos in LXX Isa 7:14 Theologically Motivated?" *Journal of Semitic Studies* 53 (2008) 211–32.
Speiser E. A. "The Creation Epic (*Enuma elish*)." In *The Ancient Near East Volume II: A New Anthology of Texts and Pictures*, edited by James B. Pritchard and translated by A. K. Grayson, 28–35. Princeton: Princeton University Press, 1975.
Spencer, Aída Besançon, "God as a Symbolizing God: A Symbolic Hermeneutic." *Journal of the Evangelical Theological Society* 24 (1981) 323–31.

Bibliography

Spero, Shubert. "Pharaoh's Three Offers, Moses' Rejection, and the Issues They Foreshadowed." *Jewish Bible Quarterly* 38 (2010) 93–96.
Spurgeon, Charles H. *Commentary on Matthew*. Carlisle, PA: Banner of Truth Trust, 2010.
Stacey, David. *Isaiah 1–39*. London: Epworth, 1993.
Stein, Robert. *Luke*. Edited by E. Ray Clendenen, Kenneth A. Matthews, and David S. Dockery. The New American Commentary 24. Nashville: Broadman & Holman, 1992.
Stuart, Douglas K. *Exodus: An Exegetical and Theological Exposition of Holy Scripture*. Edited by E. Ray Clendenen, Kenneth A. Mathews, and David S. Dockery. The New American Commentary 2. Nashville: Broadman & Holman, 2006.
Stubbs, David L. *Numbers*. Edited by R. R. Reno, Robert W. Jenson, Robert Louis Wilken et al. Brazos Theological Commentary on the Bible. Grand Rapids: Brazos, 2009.
Surburg, Raymond F. "Interpretation of Isaiah 7:14." *Springfielder* 38 (1974) 110–18.
Swanson, James, and Orville Nave. *New Nave's Topical Bible*. Oak Harbor: Logos Research Systems, 1994.
Sweeney, James P. "Modern and Ancient Controversies over the Virgin Birth of Jesus." *Bibliotheca Sacra* 160 (2003) 142–58.
Tawil, Hayim ben Yosef. *An Akkadian Lexical Companion for Biblical Hebrew: Etymological-Semantic and Idiomatic Equivalents with Supplement on Biblical Aramaic*. Jersey City, NJ: KTAV, 2009.
Tertullian. *Latin Christianity: Its Founder, Tertullian; Apologetic, Anti-Marcion, Ethical*. Vol. 3 of *The Ante-Nicene Fathers: Translation of the Writings of the Fathers Down to A.D. 325*, edited by Alexander Roberts and James Donaldson. Grand Rapids: Eerdmans, 1957.
Thayer, Joseph H. *Thayer's Greek-English Lexicon of the New Testament*. Peabody, MA: Hendrickson, 2002.
Treier, Daniel J. "The Fulfillment of Joel 2:28–32: A Multiple-Lens Approach." *Journal of the Evangelical Theological Society* 40 (1997) 13–26.
Troxel, Ronald L. "Isaiah 7, 14–16 Through the Eyes of the Septuagint." *Ephemerides Theologicae Lovanienses* 79 (2003) 1–22.
Turner, David L. *Matthew* in the *Baker Exegetical Commentary on the New Testament*. Edited by Robert W. Yarbrough and Robert H. Stein. Grand Rapids: Baker, 2008.
Turner, N. *Grammatical Insights into the New Testament*. Edinburgh: T & T Clark, 1965.
Van Groningen, Gerard. *Messianic Revelation in the Old Testament*. Grand Rapids: Baker, 1990.
Van Hattem, Willem C. "Once Again: Sodom and Gomorrah." *Biblical Archaeologist* 44 (1981) 87–92.
Van Seters, John. "The Plagues of Egypt: Ancient Tradition or Literary Invention?" *Zeitschrift Für Die Alttestamentliche Wissenschaft* 98 (1986) 31–39.
Vasholz, Robert I. "Qumran and the Dating of Daniel." *Journal of the Evangelical Theological Society* 21 (1978) 315–21.
———. "Isaiah and Ahaz: A Brief History of Crisis in Isaiah 7 and 8." *Presbyterion* 13 (1987) 79–84.
Vincent, Marvin R. *Word Studies in the New Testament*. Electronic version. Bellingham, WA: Logos Research Systems, 2002.
Vine, W. E. *Isaiah: Prophecy, Promises, and Warnings*. Grand Rapids: Zondervan, 1976.
Von Campenhausen, Hans. *The Virgin Birth in the Theology of the Ancient Church*. London: W. & J. Mackay, 1964.

BIBLIOGRAPHY

Von Rad, Gerhard. *Genesis: A Commentary.* Edited by G. Ernest Wright, John Bright, James Barr, et al. Old Testament Library. Philadelphia: Westminster, 1972.

———. *Deuteronomy: A Commentary.* Edited by G. Ernest Wright, John Bright, James Barr, et al. Old Testament Library. Philadelphia: Westminster, 1966.

Von Wahlde, Urban C. *The Gospel and Letters of John.* Vol. 2 of *Commentary on the Gospel of John.* Edited by David N. Freedman and Astrid B. Beck. Eerdmans Critical Commentary. Grand Rapids: Eerdmans, 2010.

Voss, Howard F. *1, 2 Kings.* Grand Rapids: Lamplighter, 1989.

Walsh, Jerome T. "The Contexts of 1 Kings 13." *Vetus Testamentum* 39 (1989) 355–70.

Walvoord, John F. *The Revelation of Jesus Christ: A Commentary.* Chicago: Moody, 1966.

Webb, Barry G. *The Book of Judges: An Integrated Reading.* Sheffield, UK: Sheffield Academic, 1987.

Wegner, Paul D. *An Examination of Kingship and Messianic Expectations in Isaiah 1–35.* Lewiston, NY: Mellen, 1992.

———. "How Many Virgin Births Are There in the Bible? (Isaiah 7:14) A Prophetic Pattern Approach." *Journal of the Evangelical Theological Society* 54 (2011) 467–84.

Wenham, Gordon J. *Genesis.* 3rd ed. Edited by D. A. Carson, D. Guthrie, and J. A. Motyer. New Bible Commentary: 21st Century Edition. Downers Grove: InterVarsity, 1994.

Wesselius, J. W. "Language and Style in Biblical Aramaic: Observations on the Unity of Daniel 2–6." *Vetus Testamentum* 38 (1988) 194–209.

Widyapranawa, S. H. *The Lord Is Savior: Faith in National Crisis. A Commentary on the Book of Isaiah 1–39.* Grand Rapids: Eerdmans, 1990.

Wildberger, Hans. *Isaiah 1–12: A Commentary.* Translated by Thomas H. Trapp. Minneapolis: Fortress, 1991.

Wilken, Robert L. *Isaiah: Interpreted by Early Christian and Medieval Commentators.* Edited and translated by Robert L. Wilken, Angela R. Christman, and Michael J. Hollerich. Grand Rapids: Eerdmans, 2007.

Wilkinson, John. "Apologetic Aspects of the Virgin Birth of Jesus Christ." *Scottish Journal of Theology* 17 (1964) 159–81.

Williamson, Lamar, Jr. *Mark.* Edited by James Luther Mays, Patrick D. Miller, and Paul J. Achtemeier. Interpretation: A Bible Commentary for Teaching and Preaching. Louisville: Westminster John Knox, 1983.

Willis, John T. "The Meaning of Isaiah 7:14 and its Application in Matthew 1:23." *Restoration Quarterly* 21 (1978) 1–18.

Willis, John R. *The Teachings of the Church Fathers.* New York: Herder & Herder, 1966.

Wilson, John A. *Signs and Wonders upon Pharaoh: A History of American Egyptology.* Chicago: University of Chicago, 1964.

Wilson, R. Dick. "The Meaning of 'Alma (A. V. "Virgin") in Isaiah vii. 14." *PTR* 24 (1926) 316–20.

Wolf, Herbert M. *Interpreting Isaiah: The Suffering and Glory of the Messiah.* Grand Rapids: Zondervan, 1985.

———. "Solution to the Immanuel Prophecy in Isaiah 7:14–8:22." *Journal of Biblical Literature* 91 (1972) 449–56.

Wolverton, Wallace I. "Judgment in Advent: Notes on Isaiah 8:5–15 and 7:14." *Anglican Theological Review* 37 (1955) 284–91.

Wood, D. R. W., and I. Howard Marshall, *New Bible Dictionary,* 3rd ed. Leicester, UK; Downers Grove: InterVarsity Press, 1996.

Wood, Leon J. *Distressing Days of the Judges.* Grand Rapids: Zondervan, 1976.

BIBLIOGRAPHY

Woodhouse, John. "Jesus and Jonah." *Reformed Theological Review* 43 (1984) 33–41.
Wuest, Kenneth S. *Wuest's Word Studies from the Greek New Testament: For the English Reader*. Electronic version. Grand Rapids: Eerdmans, 1997.
Yitzchaki, Sholomo. "Tanech with Rashi's Compete Commentary." http://www.chabad.org/library/bible_cdo/aid/15938#showrashi=true (Accessed November 19, 2013).
Young, Edward J. *The Book of Isaiah*. 3 vols. 1965. Reprint, Grand Rapids: Eerdmans, 1978.
———. *Who Wrote Isaiah?* Grand Rapids: Eerdmans, 1958.
Youngblood, Ronald F. *The Book of Isaiah: An Introductory Commentary*. 2nd ed. Grand Rapids: Baker, 1993.
———. *Exodus*. Chicago: Moody, 1983.
Zimmermann, Frank. "Immanuel Prophecy." *Jewish Quarterly Review* 52 (1961) 154–59.

www.ingramcontent.com/pod-product-compliance
Lightning Source LLC
Chambersburg PA
CBHW070918180426
43192CB00038B/1749